# QUEER CRAFTS

# CRITICAL CRAFT STUDIES

## Series editors:

**Susan Surette,** Concordia University, Canada
**Elaine Cheasley Paterson,** Concordia University, Canada

Critical Craft Studies presents rigorous and original research on the role and significance of craft in society and culture, past and present. Reflecting craft's shifting parameters in terms of indigenization, settler productions, interface with industry, relationships with design, Do-It-Yourself revival, maker culture and identity constructions, this series showcases craft studies as a discipline in its own right. It offers an interdisciplinary and global approach to craft, welcoming contributions from the fields of anthropology, material culture, cultural geography, heritage studies, critical race theory, architecture and design, art history, sociology, and studies in gender and sexuality, critical disability, migration, and sustainability, among others.

Books in this series demonstrate the innovative and critical edge that a craft lens may bring to bear upon a wide range of academic concerns. They form a springboard for further research and discourse in craft studies, elevating academic discussions which put craft in the spotlight.

# QUEER CRAFTS

## Material Practices and the Making of Identity

**Daniel Fountain**

BLOOMSBURY VISUAL ARTS

LONDON • NEW YORK • OXFORD • NEW DELHI • SYDNEY

BLOOMSBURY VISUAL ARTS
Bloomsbury Publishing Plc, 50 Bedford Square, London, WC1B 3DP, UK
Bloomsbury Publishing Inc, 1359 Broadway, New York, NY 10018, USA
Bloomsbury Publishing Ireland, 29 Earlsfort Terrace, Dublin 2, D02 AY28, Ireland

BLOOMSBURY, BLOOMSBURY VISUAL ARTS and the Diana logo are trademarks of Bloomsbury Publishing Plc

First published in Great Britain 2026
Reprinted by Bloomsbury Visual Arts 2026



Cover design by Louise Dugdale
Cover image: Rose Schmits, *TransForms*, 2019. Collection of 281 ceramic vessels



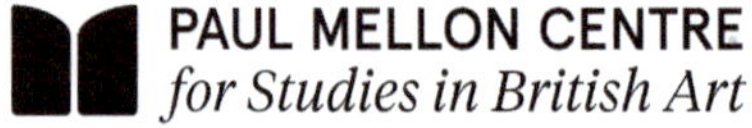 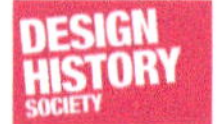

A catalogue record for this book is available from the British Library.

Library of Congress Cataloging-in-Publication Data
Names: Fountain, Daniel (Daniel James) author http://id.loc.gov/authorities/names/no2023117937
Title: Queer crafts : material practices and the making of identity / Daniel Fountain.
Description: London ; New York : Bloomsbury Visual Arts, 2026. | Series: Critical craft studies | Includes bibliographical references and index.
Identifiers: LCCN 2025015153 | ISBN 9781350359369 hardback | ISBN 9781350359352 paperback | ISBN 9781350359376 epub | ISBN 9781350359383 pdf
Subjects: LCSH: Decorative arts—History—21st century—Themes, motives | Gender identity in art http://id.loc.gov/authorities/subjects/sh97000999 | Sexual minority community http://id.loc.gov/authorities/subjects/sh2014000538
Classification: LCC NK792 .F68 2026 | DDC 745.086/6—dc23/eng/20250612
LC record available at https://lccn.loc.gov/2025015153

ISBN: HB: 978-1-3503-5936-9
PB: 978-1-3503-5935-2
ePDF: 978-1-3503-5938-3
eBook: 978-1-3503-5937-6

Series: Critical Craft Studies

Typeset by Deanta Global Publishing Services, Chennai, India
Printed and bound in Great Britain

For product safety related questions contact productsafety@bloomsbury.com.

To find out more about our authors and books, visit www.bloomsbury.com and sign up for our newsletters.

CONTENTS

# ACKNOWLEDGMENTS

Many people have helped to make this book possible. I have been grateful for the generosity of various colleagues at the University of Exeter who have supported me on the challenging journey of writing my first monograph. The usual stresses and challenges associated with this were exacerbated by the systematic dismantling of the UK Higher Education sector, funding cuts, and an increase in homophobia and transphobia, both within and beyond the academy. Whether it was sharing resources, reading drafts, co-writing, peer-reviewing grant applications, being a shoulder to cry on, or simply coaxing me out of hibernation and into the pub, special thanks to Az, Jamie, Marcus, Roz, Angeliki, Sarah, Tricia, Ina, and Jana. As an educator, I firmly believe that teaching and learning is a two-way process. I have had the pleasure of learning from many postgraduate research students, especially Sam Godfrey, with whom I have been lucky to share in many conversations around the intersections between transness, textiles, and sloppy craft.

I am incredibly grateful for the invitations I have had to speak about preliminary research for this book with staff and public audiences at the Crafts Council, Australian Centre for Contemporary Art, Common Threads Press, National Museums Liverpool, The Whitworth, and the Museum for Art in Wood. I have also enjoyed collaborating with colleagues and students at various universities. Feedback from research seminars I conducted at the University of British Columbia, Arts University Bournemouth, and the Royal School of Needlework greatly informed the book's development. Thanks to Roberto, GPat, Emma, Willem, and Amy for facilitating these conversations.

I acknowledge the support of everyone at Bloomsbury Academic, especially my commissioning editor, Suzie Nash, and editorial assistant, Joseph Skingsley. I also wish to thank the artist, Matt Smith, for facilitating the initial connection with Bloomsbury and encouraging me to write this book. I appreciate the anonymous peer reviewers who offered judicious and generous appraisals of the manuscript, and support from the Critical Craft series editors, Elaine Cheasley Paterson and Susan Surette.

Some of the material from Chapter 1 was initially published as an open-access article in the journal *MAI: Feminism and Visual Culture*, an issue I edited for *Decorating Dissidence*, and the exhibition catalog *Paul Yore: WORD MADE FLESH* (2022). I must also extend my thanks to the peer reviewers and editors who supported the development of that material.

I am very thankful for the financial support of the Paul Mellon Centre and the Design History Society, who awarded me publication grants, and the University of Exeter, which supported me via its "Project Monograph" scheme.

To all the featured practitioners, many of whom I have enjoyed working with for several years—this is for you. To my family, chosen family, and faithful canine companion, Evie—this is also for you. Most of all—this is for me. This was the book I always wanted but could never find. I guess there are some things that we must craft for ourselves . . .

# PREFACE

## *Creatively Bent*

In 2018, I traveled to Somerset House in London to see an exhibition of work by queer South African artist Athi-Patra Ruga (b.1984). *Of Gods, Rainbows and Omissions* featured a series of handcrafted petit point tapestries depicting portraits of Black, queer, and femme communities living in an imaginary queer utopian world that Ruga called Azania. Ruga's fantastical worlds are populated by original avatars of his creation, such as a recurring figure called Castrato who appears in the work titled *Castrato as [the] Revolution* (2010). Ruga describes Castrato as both a self-portrait and a tribute to figures from art and performance. It also references the historical phenomenon of castrato singers; males who were castrated before puberty to preserve their high vocal range. The central figure in the work is both captivating and enigmatic, simultaneously commanding and denying attention (Figure 0.1). The figure emerges from a backdrop of burned orange and blue geometric shapes, suggestive of towering skyscrapers and a cityscape at sunset. Vibrant hot pink elbow-length gloves stand out against a black and gold glittery bodysuit, with a clear outline of a phallus protruding from it. However, the phallus is depicted in complete silhouette, and a jagged black band conceals the figure's eyes. Through this act of self-censorship, Ruga denies a direct gaze and disrupts any attempt to objectify the figure or assume their sex or gender.

On the way to the exhibition, I was called a host of derogatory slurs by a pack of young teenagers in the tube station—"bent" being one that stuck in my memory. No stranger to receiving unsolicited homophobic hate speech, I dismissed it with a swish of the (limp) wrist. I went about the rest of the afternoon minding my own business, thinking nothing more of the specific linguistic associations of this word. Yet, as I entered the exhibition space and gazed upward at Ruga's petit point, I was struck by the fact that they, too, were bent. The textile portraits were physically crafted at an angle, inviting viewers to tilt their heads and see things anew. "Why not try to see things from a different angle?" as the hit Broadway song and Gloria Gaynor single goes. Ruga refuses to be constrained to a rectangular composition, and the process of making his work also relies upon a further deviation from straightness. This is because petit point is a form of very fine canvas embroidery where stitches go *across* the intersection of the canvas in a series of diagonal lines /// \\\ (often known as "tent stitches") rather than straight lines – – –. With every stitch, Ruga's fibrous portraits of queer desire deviate us further away from the line of heterosexuality.

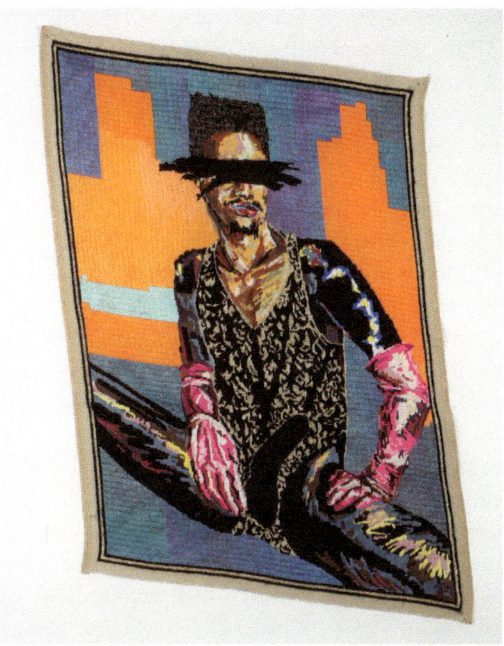

**Figure 0.1** Athi-Patra Ruga, *Castrato as [the] Revolution*, 2010. Wool and tapestry thread on tapestry canvas, 52.4 × 37.8 inches. Courtesy of Athi-Patra Ruga and What if the world gallery.

Ruga's work disrupts conventions on multiple levels. A slight tilt in the composition, from straight ||| to slanted \\\, was imbued with so much symbolic meaning, what we might call a "queering" of conventions. It was a way of asserting Ruga's own queer identity while simultaneously re-orienting the viewer, *querying* and *queering* the dominance of the rectangle as the default "normal" or "natural" way to depict the world. This critique of pictorial representation seems to extend to the rigid format of historical colonial paintings, including portraits of white oppressors and horizontal landscapes of the lands they colonized. These visual histories were key in rendering specific communities invisible and inferior, and Ruga often re-configures these in his work. By subverting the composition and using it to depict queer Black subjects in states of joy rather than oppression, Ruga provides a resistance to these legacies, envisioning an inclusive post-liberation, post-colonial, and post-apartheid society. Ruga's choice of materials—thread on canvas instead of paint on canvas—further disrupts hierarchies, particularly that of so-called "high art" (painting) and "low craft" (textiles). This division also has its roots in colonialism, where European colonizers, mainly the British, imposed these hierarchies of visual culture alongside oppressive anti-homosexuality laws. The subjugation of both craft and queerness have always been intertwined in complex ways.

When I got home from the exhibition, I looked up different meanings of the term "bent" in the dictionary and began to braid together their seemingly disparate associations. Its definitions and uses included derogatory slang historically used against gay men and queer people, the process of deflecting from the straight line, the physical shaping or "bending" of material, and also a phrase to describe that someone is determined, resolute, and devoted.[1] In the English language, a related term "creative bent" is used to describe someone with a natural penchant for creativity—someone with a strong inner drive to express themselves outwardly through making.[2] There are also many connections between bent and "queer" which often meant *across,* emerging from the "Indo-European root *twerkw'* which also yields the German *quer* (transverse), Latin *torquere* (to twist), English *athwart,*" and later appearing as "oblique, bent, twisted, crooked."[3]

These discursive formations have long fascinated me, especially their instability and ripeness for reinvention. As a textile practitioner, I explore linguistic reclamation through the material reclamation of discarded materials and found fabrics. From creating a giant "big girl's blouse" to using needlework techniques such as "faggoting" and materials such as "gimp" thread, I reappropriate derogatory words that have been hurled at me like a stone to mark my supposed "difference" (Figure 0.2).[4] Working with waste materials in "sloppy" ways that are certainly not straight, clean, or neat, I celebrate the messiness of the queer experience and challenge the designation of queer people as waste or surplus. You could say that I have both a natural "bent" towards examining language and a "creative bent" to craft works that make my identity as a queer, non-binary person visible. But bending the rules sometimes comes with the consequence of never *really* fitting in (why would we want to?). I have never truly been welcomed within craft communities because, to them, I work in an art context. I have never truly been welcomed within art communities either because, to them, I work in a craft context. Other people's perceptions and constant desire to label, define, categorize, or make things "straight" are often revealing. Although the liminal space I find myself caught in can be challenging, it can also be incredibly generative.

For me, "bent" isn't an insult anymore; it is a badge of honor. It represents the entire constellation of possibilities that unfold when we detour from the straight path and embrace being "out of line." It is about celebrating "difference," accepting failure, and challenging the status quo. In creative practices, a bent approach might mean pushing boundaries and using tools or materials in ways that are not "expected," as Ruga demonstrates with his refusal to conform to 'expected" norms in portraiture. For queer and trans practitioners like me, there is often a natural alignment between this creative approach that challenges norms around making and our identity, which inherently challenges rigid understandings of gender and sexuality.

As the following pages will articulate, this book does not approach craft head-on but at an angle—that is, queerly—conceptualizing craft not just as a creative pursuit but as something integral in shaping identity and community. It

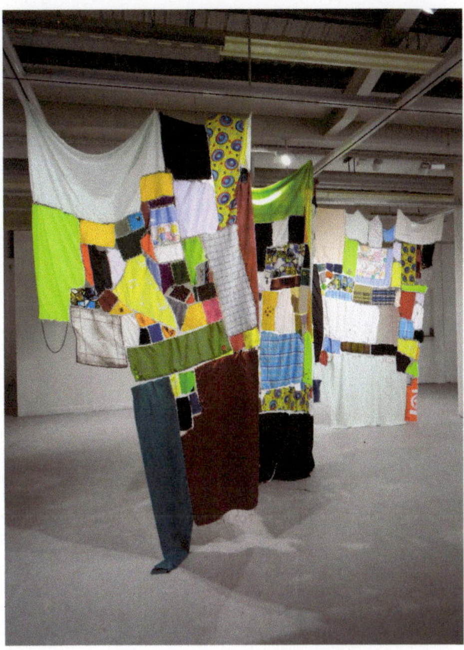

**Figure 0.2** Daniel Fountain, *Faggoting,* 2019. Found objects, discarded textiles, darning thread, 116 × 335 inches (installation dimensions variable). Copyright Daniel Fountain.

encourages you, my dear reader, to forge new relations to craft and invites you to help unravel the cisnormative binaries, heteronormative assumptions, and other falsely constructed narratives that craft has historically been tethered by. It also calls for you to value the productive space between theory and practice, acknowledging an often symbiotic relationship between thinking and doing. Ultimately, this book encourages a fresh perspective on what matters—matter. Matter matters, queer matters, and queer matters matter.

This short vignette encapsulates much of what will follow. It signals how contemporary practitioners identifying as LGBTQ+ are dismantling the binary between art and craft, how they are experimenting with traditional tools and techniques in new ways, and using craft to explore intersectional identities. More than this, it also foregrounds my personal identification with this material and my embodied relationship to some of the forms of crafting and positionalities I write about. Many critics have argued that foregrounding lived experience is crucial in queer accounts of history and criticism because it can enable the construction of kinship, empathy, affects, intimacy, and a 'knowing" that reaches beyond mere words on a page or screen.[5] I hope some of you find this is the case here. However, before we begin, let me make something very clear. I do not claim that the ways in which I live, practice, and conceptualize craft are the only way of interpreting or navigating this wide-ranging and deeply personal material. After all, to do so would not be to make things very *queer*. Craft and queerness are both multiplicitous, meaning different things to different people. I encourage you to embrace your own perspective, follow your own path, and continue bending the rules . . .

# INTRODUCTION

## UNRAVELING "QUEER" AND "CRAFT"

Queerness and craft may seem like two separate strands of inquiry, but they are, and always have been, interwoven. Both terms—"queer" and "craft"—have historically occupied marginal and subjugated positionalities in opposition to dominant hierarchies: queer in opposition to heterosexual and cisgender normativity and craft in opposition to fine art. In short, the issues of marginality that members of the LGBTQ+ community often face mirror the marginalized position of craft within the cultural canon, especially in a European and North American context. Given this, it is perhaps unsurprising that these materials and processes, which have historically been marginalized or deemed lesser, are increasingly being embraced by a range of LGBTQ+ contemporary practitioners to, quite literally, give "form" to their identities, experiences, and communities that have also been marginalized or deemed lesser. This book explores why this might be and attempts to patch together a multitude of responses to provocations such as "What is so queer about craft?", "What does it mean to make queerly?", and "How is identity made materially?".

Rather than attempt to provide a definitive or singular response to these questions, I seek to encapsulate a range of reactions, open possibilities, and bring these fields—craft studies and queer theory—together. What drives this research is an urgent need to make the relationship between craft and queerness legible, to discern how they inform each other, challenge each other, and how bringing these seemingly disparate strands of inquiry together might generate new ways of thinking, making, and being. Craft's links to the personal and the handmade allow for queerness to be made visible. Yet, queerness also allows craft's links to the personal and the handmade to be visible. As featured practitioner LJ Roberts argues, "[c]raft can gain from the methods and tools that queer theory has deployed to reclaim and reconfigure its own marginal position into a place of empowerment."[1] Equally, scholar and curator Jeanne Vaccaro speculates that "queer and transgender theory can gain from the methods and tools developed in craft."[2] Although this book builds upon existing work exploring the broader relationships between gender, sexuality, and craft practices, queer craft is a relatively new area of inquiry that is rapidly evolving. However, before giving an overview of this book and the material it covers, it first needs to be acknowledged that definitions of both "queer" and "craft" have a notoriously knotty history tied to the personal and the political.

Historically, queer has been used in several different ways: "to signify something strange [. . .] to refer to negative characteristics [. . .] to denote one's difference, one's "strangeness."[3] Although used initially as a derogatory term, primarily for gay men, the rise in use of the term "queer" in the late 1980s can be said to reflect the loss of faith in the coherence of a singular "gay" identity, and activist groups in the United States such as AIDS Coalition To Unleash Power (ACT UP) and Queer Nation began to reappropriate the term to unite a broader range of constituencies opposed to conventional notions of sexuality and gender. For the American artist and queer theorist Eve Kosofsky Sedgwick, the "always derogatory underbelly" of "queer" is precisely its source of power.[4] If the word were to lose all of its stigmatization, she argues, it would simply become an affirmative term, losing its potency as "a near inexhaustible source of transformational energy."[5] Although some people reading this book may still heavily associate the term queer with hatred and abuse, I intend to use it here as a celebratory term, a source of identification, and a symbol of collective strength. Further, although the term therefore certainly draws its politics and affective force from the history of LGBTQ+ communities, it is not equivalent to these categories, nor is it necessarily an identity. As queer theorist David Halperin suggests: "[q]ueer is by definition whatever is at odds with the normal, the legitimate, the dominant. There is nothing in particular to which it necessarily refers. It is an identity without an essence."[6] To put it more simply, and to invoke the work of American social activist bell hooks, we might think of "queer as not about who you're having sex with, that can be a dimension of it, but queer as being about the self that is at odds with everything around it and has to invent and create and find a place to speak and to thrive and to live."[7] In this sense, to be queer is to not "fit" into dominant systems and to be constantly at odds with them. Yet, "not fitting" forces someone to innovate, to *craft* ways through (and beyond) those exclusionary systems, as hooks alludes to. It is curious that queer theorists have been using the vernacular of craft for years to emphasize the construction of queer identity and community, and this will be made evident in the pages that follow—from hooks' acknowledgment of the importance of invention and creativity as forms of queer survival, Sara Ahmed's aphorism of "*crafting* a life," and José Esteban Muñoz's theorization of disidentity as "a version of self that is crafted," among countless other examples.[8]

In recognition of the differing approaches to the term queer, it is used throughout this book with a dual referent. First, as a noun relating to non-normative genders and sexualities (as in queer identity or the queer community). Second, as a verb that represents a movement toward queer as a process of "doing" that deconstructs and interrogates (as in queering craft or queering material). This dual approach is vital because in the process of queering something, queer, in turn, can operate as a form of intellectual activism that challenges presumptions and schematic binaries, particularly concerning gender and sexuality, but not merely there. The process of queering can also operate as a "broad critique of social antagonisms, including race, gender, class, nationality, and religion, in addition to sexuality," to name but a few, allowing for more intersectional and fluid interrogations to emerge.[9] Queerness is not a monolithic identity, and this book aims to take an intersectional approach. The intersections between sexuality, gender identity, class, race, ethnicity, religion, disability, and migratory experience, among many other factors, create nuanced complexities that enrich the archive of queer experience.

As with definitions of queer, definitions of craft have significantly been contested, so much so that woodworker and writer David Pye referred to it as "a word to start an argument with."[10] Indeed, I have started many. Today, craft is commonly used as an all-encompassing term to refer to a broad set of materials and processes that usually involve making something by hand. Often grouped under the category of "the crafts" are "ceramics, glass making, metalsmithing, woodworking, and the various combinations of process and material that fall under the heading of the textile arts."[11] However, in recent years, creative engagements with paper have started to be considered within, or at least adjacent to, this rubric. Usually, these craft materials and processes require the maker to possess a certain level of skill, and they are typically associated with producing functional or decorative objects. Craft's associations with the "decorative," "amateur," and even more problematic, the "ethnic" or "primitive" have been central to its marginalization within the Western cultural canon and, by extension, the bodies of those who practice such crafts. It is no secret that the craft world is often highly conservative, steeped in rigidity and tradition. Still, as craft historian Glenn Adamson acknowledges, "craft's inferiority might be the most productive thing about it," prompting critical dialogue about its use and increasingly shifting parameters.[12]

At first, then, queer theory and craft may seem to be in tension with one another; they are not necessarily perfect bedfellows. Queerness is often about *dismantling* norms of gender and sexuality, while craft is typically associated with *maintaining* norms around making. However, the regulation of "normal" ways of making or the "proper" use of techniques can rapidly extend to what bodies and identities are allowed to produce work and what this work can or "should" look like. Yet, these rules can easily be bent or even broken. This book explores the materiality and queer potential of traditional craft materials and practices. Still, the practitioners featured here often adapt and subvert material traditions, experimenting with form and function, examining both skilled craft and "sloppy craft" approaches, and blurring the boundaries between art and craft.[13] Consequently, rather than reinforcing hierarchies or imposing labels, we might more usefully conceive craft here as a broader process, an activity, attitude, or habit of action. Adamson attests that craft "only exists in motion. It is a way of doing things, not [just] a classification of objects, institutions, or people."[14] This broad conceptualization of craft ultimately allows for a breadth of activities to be considered under this rubric. It also underscores how crafting, as an expanded practice, is evident in the fabric of everyday life for many people, and it is not just something enacted within the confines of a workshop or studio.

Just as both "queer" and "craft" defy neat categorization, so does the compounded term "queer craft." When placed in conversation together, the already knotty definitions of queer and craft become even more tangled. This is fundamentally messy work. To engage with queer craft is to step into a tangled web. Rather than being bound by this, those involved in the study and practice of queer craft delight in its multiplicity, its slipperiness, and its refusal to conform. Broadly speaking, the term "queer craft" might be used to describe the practices of self-identifying queer practitioners who are utilizing traditional craft skills and techniques to create work that expresses queer identity and community. Put simply, this book focuses on objects made by, for, and about queer people, demonstrating how the act of making and the chosen materials give form to specific concepts and lived experiences. Queer craft can also create a sense of connection and kinship, enabling the sharing of stories, knowledge, and experiences. For many queer practitioners, the process is just as crucial as any "final" object. After all, crafting is not just an engagement with materials and techniques but often an encounter between people and places. This is also true of queerness, which primarily exists in connection with one another and the world around us.

While "queer" offers a sense of unity, scholars warn that its expansiveness can obscure the real differences and sometimes even conflicting needs and priorities among the diverse identities housed under the LGBTQ+ "umbrella." In this sense, to describe a set of practices under the rubric of "queer crafts" might also be at risk of homogenizing aspects of the queer experience and, in doing so, subsuming specific practices and practitioners—especially of trans people who may identify dually as both queer and trans.[15] This is a fraught issue within the field, felt through many conversations across theory and practice. For instance, several scholars have voiced concerns over the field of trans studies being "relegated to the role of a fractious "special guest" within queer studies."[16] Similar to this, trans practitioners frequently raise concerns that their work is often categorized *within* queer art or queer craft or treated as tokenism rather than a distinctive field worthy of individual attention. Yet, putting it in a distinctive "box" of its own accord, such as "trans craft," and severing it from queer craft is also at risk of further marginalization, essentializing, flattening both terms, and erasing both practitioners and practices "that don't fit into the artificial category in the first place," as artist and researcher Sam Godfrey has argued.[17] In short, this is a highly complex and deeply personal topic where people will have different opinions and unique experiences. I respect certain limitations of my focus and my use of terms as not being complex enough to account for the fullness of LGBTQ+ experiences or the entire field of queer crafts. Yet, we currently find ourselves in a moment of crisis where queer and trans bodies (especially bodies of color) face the systemic dismantling of their civil rights and bodily autonomy, the threat of violence, and the removal of their visible presence from public life. In addition, although the "T" (Transgender) is part of the same "LGBTQ+" acronym and community, many people would have it otherwise. When the voices of trans-exclusionary radical feminists, or so-called "gender critical" people, are becoming increasingly amplified, it is easy for these identities to be rendered invisible.[18] Craft—as a physical, visible expression of identity—challenges this idea. The need for creative expression and equitable visibility of these practices has never been more vital.

## *Feminist Legacies, Queer Futures*

Although this book is focused on contemporary examples of queer craft, ranging from the late 1980s to the 2020s, it is important to sketch out a broader historical context, especially concerning the gendering of craft and the binary between art and craft. Several scholars have persuasively argued that the development of a hierarchy of the arts coincided historically with a similar one between the categories of male and female. For instance, in *The Subversive Stitch: Embroidery and the Making of the Feminine* (1984), the art historian Rozsika Parker argues that "the development of an ideology of femininity coincided historically with the emergence of a clearly defined separation of art and craft," particularly in Britain and America.[19] This dichotomy, Parker argues, is most visible in textiles. Deemed "outside" the modes of masculine, capitalist production, Parker explains that since the Renaissance, textile practices were especially considered unproductive and passive activities or "hobbies," mainly due to their ability to be conducted in a domestic environment. She also observes that the wider gendering of craft extended well into the eighteenth century, where tasks were "consigned to the "appropriate gender"" within the academy.[20] Even later, she observes how this division persisted at least into the 1980s, particularly in Britain, where "boys" would be expected to study carpentry or metalwork (which were seen as "masculine") and "girls" would be expected to study embroidery (which was seen as "feminine").[21]

Many contemporary artists who formed part of the second-wave feminist movement sought to deliberately exploit this relationship between craft and gender, using craft (namely textiles) as a "weapon of resistance" to unpick and unravel the very binaries between high/low, art/craft, male/female, masculine/feminine.[22] This was marked by the revolution of what became known in the American tradition as "fiber art" (or "textile art" in the British tradition), which by the late 1970s had come to signal any work that utilized techniques such as stitching, quilting, knotting, knitting, braiding, beading, and so on.[23] These practitioners recognized the potential for the creation of new categories to traverse the divide separating craft from fine art, often referring to themselves as "fiber artists," "textile artists," or "soft sculptors."[24] In short, feminists during this period saw textiles as "a highly productive force in the art world by virtue of its perceived inferiority," actively using these techniques to push back against the stereotyping of textile crafts as domestic, passive, and inherently feminine.[25]

It is evident that the feminist recuperation and evaluation of textile traditions as gendered practices have been incredibly influential, particularly in the contemporary art world, and we must honor the work of our feminist forbearers, without whom this notion of "queer craft" would not be possible. Despite the importance of these histories, women's engagement with craft has been studied by academics at length, and it has been argued that "nearly all of the documenting and theorizing around such practices still seems to suggest that this is an exclusive realm of women."[26] Scholars such as Joseph McBrinn have now begun to explore the construction of masculinity as "the asymmetrical pendant to the more critically investigated femininity" and to extend feminism's critique of "the fixity of all subject positions."[27] In his book *Queering The Subversive Stitch: Masculinity and The Culture of Needlework* (2021), McBrinn sensitively acknowledges that while Parker's re-evaluation of crafts historically practiced by women continues to be influential (having been reprinted fourteen times since I. B. Tauris first republished it in 2010), there is potential for it to be *queered* to counteract the "complete omission or the covert marginalization of men within the culture of needlework."[28]

While recent scholarship has begun to dismantle the gendered binaries within craft and the artificial divide between art and craft, the overwhelming emphasis on textiles persists. This is particularly striking given Parker's own acknowledgment of the gendered nature of other materials like wood and metal, which have received comparatively little attention. Furthermore, existing scholarship still often upholds a binary knowledge system between male/female, masculine/feminine, and as a result, it typically excludes the crucial contributions of trans practitioners who have been central to deconstructing these very binaries. Therefore, while I respect the importance of existing sources and occasionally draw upon them here to situate my thinking in a broader context, it is essential to note that scholarship in this field is not without its limitations, complexities, or issues. The same goes for the craft sector itself. As a queer, non-binary practitioner, writer, educator, and curator of craft, I have personally experienced homophobia and transphobia across all these spaces, and I am sure many reading this book will have had similar experiences. There is—against all these forces—a thriving and growing dialogue of diverse voices and inclusive conversations which are often healing, empowering, and radical. There is an urgent need to consider how craft's historic position as "other" might intersect with various genders, sexualities, and identities in the contemporary climate. Likewise, by considering a range of other materials and processes that have also been highly gendered, as opposed to just textiles, I hope to encourage further conversation on the topic of queer crafts and encourage other scholars to consider a greater range of practitioners, materials, and processes, especially from an intersectional, interdisciplinary, and international perspective.

Even though these conversations about queer crafts are only just beginning to emerge in scholarly literature, it is worth signaling that there has been a wealth of public programming in recent years, indicating a broad and eager audience for work in this field. This is hardly surprising given that the do-it-yourself (DIY) concept is becoming increasingly pervasive in the current cultural landscape. More broadly, many have cited a craft renaissance or "return" to the handmade during the Covid-19 pandemic, and we have witnessed a rise in the number of reality TV shows dedicated to material-specific practices, including competition shows such as *Blown Away* and *Metal Shop Masters*. Few mainstream exhibitions have explicitly focused on queer crafts, but several dedicated and medium-specific exhibitions have recently taken place, most notably in the United States. These include *Queer Threads: Crafting Identity and Community* at the Leslie Lohman Museum (2014), *SEXUAL POLITICS: Gender, Sexuality and Queerness* at the Northern Clay Center (2015), *Transparency: An LGBTQ Glass Art Exhibit* at the

Museum of Glass (2019–2021), *Queering Masculinity: NYC Jewelry Week* (2020), and *Cock, Paper, Scissors* at the ONE Archives, USC Libraries (2016), among others. While largely limited to a North American context, this wealth of cultural activity demonstrates that there is indeed a range of LGBTQ+ practitioners working with a range of materials and processes that have hitherto been overlooked, at least in academic scholarship. This book explores new, more conducive approaches to making, thinking, and writing about craft, especially by integrating practice and theory, recognizing that craft exists within a broad and active framework.

## Beyond the Binary

As briefly outlined above, "art" and "craft" have been used throughout history to distinguish between different types of creative work. Still, in recent years, many have argued that there is no clear dividing line between them. In a very rudimentary sense, scholars have theorized that contemporary artists have appropriated traditional craft tools and techniques, and craftspeople have begun experimenting with more expressive and experimental forms of work with conceptual agendas. However, to try and "elevate" craft to the status of art, or to claim that art has now appropriated the languages and logic of craft, only reinforces that very binary and the systems of power and oppression surrounding it. This approach does nothing to dismantle the canon itself, despite countless warnings from feminist art historians, such as Linda Nochlin and Griselda Pollock, about the ideological underpinnings of art history and its systems of exclusion, especially along the lines of gender, race, and class.[29]

Certainly, the increasingly blurred boundaries between art and craft have broadened appreciations for both, while also offering enhanced visibility to the work of practitioners who have previously been excluded. However, more important than this, it has prompted us to question the very need for such categorization and to imagine a world beyond an incessant and irrational need to label and define. Many queer scholars and practitioners, including myself, find the constant rehashing of this debate tiresome, boring, and unproductive. Publications and exhibitions frequently push this narrative without acknowledging that the binary itself is falsely constructed, tied to patriarchal, capitalist, classist, and colonial knowledge systems. In fact, the art/craft binary has little to do with distinguishing between types of creative activity and everything to do with power. It mirrors and reinforces a whole host of limiting binaries, including male/female, masculine/feminine, superior/inferior, and is also reflective of harmful Western European constructs imposed globally through colonialism, such as between dominant/subordinate, good/bad, oppressor/oppressed, as Audre Lorde has warned.[30] Rather than perpetuating an "us-versus-them" debate that only serves to "other" certain practices, bodies, and identities, we need to move towards a more inclusive, fluid, and dynamic community of making that resists a process of labeling or neat categorization.

Queer and trans practitioners and writers, including matt lambert and John Paul Morabito, have embraced this manifesto, interpreting "beyond the binary" as a move beyond both disciplinary and gender boundaries.[31] Today, *trans*, a shortened version of the word transgender, is a "hyper-inclusive category under which a constellation of gender identities and styles are meant to find their home," with many non-binary and gender nonconforming people identifying under this umbrella.[32] Moreover, Jules Gill-Peterson notes that as a prefix, trans is already imbued with "a kind of boundary-crossing energy, a refusal to be contained by binaries."[33] Many practitioners featured in this book, especially those identifying under the trans "umbrella" often see the physicality and malleability of craft materials as a productive avenue to deconstruct the archaic gendering of craft. This is often a process of unmaking, undoing, and unthinking, just as it is a process of making, doing, and thinking.

The ways in which categories of making are now being dismantled and even transcended have also been the subject of much discussion in recent craft scholarship as part of much broader contemporary debates on "post-craft" or "postdisciplinary" practices.[34] For example, Kenji Kaneko suggests that compared to countries such as Japan, the British and Eurocentric debate on art and craft has reached a "cul-de-sac," or a dead end, endlessly trapped in a binary system that is labeled as "outmoded" and too "simplistic" for more fluid and dynamic forms of making that center materials and materiality.[35] In *Fray: Art and Textile Politics* (2017), American art historian Julia Bryan-Wilson deliberately evokes the term "fray" to metaphorically explore how, just like a frayed edge on an unhemmed piece of fabric, the borders between art, craft, and design are now blurred and jagged, but still constantly "in the fray" of debates about gendered labor and material production.[36] This discourse has also been echoed within conversations about "critical craft" approaches, where many scholars, practitioners, curators, and educators have discussed the ever-shifting identity of craft in contemporary culture, tied up with differing global definitions of craft, as well as changes in technology, globalization, ecological crisis, capitalism, colonialism, and more—as other publications in the *Critical Craft Studies* series illustrate.[37] For Adamson, craft now inhabits a "post-disciplinary" world where "no one activity has any more right to be called art than another" and practitioners are free to call themselves whatever they like or not to call themselves anything at all.[38]

These conversations are fundamentally linked to identity and a sense of self. Choosing a label—such as artist, craftsperson, designer—or rejecting labels altogether can be a powerful act of self-definition. For some practitioners, adding "queer" as a prefix before their chosen term (such as "queer designer") emphasizes the role of queerness in their work and asserts their presence as the person who made it. However, others may resist this, fearing their work will be seen only through a queer lens, potentially leading to bias or even censorship. This is especially true for those in hostile environments where being open about their identity might risk personal safety. Not wanting to impose definitions, I use the terminology and pronouns each practitioner used at the time of publication. Recognizing that disciplinary and personal identities are fluid, while also respecting practitioners' self-identification, I adhere to the terminology and pronouns they used at the time of publication. I use the overarching term "practitioners" for the collective, avoiding potentially limiting discipline-specific terms.

## Materializing the Self

My expansive use of "craft" and "crafting" reflects how the featured practitioners often move beyond mere object creation, emphasizing craft's presence in daily life as a lived and embodied practice. It is important to note that craft offers a mode of thinking with and through materials and processes: "craft allows us to make what we need, not rely on what others make for us."[39] Craft is something so ubiquitous to all lives, but especially to queer lives, which depend on a sense of resourcefulness, a craftiness in both senses of the word—both cunning and inventive by approach and often moving through the world with a do-it-yourself approach. As lambert suggests, "there is a proposal to be made that craft is a way of looking and living that is learned through material or process specificities, but not contained by them."[40] The crafting inherent in queer life takes many forms, both physical and symbolic: from the threads of kinship that bind us together to the creation of objects that reflect our identities, including clothing, badges, banners, quilts, zines, and more. In *Crafted with Pride: Queer Craft and Activism in Contemporary Britain* (2023) I gathered contributions from activists, academics, archivists, curators, and practitioners. We argued that the democratizing power of craft fosters community, camaraderie, and repair, facilitating the sharing of knowledge, skills, and lived experiences through discussions of sociopolitical issues in Britain and its diaspora. In my article *Survival of the Knittest: Craft and Queer Feminist Worldmaking* (2022) I drew upon a range of objects and collections—from the NAMES Project AIDS Memorial Quilt to the Museum of Transology (MOT)—to forward the idea of queer craft as a process, and especially as a mode of survival.[41] While similar sentiments resonate throughout this book, its focus, unlike previous publications, centers primarily on material practices rather than material culture or "craftivism."

Craft objects are often defined by their intimate connection to the body, serving physical purposes, functions, and needs. Making is an inherently embodied experience, and the queer nature of many material practices in this book arises from this close relationship, sometimes even acknowledging the body itself as a material to be crafted. This bodily connection to craft is particularly salient within trans communities, and the book features several trans practitioners who use craft as a metaphor to explore the crafting of the body. In a short section in her book *Fray* called "queer handmaking," Bryan-Wilson acknowledges that "non-gender conforming folks like drag queens, drag kings, butch lesbians, and femmy fags (as well as transgendered folks who aim to pass "seamlessly," to invoke a sewing metaphor) have had to make their own clothes, significantly tailor garments, and invent body-altering modification."[42] While by no means exhaustive, such a long list reminds readers that we need to acknowledge the complex role that craft has for those who identify as trans—not just in the process of making craft objects, but as a way of being and as a mode of survival. This concept has been echoed by Vaccaro, who has outlined the affinities between textile art and the everyday process of "becoming" and "crafting identity" that trans life particularly necessitates, a process she refers to as the "felt configuration of the "handmade."[43] Approaching craft as a "theoretical process and method," she observes:

> Deploying ideas of craft—too frequently dismissed as low art, skilled labor, or 'women's work'—the handmade connects transgender to collective process and quotidian aesthetics. As the material is marginalized by discursive forms of legibility, the performative dimensions of craft privilege the politics of the hand, that which is worked on, and the sensory feelings and textures of crafting transgender identity.[44]

From this perspective, craft is fundamentally "a mode of knowing and doing objects and bodies," particularly for trans bodies.[45] It allows us to reflect on the materiality of the body and its sensual affects: "the felt labor and traces of making and unmaking identity and the performative doing of gender"—including (but not limited to) "wood, wool, skin, sweat, rubber, foam, cloth, and scar tissue."[46] Craft fundamentally makes identity "felt and legible."[47]

## *Overview and Structure*

With much at stake, I have designed this book with a range of audiences in mind, hoping that it will be both a useful pedagogical tool and a personal guide through which to navigate the spectrums of queerness, crafts, and queer crafts. It will be most relevant to scholars and students working in fields such as craft studies, art history, design, queer theory, and trans studies, as well as practitioners who may use it as a helpful resource book or a kind of studio companion. It may also interest curators who need an accompaniment to creative programming or a critical apparatus. More broadly, I hope it may offer both a source of creative inspiration and personal identification for members of the LGBTQ+ community. The book deliberately features a broad range of contemporary practitioners, from established and well-known names to more emerging practitioners, allowing for multiple perspectives and equity in visibility across career stages. Many chapters are especially grounded in oral history and personal reflections from the featured practitioners, drawn from interviews and archival research, and some long-standing professional relationships. This attempt to privilege communication through the natural grain of the community itself is a key methodological design that enables personal experience to shine through, avoiding taxonomizing the queer experience. Instead, it offers significant opportunities to debate and expand conceptions of queer crafts within academic discourses as they are lived through individuals and institutions. While many of the featured practitioners are from the United States, where conversations surrounding queer crafts have been most active, the book also aims to start generating wider conversations across other locales, featuring work by practitioners from China, Pakistan, Mexico, the Netherlands, and Australia, as well as those who are part of the Vietnamese and Nigerian diaspora. The intent was never to write a comprehensive compendium of contemporary queer crafts, itself a rather impossible task. Instead, I aim to *cruise* the corpus of contemporary queer crafts to find a selection of practitioners and scholars whose work, I believe, captures a diverse array of experiences and demonstrates how queerness might inform a critical, social, and political engagement with a range of craft practices. Naturally, there is much left to explore and share, whether by myself or others.

Given that craft is fundamentally shaped by the materials used, the book adopts a material-led structure. Each chapter delves into a distinct set of practices—textile, ceramic, wood, paper, metal, and glass—and examines the work of two contemporary practitioners. Here, the focus is on how these practitioners utilize these materials and techniques to explore queerness and intersectional identities. However, several practitioners have resisted confinement to a singular material or process. Except for Hamad Butt (featured in Chapter 6), all featured practitioners are living at the time of publication, and their practices continue to evolve. For example, LJ Roberts is best known for large-scale knitted works and is grouped under "textile," but they worked with paper and collage early in their career. Similarly, Antonius-Tín Bui is grouped under "paper" due to their interest in the cultural histories of paper, but they initially engaged with textiles and performance. Therefore, rather than focusing on their career-long practices, I have chosen to focus on specific aspects of their work that showcase the power of materiality. There are also shared themes and concepts that transcend material specificities. These broadly include worldmaking, subversion, crafting the body, craft as a form of archiving, healing through making, "sloppy" craft, the politics of visibility, joy as resistance, the erotic, and digital cultures, to name but a few key themes. Therefore, readers are encouraged to explore the chapters in any order, seeking their own connections and resonances.

The origins of many of the materials and processes I discuss in this book can be traced to prehistory, and their respective histories have been picked up by many scholars elsewhere. Given my focus on contemporary creative production, it is also essential to note that the intersections between craft and queerness are not an ahistorical phenomenon. Each chapter is often contextualized within a broader, historical, and theoretical framework that talks about the traditions of these materials and processes and how these practitioners are referencing or reinventing them as sites of queer possibility. Where relevant, I have included comprehensive footnotes that serve as both a series of thank you letters, acknowledging the contributions of numerous individuals across diverse fields, and as a resource for readers seeking to explore specific aspects of queer crafts in greater detail.

Recognizing that the book potentially has a wide-ranging readership, there is a two-part glossary at the back. The first includes terms used concerning LGBTQ+ identities and communities at the time of publication, including those mentioned in the book. These terms are highly subjective, vary across cultures, and are continuously contested, re-evaluated, and added to over time. The terminology will likely be outdated when these words go to print and again by the time you read this. Therefore, it is essential to note that the interpretations offered here are not definitive. The second part of the glossary contains a series of basic technical terms associated with each material practice featured within this book. Again, these are not exhaustive, but they are intended to give non-specialist readers a better insight into the materiality and technical processes behind the works featured herein.

## *Chapter Summaries*

Chapter 1 focuses on the textile works of American artist LJ Roberts and Australian artist Paul Yore. Historically relegated, and as material processes that are perhaps most ripe for being worked and reworked, textiles seem to offer particularly fertile ground in which to queer imagery and materials. As works by both Roberts and Yore demonstrate, textiles are fitting for exploring the "open *mesh* of possibilities, gaps, overlaps, dissonances and resonances, lapses and excess of meaning" concerning gender and sexuality.[48] This chapter relates to ideas of queer worldmaking, including its intersections with nomadism, gentrification, and colonialism.

Although trans, non-binary, and gender nonconforming practitioners are represented throughout the book, Chapter 2 specifically explores how trans practitioners have seen affinities between their own identity and the physical process of "transition" that happens while creating ceramics. This includes the molding and sculpting of the clay as analogous to the crafting of the body and the high-pressure and extreme conditions the clay endures in the kiln as analogous to the resilience of trans communities thriving in a hostile society. As art historian and craft scholar Jenni Sorkin notes, "clay is key to rendering the body metaphorically, but also [to] create a morphology of form itself, that, is revising and re-shaping form."[49] The chapter focuses on the work of Dutch ceramicist Rose Schmits and the American artist Nicki Green, who primarily work with clay. Both practitioners use vessels to stand in for transgender bodies and comment on how they can grow, change, and be sculpted into the maker's desired shape and form. More than this, Green and Schmits create work that aims to document the trans experience, so this chapter specifically looks at the role of craft as a form of archiving.

Chapter 3 explores queer woodworking, specifically focusing on how contemporary practitioners have explored techniques traditionally associated with furniture making. Queer bodies, through their failure to reproduce norms, certainly do not easily (or comfortably) "fit" into heteronormative spaces, which are often hostile and unwelcoming. These notions of queer (dis)comfort are reflected in works by Mexican sculptor Raul De Lara and American-Nigerian designer of "functional sculptures" Nifemi Ogunro.[50] This chapter explores how they use pre-industrial furniture techniques to investigate how furniture can operate as orientation devices.

Reflecting on queer theorist Sara Ahmed's assumptions that "[p]aper matters . . . [p]aper can also be queer; paper can be used queerly," Chapter 4 focuses on the queer use of paper, using the collage works of American artist Troy Montes-Michie and the papercut works of Vietnamese-American "shapeshifter" Antonius-Tín Bui as sites for analysis.[51] I concentrate on Troy Montes-Michie's appropriation of printed pornographic ephemera in woven paper works and large-scale collages. These works utilize found materials to disrupt the gaze and explore shifting narratives of identity relating to ethnicity, race, gender, class, and sexuality. Bui's papercut works are large-scale and labor-intensive portraits of their biological and chosen families. Bui deconstructs the whiteness of paper through their reductive cutting process, metaphorically carving out space for the narratives so often omitted from history. The chapter reflects on the deconstructive logic of paper cutting and collage, centering on an endless dismantling and reconfiguring, a dually destructive-creative act of unmaking-making. Although the deconstructive process of paper cutting and collage might therefore be seen as one of aggression (to rip, to tear, to cut)—I focus on how the act of reconfiguring (to piece together, to glue, to make new) can also be both reparative and therapeutic.

In Chapter 5, I turn to the work of Chinese jeweler Hansel Tai and the wearable "queer armor" produced by the company Affect Metals, founded by LA-based metalworker Abe Heath. Metal symbolizes permanence, strength, and support, unlike textiles, clay, wood, or paper, which can be reworked and deconstructed at will. It is often associated with weaponry and protective gear, but it can equally be refined and delicate when used in jewelry making. Both Affect Metals and Tai experiment with metal's function and inherent tensions between its use as protection and a glamorous form of luxury and camp adornment. Central to discussions in this chapter are themes of the erotic and crafting fetish.

Chapter 6 looks at two contemporary practitioners who explore the different properties of glass to comment upon the fragility of the body, namely ideas of corporeality and containment, and explore biological processes to intervene with medical epistemologies. Firstly, I present the work of American glass sculptor Tim Tate. The same year as starting a degree at Penland School of Craft in 1989, Tate was diagnosed as HIV+. Since then, his glass works reflect how his life changed because of this diagnosis. Secondly, I discuss the work of British-Pakistani artist Hamad Butt. Butt is the only person featured in this collection who is sadly no longer living, but his work is often an important touchstone for many scholars and practitioners working on queer glass. Like the discussion of Tate's work, an examination of Butt's remaining archive will be central to this discussion. I will predominantly focus on the *Familiars* (1992) series, which was created during the same period his health began to worsen from HIV/AIDS. This serves as an important reminder of this work as a form of "at-risk" history, indicating the urgent need to document and archive these practices so their legacy lives on and that their work can continue to enthuse and inspire a future generation of practitioners.

Taken together, these chapters form a meaningful *patchwork* of identities and communities, as articulated, felt, and made material through a range of crafted objects. Patchwork is an apt metaphor for compiling this book: a way of making something whole out of previously disconnected fragments, born out of material necessity and urgency. In sewing this patchwork together, I aim to assemble a field and provide a platform from which those engaged with the study, practice, and preservation of queer crafts might build upon. The resulting patchwork is bright and colorful, capturing the spirit, beauty, and diversity of the field, and I hope it provides a source of comfort and warmth for many. This process of patching also emphasizes the multifaceted use of craft in queer culture, echoing how queer subjectivities are often formed out of an eclectic array, or patchwork, of (sub)cultural references and reworkings of dominant cultural representations. The book finishes with Chapter 6 and offers no formal conclusion. This was a deliberate choice and perhaps a queer one. I do not wish to tie off the threads here; they remain loose and unfixed. There is scope for the patchwork I lay out here to be added to or even for its patches to be unpicked and rearranged in different variations. The examples that follow serve as templates for developing and exploring new approaches to understanding and undertaking the represented craft practices, rather than a final word on the subject. This book is not the end but rather the beginning of what I hope will be a very long and generative dialogue that will enable a broader appreciation for the production, reception, and preservation of queer crafts.

# Chapter 1

## TEXTILE

### THREADS OF KINSHIP: QUEER WORLDMAKING AND CRAFTING COMMUNITY

*Introduction*

Textiles are woven into the very fabric of society. We sit on textiles, lie on them, and wrap, cover, or adorn our bodies with them. In the English language, the idiom *social fabric* is even used to describe the interweaving of people and systems—the common threads that connect us. The material and metaphoric qualities of textiles can provoke a range of feelings—they can be comforting, intimate, nostalgic, melancholic, erotic, and much more.[1] Because of the ubiquity of textiles in daily life, their connections with forms of worldmaking, and their affective potential, textiles remain a valuable form of creative expression. Textile crafts encompass many practices that involve working with natural or synthetic fibers. In studio crafts, the broader umbrella of "textiles" is primarily divided into a series of process-specific categories such as weaving, patchworking, braiding, binding, and stuffing, as well as a host of practices commonly grouped under the equally broad classification of "needlework," encompassing sewing, needlepoint, knitting, crochet, macramé, embroidery, and more. Of course, many textile practitioners now move nimbly between and beyond these categories, defying neat categorization.

As the Introduction acknowledges, textiles have historically been considered "low" forms of making in much of Europe and North America compared to so-called "high" art such as painting. Textiles, in particular, were largely gendered as "feminine" crafts carried out within the home, thus associated with the "passive" and the "private."[2] However, there is now potential to unpick these falsely constructed binaries, showing how textiles can be "active" just as much as "passive," and "public" just as much as "private." In an updated introduction to the 2010 reprint of *The Subversive Stitch,* Parker observes that since she first published her book in 1984, there has now been a "cross-pollination of arts and crafts" that require further examination.[3] Literary scholar Amy E. Elkins has also called for a more inclusive understanding of craft—one that moves beyond its traditional association with "housewives and white feminists" and recognizes "its global, collaborative, and *queer* networks."[4] This perspective is shared by McBrinn, who also advocates for a "queering" of textile history.[5] While the study of textiles and the position of women within society is long-standing, such a link between textiles and queerness remains a relatively unexplored area in academic scholarship. Yet, as highly gendered materials and physical processes that offer malleability, flexibility, and decorative potential, textiles seem to provide the most immediate possibilities for queer work. This chapter addresses these omissions, showcasing the crucial synergies between queerness and textiles in creative expression, daily life, and activism.

Recently, there has been a growing public and academic interest in textile crafts. This has led to a resurgence of interest in textile techniques as well as a renewed appreciation for the history and cultural significance of textiles in queer culture more broadly. Central to this discussion is the role of "craftivism" (a term combining "craft" and "activism"), which describes a mode of crafting especially motivated by social or political activism.[6] Textiles are inseparable from a history of rebellion and resistance; from customized and handmade clothing, protest banners, community quilts, and the coming together via dedicated craft collectives, there is a rich history of textiles and its intersections with LGBTQ+ activism.[7] As a result of this, textiles have become the most visible in the arena of queer crafts, and there has recently been a wide range of cultural programming foregrounding the work of LGBTQ+ practitioners working with textiles. One of the first and largest public exhibitions of queer textiles to date was *Queer Threads: Crafting Identity and Community*, which initially took place at the Leslie Lohman Museum in New York in 2014. It has since toured across the United States in different variations, accompanied by a range of public programming and an illustrated catalog.[8] The exhibition was organized by independent curator John Chaich and his initial aim was to explore how contemporary artists engage with themes of queer identity through thread-based materials, techniques, and processes. This is mainly because in the 1960s, when textiles entered the language of late modernist and contemporary art in Europe and North America, they did so as radically feminist *and* often queer, tied to debates around both gender *and* sexuality—though the latter had largely been ignored.[9] For Chaich, the driving force behind *Queer Threads* was a simple question: "Why are so many queer artists drawn to working in fiber and textiles?"[10] Having used textiles in my practice for many years, this question was similar to my initial research into queer crafts. In the exhibition catalog, Chaich went as far as declaring that "craft has been long considered the queer stepchild of fine art."[11] But why so? What makes craft, especially textiles, inherently *queer*? In the exhibition handout, Chaich attempted to map out a response, stating:

> Loaded with gender connotations and power hierarchies, fiber and textile traditions [. . .] provide a fitting platform for examining tastes, roles, and relationships socialized within and around gay and lesbian culture. And thread—be it yarn or embroidery floss—parallels the potential for connectivity in our lives as same-gender-loving and gender-non-conforming peoples. Our commonalities may be as thick as a knot or as thin as a string. As individuals, we are strands; as communities we are interwoven. Both can be broken or braided.[12]

Because textiles are more open to being physically worked and reworked, they are especially ripe for queer practices that explore processes of crafting a community which, as Chaich notes, can ultimately be braided or broken. Chaich's statement provides a poignant metaphor to reflect upon concerning processes of queer worldmaking, a theme that is explicitly in this chapter but one which transcends specific material choices and broadly relates to many of the other works featured within this book. Queer worldmaking is about imagining the alternative possibilities that could exist outside of exclusionary ideologies, systems, and processes if cisgender and heterosexual identities were no longer privileged or regarded as "normal." Although the term "worldmaking" has been discussed for decades, the concept of "queer worldmaking" appeared within queer theory in the late 1990s and has largely been credited to the essay *Sex in Public* (1998) by queer theorists Lauren Berlant and Michael Warner. The aim of their text, Berlant and Warner argue, is to describe "the radical aspirations of queer culture building: not just a safe zone for queer sex but the changed possibilities of identity, intelligibility, publics, culture, and sex that appear when the heterosexual couple is no longer the referent or the privileged example of sexual culture."[13] The project of queer worldmaking is fundamentally a creative one—it encourages us to imagine, dream, and critically consider how sites of oppression and violence can be transformed into sites of resistance and safety, further calling for a steady engagement with multiple politics that eventually espouse a world that sustains not on structure, but instead on endless possibilities and re-configurations.

This chapter specifically focuses on the work of LJ Roberts and Paul Yore, both of whom explore ideas of queer worldmaking through knitted, stitched, woven, and quilted works. In their work, Roberts and Yore celebrate intersectional queer communities, but they also ruminate on gentrification, colonial legacies, and the politics of crafting queer worlds—emphasizing how these worlds can be unpicked, unwoven, or cut, just as they can be interwoven, braided, and pieced together.

## *LJ Roberts (b.1980, USA)*

LJ Roberts explores queer-feminist politics through large-scale knitted installation works and intimate embroideries. They declare that the issues of marginality they encounter as a queer, gender nonconforming, and non-binary person mirror the historical position of textiles and craft within American visual culture.[14] Reflected at both a material and conceptual level of their practice, they seek to explore ideas of marginality *through* processes that have also been marginalized. In 2003, they created their first textile piece while studying at the University of Vermont. It was a hand-knit pink triangular banner that read "Mom Knows Now." The banner was dropped from the Steeple of the Ira Allen Chapel, where the act served as an act of coming out to their mother and as a homage to the activism of AIDS Coalition to Unleash Power (ACT UP), whose members often used forms of creativity and craft as tools for resistance.[15]

The pink triangle is an important symbol in queer visual culture, having been inverted and reclaimed by queer activists such as ACT UP in the 1980s as a source of strength from its origins as a Nazi concentration camp badge during the Second World War, where the downward-pointing triangle was primarily used to identify homosexual men.[16] *"Mom Knows Now"* marked the beginning of Roberts's investment in exploring themes of activism and queer worldmaking through textiles. This is perhaps best exemplified in their knitted work *The Queer Houses of Brooklyn in the Three Towns of Breukelen, Boswyck, and Midwout during the 41st Year of the Stonewall Era* (2011), which was exhibited as part of the first iteration of *Queer Threads* at the Leslie-Lohman Museum.[17]

*The Queer Houses of Brooklyn* (Figure 1.1) celebrates the crafting of alternative kinship structures. It takes the form of an abstract knitted map of Brooklyn, and the locations of twenty-four queer collective houses are marked by upward-pointing pink triangles, each adorned with a badge to represent its respective house name. The map is based on an original drawing by Roberts's close friend, Rosza Daniel Lang/Levitsky, which plots the locations of queer collective houses across Brooklyn between 2010 and 2011. Lang/Levitsky designed the map as part of Queer House Field Day, an event organized by Queers Organizing for Radical Unity and Mobilization (QuORUM) to make the local geographies of these houses visible and to connect them to the broader underlying colonial history and gentrification of Brooklyn; hence the Dutch names present within the work's title (*Breukelen, Boswyck, and Midwout*), highlighting the impact of European colonization and its lasting effects on the area today.[18]

The knitted map is often displayed in an installation setting, hung against a wall. The stuffed, knitted patches cascade down the wall and sprawl across the floor. At the end of the fringes is a sea of scattered badges designed by another collaborator and friend, Buzz Slutzky, which viewers can take home. This encourages a playful, queer form of participation where viewers must "go down" or "bend over" to receive the goods.[19] The participatory element also provides a homage to the work of queer artist Félix González-Torres (b.1957, Cuba – d.1996, USA), who is well-known for his use of multiples through works such as *Untitled (Portrait of Ross in L.A.)* from 1991, and whose work remains a personal source of identification and inspiration for Roberts.[20] Each of the twenty-four different badge designs by Slutzky corresponds to a house on Roberts's map and features its own characteristic name and symbol, which subvert traditional iconography associated with coats-of-arms and archaic heraldic devices. Rather than lions, crowns, and shields, there are vulvas, leather daddy devils, and pansies to illustrate respective house names: Le Pouse Palais, Den of Sin, and Pansy Commons, for instance.

Roberts' *The Queer Houses of Brooklyn* is ultimately crafted in a community made in collaboration with their queer kin, including Slutzky and Lang/Levitsky. The work and its collaborative construction emphasize how craft plays an essential part in many queer lives, that spaces, homes, and "chosen families" are all something that is crafted outside of the confines of cis-heteronormativity. Here, the term "house" is often used not to signify a physical site made from bricks

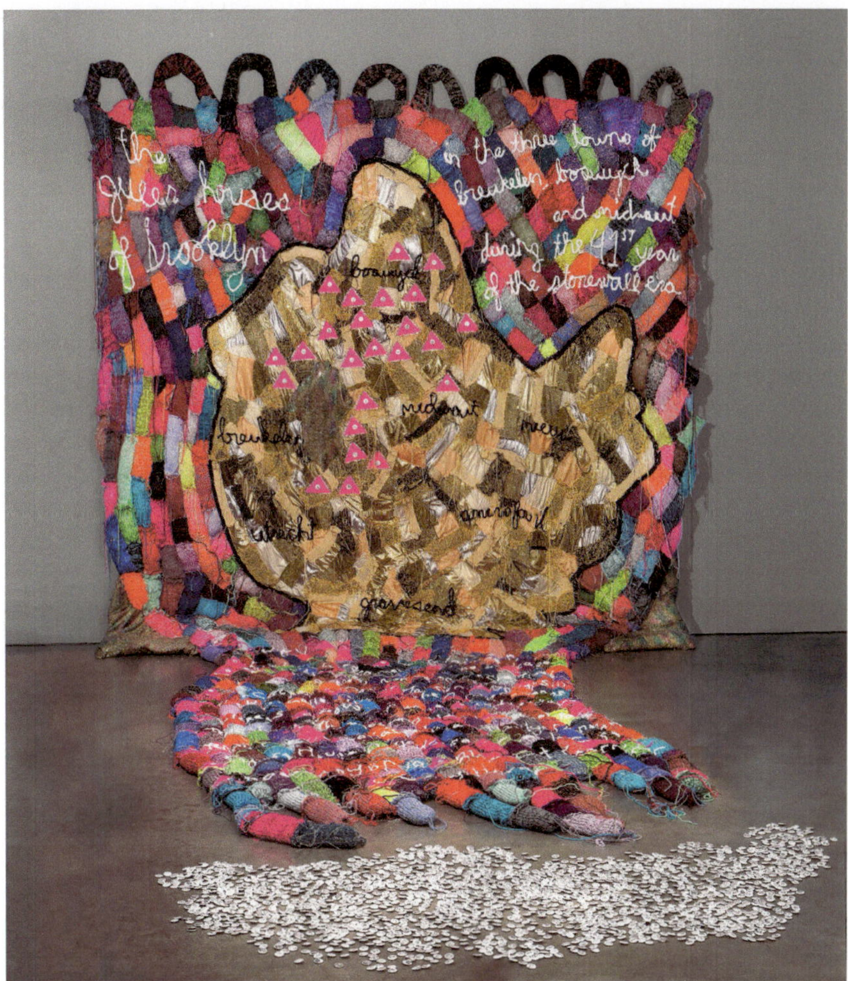

**Figure 1.1** LJ Roberts, *The Queer Houses of Brooklyn in the Three Towns of Breukelen, Boswyck, and Midwout during the 41st Year of the Stonewall Era*, 2011. Based on a 2010 drawing by Daniel Rosza Lang/Levitsky with twenty-four illustrations by Buzz Slutzky on printed pin-back buttons. Poly-fill, acrylic, rayon, Lurex, wool, polyester, cotton, lamé, sequins, and blended fabrics with printed pin-back buttons, 138 × 114 × 108 inches. Courtesy of the artist and the Smithsonian American Art Museum. Copyright LJ Roberts.

and mortar, but it is often used to describe a group or "chosen family," a form of familial worldmaking beyond the confines of biological reproduction and inheritance. The term is most used as part of the ballroom scene in the United States. This is a subculture that primarily consisted of queer African American and Latinx communities who found themselves ostracized in society and many of whom experienced overt forms of racism, transphobia, and violence, even among the drag queen pageant circuit. The origins of ballroom extend back to the late twentieth century, but the culture was widespread in the 1980s and is now an international phenomenon. These balls saw participants compete in various categories with events usually including "walking" (as in walking a fashion runway) or "voguing" (a highly stylized form of dance). Members often competed in their "houses," which functioned as alternative familial systems where people frequently lived together or supported one another, usually presided over by an older member of the community who would be referred to as the "house mother" or "house father." Writing from the position of a "queer femme, a housing organizer in New York City, and a founder of a queer home in Brooklyn," Katie Goldstein rightly notes that "home can be a fraught place for many queers."[21] They add: "[t]he act of creating queer homes redefines what home is and can be, and it challenges the invisibilisation and marginalisation of queer community."[22] In Goldstein's view, "[c]reating queer homes puts a queer mark on a non-queer landscape and, through that act, demands that queerness be recognized as an identity that must be seen."[23] Roberts's work, therefore, quite literally enacts this process of making queer homes visible, using the iconic symbol of the pink triangle to put a queer mark on a non-queer landscape and show how these communities and homes are crafted.

To make the work, Roberts revealed that they utilized a wide range of methods and techniques such as a bright pink toy Barbie knitting machine ("Barbie Knit Magic"), single-strand hand embroidery, a small sock-making machine, quilting, and forms of appliqué. Roberts notes that as a queer person who struggled with being raised in a conservative suburb just outside of Detroit, textiles have been a pertinent material through which to work through such ideas. The use of highly gendered objects, such as the Barbie knitting machine, to create works that celebrate life and structures outside of the gender binary acts as a further queering of textile practice. Most of these textile methods, tools, and techniques are portable, accessible, and can adapt to various circumstances, which Roberts confesses "is also how I aim to move through life."[24] The likes of crochet, knitting, and embroidery can all be worked upon outside a private space, such as a studio, and carried out in public, such as at a picket line or protest. For over a decade, Roberts has crafted *Portraits* (2011–), a series of incredibly intricate 4" × 6" single-strand embroideries depicting their chosen family. These intimate works, often stitched on the subway, are then nestled into their tote bag, symbolically carrying their chosen family with them as they move through life, and cradling them close to their body.[25] Speaking about the portraits, Roberts notes: "[t]he embroideries are a ten-year record of my friendships and relationships, the politics that marked the decade, the fun I had with friends, the everyday action and resistance that these people practice, those who influence and inspire me, the elders who have mentored me, people who have collaborated with me."[26] Roberts sees these portraits as a way of dismantling the heteronormative tendencies of portraiture, and the choice of thread (as opposed to paint), complete with its metaphors of connectivity, is integral to this.[27] Further, the portraits are often intentionally exhibited with both sides visible, contrary to traditional embroideries which are often framed or displayed in embroidery hoops to conceal the reverse. Celebrating the unadorned surface on the back of the work emphasizes how the "snags" or "imperfections" are often just as significant in queer life as the "polished" side and play a key role in the making of the self—queer life is not always "straight" or "neat" but marked by mess and disarray as we struggle against the status quo. In *The Queer Houses of Brooklyn,* threads dangle from the surface of the work, and the stitching is equally visible. *The Queer Houses of Brooklyn* is, therefore, particularly fitting for such a commentary, serving as a metaphor to express how queer people often *craft* the houses they are "born" into. The piece is also assembled, patched, and unites a variety of individual knitted pieces, which can be seen as a poetic metaphor for the politics of queer community building.

Roberts explains that the large-scale of *The Queer Houses of Brooklyn* and its patchworked nature directly references The NAMES Project AIDS Memorial Quilt, which greatly inspired them when they were coming to terms with their gender and sexual identity as a teenager (Figure 1.2). At the age of fifteen, they were the only student who opted to attend a school field trip to see the Quilt displayed in its entirety on the Washington Mall. "It was the first time I had seen a queer collection of symbols…seeing rainbow flags and pink triangles and a lot of love expressed was a really profound thing," Roberts recalled.[28] The AIDS Quilt, as it is more commonly known, was initiated on November 27, 1985, by the activist Cleve Jones at an annual candlelight vigil in the Castro District of San Francisco to mourn the murder of Harvey Milk, the first openly gay man to be elected to public office in California.[29] Given the increasing numbers of people dying in the District, Jones and his friend, Joseph Durant, handed out blank placards and marker pens so that attendees could inscribe these with the names of their kin who had died from AIDS-related illnesses.[30] Rather than discarding the placards after the vigil had ended, demonstrators began to stack their boards against the walls of the San Francisco Federal Building as a symbol of resistance against President Reagan's administration and its lack of action surrounding HIV/AIDS. Jones recalled an epiphany in front of the growing patchwork of names: "[s]tanding in the drizzle, watching as the posters absorbed the rain and fluttered down to the pavement, I said to myself, It looks like a quilt. As I said the word quilt, I was flooded with memories of home and family and the warmth of a quilt."[31] Quilts are primarily associated with milestones in cis-heteronormative culture—birth, marriage, and death—and they are typically passed down through generations of biological family members, usually through matrilineality. By creating a memorial through the medium of quilting, Jones seemed to make a statement that notions of warmth, care, and compassion (which we would ordinarily associate with a quilt) were so far removed from how society was responding to LGBTQ+ people with HIV/AIDS at the time. Instead of receiving a warm embrace or being wrapped in a comforting quilt, these people were primarily left to die in hospital corridors, were cast off by their biological families, and even thrown out of their apartments by landlords.

Since its inception, the project has been dedicated to a wide range of individuals who have died of AIDS-related causes, inviting people to create their own textile memorial panels. Some of the panels are made by biological family members, but my archival research revealed that it was more often people's chosen families, friends, neighbors, colleagues, and general acquaintances who more often provided

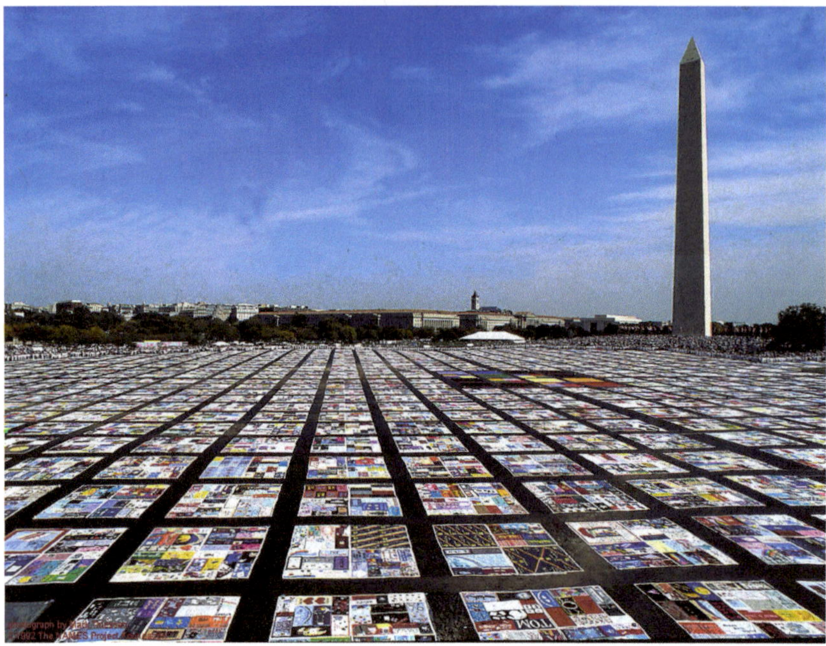

**Figure 1.2** The NAMES Project AIDS Memorial Quilt in front of the Washington Monument. Courtesy of National Institutes of Health.

a dedication—usually in the knowledge that the individual's biological family would not recognize their sexuality, let alone come to terms with their diagnosis or craft a quilt panel to commemorate them.[32] More harrowing, some people crafted a panel to memorialize themselves, and others have surnames cut out or censored with an extra layer of fabric. For instance, one panel reads: "My name is Duane Kearns Puryear. I was born on December 20, 1964. I was diagnosed with AIDS on September 7, 1987 at 4:45pm. I was 22 years old. Sometimes, it makes me very sad. I made this panel myself. If you are reading it, I am dead…."[33]

Although referred to as a "quilt," the AIDS Quilt does not follow the formal logic of quilting, which, by definition, is two layers of fabric with a layer of wadding or batting between them. Instead, most panels are only a single layer of fabric, and all manner of objects are sutured onto the quilt, including clothing, teddy bears, photographs, vinyl records, and even cremation ashes. The quilt is an ongoing project, and at the time of writing, it is the largest community art project in the world, estimated to consist of over 48,000 individual memorial panels.[34] Although there are no formal requirements, the foundation suggested that each panel measures 3 ft × 6 ft, the average size of a human grave.[35] Eight of these panels are then sewn together by the Foundation to create a 12 ft × 12 ft "block" primarily to make the quilt easier to store and categorize. Although the blocks could be shown independently, each panel would therefore never be shown alone; the intention is "to see each name—each life—not as isolated, but as ensconced in a 'visual dialogue'" with one another, even after death.[36] The interdependency of the blocks is, therefore, vital to how the AIDS Quilt operates on a formal level. The fact that the names are memorialized in transitory textiles instead of being etched permanently in stone is also crucial; "cloth fade frays with time; its fragility, its constant need for mending, tell the truth about 'material' life."[37] This sense of community building, textile activism, and remembrance is echoed in the patchworked nature of *The Queer Houses of Brooklyn*. Here, Roberts unites many disparate sections together through the reparative stitch. Like the AIDS Quilt, the use of thread parallels the potential for connectivity. It signals how craft can operate as a form of healing and catharsis, a mode of coming together and processing grief, and a unifying tie, the stitches that bind us. To be bound together as a community is to build emotional, social, cultural, political, and spiritual ties that we don't always "see"; these facets are often just as important in worldmaking as considering physical space.

Although Roberts's works effectively map queer worlds and communities, the notion of the queer world as ever-changing must not go unacknowledged, particularly given that many of the collective houses the work illustrates have since disbanded or have had to relocate to new apartments because of rising rents and the continued gentrification of queer spaces since the early 1980s. This has been echoed and evidenced by many scholars. For example, *The Gentrification of the Mind* (2012), by American novelist and playwright Sarah Schulman, charts the intense gentrification that New York faced from 1981 to 1996 when the AIDS epidemic swept through the city. In the book, Schulman names the most gentrified neighborhoods in Manhattan (East Village, West Village, the Lower East Side, Harlem, and Chelsea) and compares them to the findings of a report on the social impact of AIDS published in 1993 by the National Research Council, which recorded that Manhattan's highest rates of infection were also in these areas.[38] The horrific reality was that the sheer number of AIDS-related deaths meant that there was a drastic turnover of apartments, particularly given the fact that people's partners or kin often had no legal right to these residences. Rebellious queer culture and a vibrant underground arts scene were annihilated—apartments were sold off and replaced by a predominantly White, middle-class cohort. This is a crucial point; for Schulman, gentrification has a dual referent. While she explains that gentrification is a literal "concrete replacement process" in which communities are displaced, she also suggests that it is simultaneously a process of spiritual gentrification, an "internal replacement that alienated people from the concrete process of social and artistic change"—essentially a destruction of queer space, collectivity, and creativity.[39] Many members of the LGBTQ+ community therefore flocked toward cheaper areas of inner cities, such as Williamsburg in Brooklyn, which had more affordable rents and an emerging queer culture, which Roberts's map depicts. Although this did give rise to new opportunities for social and cultural connectivity, scholars such as Goldstein have written first-hand accounts that demonstrate how gentrification is still rife within these neighborhoods in Brooklyn, causing an ever-increasing divide between social classes and posing a threat to many queer communities.

The queer world must therefore be thought of as a transient space that is not locatable by a fixed concept of "home." Instead, it is more accurately a complex web of "entrances, exits, unsystematised lines of acquaintance, projected horizons, typifying examples, alternate routes, blockages, [and] incommensurate geographies."[40] In this sense, queer spaces are almost always acts of appropriation, a process of "queering" that involves a calculated repurposing of existing typologies of building and a (re)claiming of space that offer new ways of thinking, living, loving, and belonging. As historian George Chauncey suggests, there is "no queer space"; there are only spaces "put to queer uses."[41] These structures become queer only in the sense that they are activated, inhabited, and transformed for queer purposes by queer-identifying individuals. *The Queer Houses of Brooklyn*, completed in 2011, therefore marks a specific snapshot in time when queer individuals could afford to live in closer proximity to one another. Looking at the work retrospectively, the loose threads that dangle down from each of the knitted sections seem to foretell the fate of many of these communities that have since come undone and no longer exist as gentrification remains rife in the area and rent prices continue to rise, meaning that queer culture and community continues to be decimated. Although the queer houses of Brooklyn continue to "live on" through the endless supply of badges supplied with the work, the textile materials and techniques Roberts uses are "malleable and ever-changing," and therefore convey how queer worldmaking is also always "fragile" and certainly "ephemeral."[42]

Queer worldmaking is often conceptualized as a broader cultural project, a way of critiquing and imagining wider systems of connectivity beyond fixed sites. As spaces in which queer people gather, create kinships, mobilize, and build worlds, are always in flux, then that demands a certain degree of inventiveness, of being "crafty"—both cunning and creative. After all, Berlant and Warner suggest that queer worlds exist in the form of *counterpublics*—fleeting worlds that consciously subordinate the dominant public sphere, including through music, dance, cruising sites, and drag, not just physical spaces. In some cases, queer space becomes a complete rejection of these typologies—refuting the idea that queer space is determined by a building or fixed site altogether. At the time of writing, Roberts recently completed a large-scale work titled *VanDykesTransDykesTransVa nTransGrandmxDykesTransAmDentalDamDamn* (Figure 1.3), which they began constructing in 2014 and finally completed in 2020. They describe the work as a "fiber collage of a post-apocalyptic speculative conversion van" which meditates on the promises and problematics of queer worldmaking and alternative kinship structures that exist beyond a fixed or locatable concept of "home."[43] Like *The Queer Houses of Brooklyn*, this work also reflects upon the transitory nature of queer spaces by continuing to ruminate on both the promises and problems of crafting these systems. Within the work, Roberts pays homage to pioneering feminist, lesbian, queer, and transgender histories and themes of nomadism, landlessness, movement, and identity by drawing influence from the so-called conversion van culture. Alongside their colorful use of textiles, Roberts includes LED lights and uses other materials, such as shoelaces, leather, zippers, and metal studs, as a nod

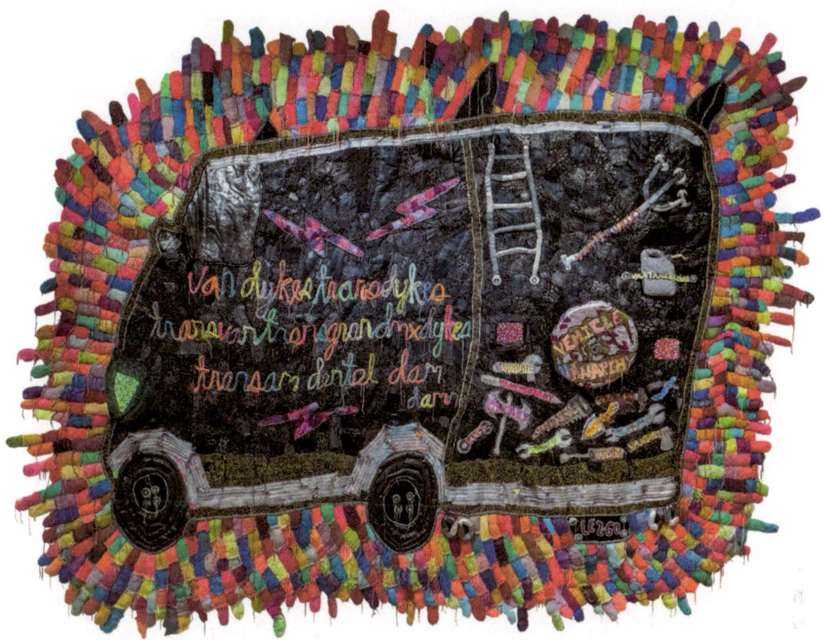



**Figure 1.3** LJ Roberts, *VanDykesTransDykesTransVanTransGrandmxDykesTransAmDenta lDamDamn,* 2014–2020. Yarn, leather, lace, upcycled bike inner tubes, metal studs, zippers, shoelaces, Lite Brites, lurex, thread, spray paint, 168 × 240 inches. Courtesy of LJ Roberts. Courtesy the artist and Hales, London and New York. Photo by Madhouse Creative. Copyright LJ Roberts.

towards the iconography associated with these queer subcultures. The work was inspired by a 2009 article by Ariel Levy which appeared in *The New Yorker* and discussed the Van Dykes: a lesbian "van gang" that traversed North America in the late 1970s.[44] The Van Dykes were founded by Heather Elizabeth and Ange Spalding in 1977 and quickly grew to become a much larger collective of lesbian separatists and non-monogamous women, all of whom took on the surname Van Dyke.[45] Living life together on the road, the group was totally "devoted to living in an alternate, penisless reality" and would only stop at outposts of Women's Land over the United States and Canada.[46] These were places that were owned by women, and where only women would be welcome—so much so that they were more commonly referred to as "wimmin's land" or "womyns land" in an attempt to "keep men out of their words as well as their worlds."[47] As Levy (2009) suggests, their attitude was: "Why capitulate, why compromise, when you could separate, live in a world of your own invention?"[48]

These traditions continue today but are far less separatist, with many queer and trans people reviving the transient and creative culture of these van gangs to craft more inclusive and communal traveling kinships. As Roberts states, despite drawing influence from these cultures of worldmaking, it is "important to remember that 'feminist' spaces can create margins, whether [they are] excluding trans people or people of color."[49] Examples of contemporary van gangs are documented in zines such as *Vanifesto* (2011), produced by Damien Luxe, which even contains an instructional guide and a list of recommendations of places to purchase vans, receive customized "body work," and suggest DIY (do-it-yourself) customizations such as "exxxtra plush seating" for the bed-cum-bench area: echoing the idea that just as the vans can be customized, so can we.[50] The culture has extended far beyond just a process of living or loving otherwise but has become an entire way of life. For example, the Heels on Wheels Glitter Roadshow is a "dazzling cabaret of performance art works by queer folks on femme/inine spectrum genders" that tours the United States annually to re-vision ideas of what "thriving and surviving as femme folks can be."[51] These collectives show how ideas of domesticity can be untethered from a fixed position, allowing for new relationalities to be constructed. Roberts celebrates the queer-feminist legacy of nomadic worldmaking but critically considers its current relevance to communities that have also had to use resourcefulness and imagination to craft alternative ways of living and being. Given the time it took to construct the piece, Roberts's work has also traveled with them across the country, from various residencies to house moves. Roberts revealed that a family of scorpions once took refuge within the work when there were significant forest fires near where they completed another residency, and their two dogs—Ziggy and Sparky—even loved to use the padded knitting as beds on many occasions. Roberts also talks about how dirty the textiles get because they are continuously transported with them and used by humans and non-humans alike: "[t]here is always a ring of dirt, of detritus…my embroideries have stains, subway grime, pet hair, and my blood on them…I accept and embrace that grime. It's part of the story, the practice."[52] The work itself becomes a repository of hidden histories and is a testament to the themes of queer worldmaking that it reflects, carrying the material memory of the sense of community embedded in its very fibers, including the smells, stains, textures, and traces of everyday life.

In short, Roberts's experience in the world "requires flexibility, adaptability, resilience, and resourcefulness," and this is reflected at the very level of their material choices, which are accessible, portable, and malleable.[53] Their work serves as an important reminder of the role that crafting has for many members of the queer community—beyond heteronormative and cisnormative concepts of home and family. In addition to the role of crafting spaces and communities, which Roberts's work exemplifies, Berlant and Warner also highlight how making a queer world has required the "development of kinds of intimacy that bear no necessary relation to domestic space, to kinship, to the couple form, to property, or to the nation."[54] This is particularly evident in the work of Paul Yore, who uses textiles to move beyond a process of mapping existing spaces and communities, and towards an entire process of imagining new utopian queer worlds.

## *Paul Yore (b.1988, Australia)*

Born and raised in Naarm/Melbourne and currently living and working on stolen unceded Gunaikurnai land, Paul Yore explores queer worldmaking and its intersections with colonial resistance using needlepoint, appliqué, cross-stitching, tapestry, and soft sculpture. However, Yore describes all his work as quilting: "[m]y textile works are essentially quilts comprising many thousands of individual fragments of fabric which are laboriously hand-sewn together. This is a very traditional methodology taken to extreme ends."[55] He acknowledges the radical potential of textiles and, like Roberts, has also referenced the AIDS Quilt and other activist quilting projects because they embody ideas of community, memory, and resistance.

Yore recalls developing an interest in textiles from an early age. However, the rigid art/craft divide in the educational system shaped his experience differently. He reflects on how his sister, attending an all-girls school, was required to study embroidery, while he, at an all-boys school, was made to study woodwork. They often joked that each would have preferred the other's discipline.[56] Yore began working with textiles around 2010 during a period of involuntary hospitalization in a psychiatric facility. While confined to his bed and gradually reducing his reliance on heavy medications prescribed to "treat" his mental health, he taught himself needlepoint—a practice that became both a creative outlet and a form of personal resilience.[57] From the beginning, Yore's work has been about survival and speaking out against oppressive systems. He has shown a commitment to the textile traditions of handiwork and often delights in the slow and meditative process that working with textiles offers. However, these techniques, historically associated with idle crafting on laps, are transformed into a chaotic and transgressive method. His work is characterized by its vibrant colors, intricate patterns, large-scale, bricolage-like approach, and bold use of text, often playfully exploring the relationship between text and textile, which both originate from the Latin word "texere" meaning "to weave," echoing how we weave our words just as we weave textiles. Many of Yore's works utilize the visual language of landscapes, maps, and cartographic representations of his home country. However, describing them as landscapes, maps, or cartographic representations is a major disservice. They are, perhaps more accurately, psychedelic queer worlds that critique the current status quo and imagine new utopian futures.

These concepts were echoed in Yore's 2022 exhibition titled *WORD MADE FLESH* at the Australian Centre for Contemporary Art, for which I wrote interpretation material and a catalog entry.[58] The exhibition was structured as an early career survey, bringing together work from a roughly 15-year period of production and featuring over 100 textile pieces. One of the displays was titled "Horizon" and grouped several of Yore's works exploring worldmaking themes. Stepping into the room of the gallery felt like being Dorothy in *The Wizard of Oz*: "I've a feeling we're not in Kansas anymore." Instead of a classical rural idyll or traditional painting of a horizon, as one may expect from the room title, the room hosted several large-scale quilts in various shapes and sizes. Several of the quilts, such as *The Rule of Lore* (2021) and *Picnic at Hanging Rock* (2021), also took the form of triangles, which might be read as a subtle critique of the ubiquity of the rectangle as the default form through which we understand pictorial representation and the format in which historic colonial paintings emerge (as with Ruga's work briefly mentioned in the Preface). However, while Yore certainly refuses to conform to the "straightness" of the rectangle, he also uses the format of the triangle to reference the queer history of the pink triangle. This symbol is repeated throughout his oeuvre, much like the work of Roberts.[59] The multi-layered nature of the work, featuring bulging textiles and unhemmed edges, also eschews straightness. All of Yore's quilts have a base layer (often a heavy blanket) that is then layered upon using sewing, cross stitching, and forms of patchwork, providing the ground upon which he builds his sprawling worlds. Second-hand bedspreads, blankets, clothes, tea towels, and other fabric remnants are most frequently used, with patterns and images being cut and torn from their original surface before being transplanted onto Yore's quilts. These materials are hastily applied to the surface, and often, "anomalies, slippages, and decisions made through necessity can be really vital parts of the creative process," Yore attests.[60]

In the work *Heads Are Spinning* (2015) we see an imaginary landscape that Yore calls "Faggot Land" (Figure 1.4). Here, the viewer sees a world in which rainbows shine, various members of the now-disbanded pop group One Direction run about guzzling semen, police are either dead or beheaded, and the two queer-coded Muppets, Bert and Ernie, live out their lives in blissful harmony. There is no denying that the quilts are often homoerotic (or "homo-erratic," a term Yore prefers). These works enact what queer theorist José Esteban Muñoz terms a form of "utopian performativity" which can signal "another modality of doing and being that is in process, unfinished."[61] After all, Muñoz reminds us, queerness itself "is a structuring and educated mode of desiring that allows us to see and feel beyond the quagmire of the present."[62]

Muñoz has explored concepts of queer futurity, worldmaking, and utopian performativity at length; essentially, the idea that queerness is not simply a fixed identity or set of experiences in the present but rather a potentiality for a different way of being in the world that is always in the process of becoming and connected to both past and present. In *Cruising Utopia: The Then and There of Queer Futurity* (2009), Muñoz draws on the work of Ernst Bloch, a German philosopher who argued that utopia is not a perfect future to be achieved but rather a *horizon* of possibility that guides our present actions and desires. He especially takes up this idea of the "horizon" and applies it to queerness, suggesting:

> Queerness is not yet here. Queerness is an ideality. Put another way, we are not yet queer. We may never touch queerness, but we can feel it as the warm illumination of a horizon imbued with potentiality. We have never been queer, yet queerness exists for us as an ideality that can be distilled from the past and used to imagine a future. The future is queerness's domain.[63]

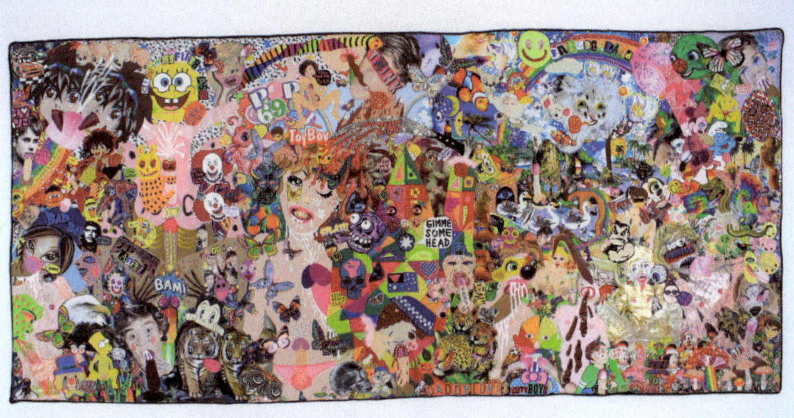

**Figure 1.4** Paul Yore, *Heads Are Spinning*, 2015. Mixed media textile appliqué comprising found materials, reclaimed fabrics, wool, beads, sequins, buttons, marker, acrylic paint, 74 × 157 inches. Courtesy of Paul Yore. Photo credit: Devon Ackermann.

Here, Muñoz likens queerness to a site of possibility, the "warm illumination of a horizon."[64] He articulates that this horizon is visible, but it is in the distance. Its warmth represents hope, a place where things can change for the better. However, work is still to be done; although we can feel its warmth, it is not quite "here" yet. This assertion provides a poignant metaphor for explorations of identity and queer worldmaking in Yore's work. He imagines spaces and places in which normative ideas of gender and sexual identity are disrupted, fragmented, and inherently "messy." The crown, the state, and the Church are all institutions of power and knowledge that Yore dismisses within his work. In their ruin, Yore builds a new queer world, or rather multiple queer worlds, where new ways of living, thriving, and desiring are made manifest, bringing this warm horizon ever closer. In this sense, Yore's work is not just about dreaming of a better future but also about the practices and performances that can help us bring that future into being. Muñoz also emphasizes the importance of joy, failure, and ephemerality as key elements of queer futurity. Joy, he argues, is a form of resistance against the negativity and violence that often surrounds queer life—a concept that reverberates throughout queer and feminist literature.[65]

Despite Yore imagining utopian visions through a playful, humorous approach to materials and subject matter, his visual rhetoric is no less political. Although the worlds that Yore crafts might seem joyful or frivolous at first glance, there is a much darker underbelly to many of these candy-colored imaginaries, which attack capitalist ideology and expose traumatic colonial histories, the ongoing effects of which are still felt by many communities today. In many other works on display, Yore appropriated and subverted the visual language associated with colonial landscape painting, such as in *The Darkest Secret of Your Heart* (2016). Looking beyond the bouncing kangaroos, plush koala bear, and appropriation

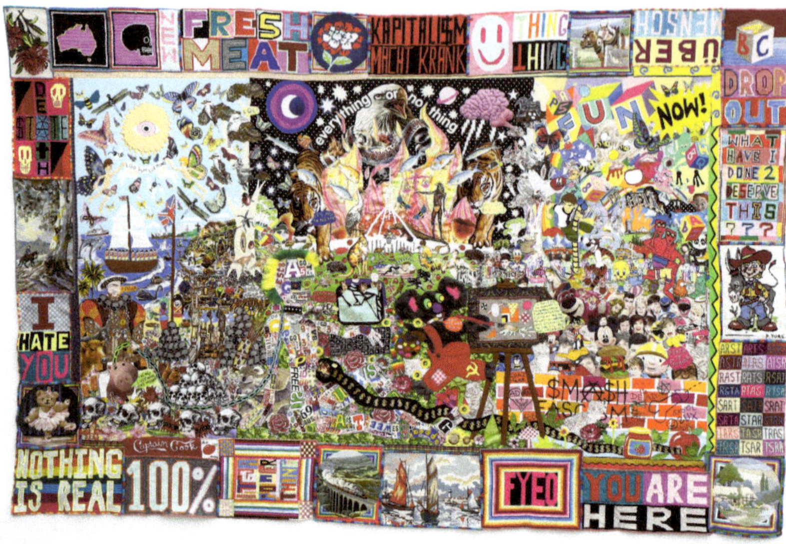

**Figure 1.5**  Paul Yore, *The Darkest Secret of Your Heart*, 2016. Mixed media textile appliqué comprising found objects, recycled fabric, sequins, beads, buttons, 94 × 153 inches. Courtesy of Paul Yore.

of cutesy cross-stitched pastoral scenes, viewers can see that in this quilt, Yore depicts the violent colonization of Australia at the hands of British forces, namely Captain Cook, whose name is appliquéd here in the style of the Coca Cola logo; simultaneously critiquing both colonialism and capitalism in one fell swoop (Figure 1.5). To the left of the work, in the background, we see these colonial forces arriving by boat. In the foreground, we see a massive pile of skulls and a long chain wielded by a fuzzy-felted King Henry VIII. The composition bears a striking resemblance to an 1865 engraving by Samuel Calvert (based on an original painting by John Alexander Gilfillan), which depicts a scene from 1770 in which Cook claimed sovereignty over the coast of Possession Island (known as Bedanug or Bedhan Lag in the Kalaw Lagaw Ya language) and oppressed the Indigenous Kaurareg people. British forces also began to impose many of Britain's strict moral codes as part of their colonizing missions. They introduced archaic anti-homosexuality laws across Australia and its colonies, such as the Buggery Act of 1533, which was first passed during the reign of King Henry VIII. The British Empire criminalized male-to-male relations in Australia, imposing the death penalty up until 1890 and life imprisonment after that until 1949. By using iconography associated with these histories, Yore brings attention to these histories and ongoing systematic violence against marginalized peoples (both Indigenous and queer), who are quite literally treated as trash, human waste, or "abject" by dominant social forces and using materials that are also designated as such.[66] The tactility of textiles implies sensuousness, a sense of warmth and intimacy embedded in the medium itself, which is often connected to the idea of the quilt as an object of comfort or safety. Yet, when combined with serious subject matter, this causes a somewhat jarring effect. By critiquing British colonialism with "softness," while also using trash and "low" pop cultural references, Yore thinks of his work as having a "disarming" effect, a way to connect with the viewer in a very direct and immediate way before revealing a darker, more serious narrative.[67] For him, this strategy is a "camp call to arms against the conservative pink-washing of mainstream gay 'politics' which has centered on same-sex marriage, and see the future of queerness as indistinguishable from the struggle against capitalism, colonialism, and ecological destruction."[68]

In physically recuperating society's cultural detritus and utilizing found objects in his work, Yore transforms this detritus of late capitalism into something sexy and glamorous, not as the pathetic and debased spectacle that it appears to be in the dominant eyes of heteronormative culture. Countless other works such as *Heads Are Spinning* (2015) imagine a queer alternative reality of sorts, erected from the wasteland of the Anthropocene, knowingly implicating themselves into the debased spectacle of mass society in a performative way. The use of found and waste materials here is based on a central critique of capitalism, imperialism, consumerism, and ecological upheaval. However, he establishes a parody, a camp *détournement* that recuperates the deprecated into a source of strength and identity. Despite its underlying sincerity, I would conceptualize Yore's work as a distinctly "camp" craft practice because of its interest in waste's convergences, alignments, and reverberations with the camp produced by sexual minorities as a form of "cross-generational, cross-cultural *recycling*."[69] While the influence of Susan Sontag's famous 1964 essay *Notes on Camp* means that camp is often associated with glamour and an ostentatious display of chic, associated with "decorative art [...] texture, sensuous surface, and style," I argue that there is an underside to it that has often gone unnoticed: camp's simultaneous investment in the discarded and rejected, the abject.[70] For sociologist Andrew Ross, camp is fundamentally a "rediscovery of history's waste," and he has persuasively argued that a "camp sensibility" occurs when products that have lost their power to produce and dominate cultural meanings "become available, in the present, for redefinition according to contemporary codes of taste."[71] While some scholars may see camp as being the opposite of sincerity, others suggest that camp aesthetics and the queer politics of "bad taste" are important bedfellows and have provided a valuable archive of camp's performative practices and its alliance with abjection. In conceptualizing camp as an "aesthetic phenomenon" which is "disengaged, depoliticized – or at least apolitical," Sontag effectively erased the binding referent from the subject of camp—the queer—thus allowing it to become "downplayed, sanitized, and made safe for public consumption."[72] In contrast, Yore's form of camp nurtures an attitude that pays attention to waste, sees waste as beautiful, exciting, and personal (even when it is simultaneously dangerous, disgusting, or industrial), and uses this as a vehicle through which to explore queer politics.[73] As Muñoz has suggested, "disidentification" is a particular mode of cultural production that operates by quite literally recycling damaged stereotypes into sources of power and self-creation, often employed by minoritarian subjects as a survival strategy.[74] His notion of recycling or "scrambling" the raw material of majoritarian culture to represent a positionality that has been "rendered unthinkable by the dominant culture" is evident at the very material level of Yore's work, which quite literally recycles materials as a way in which to recycle meaning.[75] Yore studied archaeology and anthropology as part of his Fine Arts degree at Monash University and sometimes describes himself as an "archaeologist" as opposed to an "artist" or "craftsperson" due to his rag-picking approach.[76] Through his use of materials and techniques, Yore crafts his system of value through an affective methodology of scavenging; one that values the broken, the worn down, the unloved, and the discarded.

A staunch traditionalist would argue that craft is solely defined by skilled making, all about becoming a "master" of one's craft. Yet, Yore has discussed how his work engages with forms of "sloppy craft." Although the term "sloppy" is usually associated with something careless, sloppy craft denotes an intentionally "messy" approach to making and is a particular hallmark of many queer textile practitioners. Many attest that this enables resistance to the commercialization and commodification of craft, questions hierarchies of taste, and challenges the archaic idea that craft should denote a form of "mastery" over material. In this sense, Yore and other self-disclosed sloppy crafters often see value in the "poorly done," the "trashy" and forms of "failure," at least by conventional standards of technique and social preconceptions—itself a rather camp approach. Coined in 2007 by Anne Wilson, an artist and educator at The Art Institute of Chicago, the term "sloppy craft" was developed in response to the purposefully "messy" techniques used by one of her students at the time, Josh Faught (b.1979, USA).[77] In Faught's woven textile works, threads protrude and are left to dangle, scraps of fabric and woven panels are hastily pieced together, nail polish is sometimes splattered onto the yarn, and materials such as hemp, cotton, and wool are bleached or dyed haphazardly. Further, in Faught's works such as Triage (2009) and *It Takes a Lifetime to Get Exactly Where You Are* (2012), all manner of objects are incorporated into the weavings, including activist pin badges, greetings cards, sequins, photographs, back issue magazines, and other forms of "pop cultural detritus" (Figure 1.6).[78] The reference to sloppy craft was originally used concerning textiles, and it is most used within this arena, but examples can be found in all the crafts. Adamson describes sloppy craft as the "calculated sloppiness" embraced by post-disciplinary craft education, and he aligns it with early feminist reclamations of domestic craft, the fascination with low or "abject" art forms in the 1990s, and the growing popularity of the DIY movement today.[79]

There has since been a rise in the use of the term sloppy craft, particularly in line with emerging discussions on the idea of "post-craft" in Western craft production, which has attempted to chart how new economies of making in a post-disciplinary and post-industrial landscape are further reconfiguring craft's relationship to art, design, and industry. Yet, even though the term was first used about the work of a queer practitioner, Faught, it has often been overlooked as a significantly "queer" approach to making in current scholarship. Taking as a starting point the

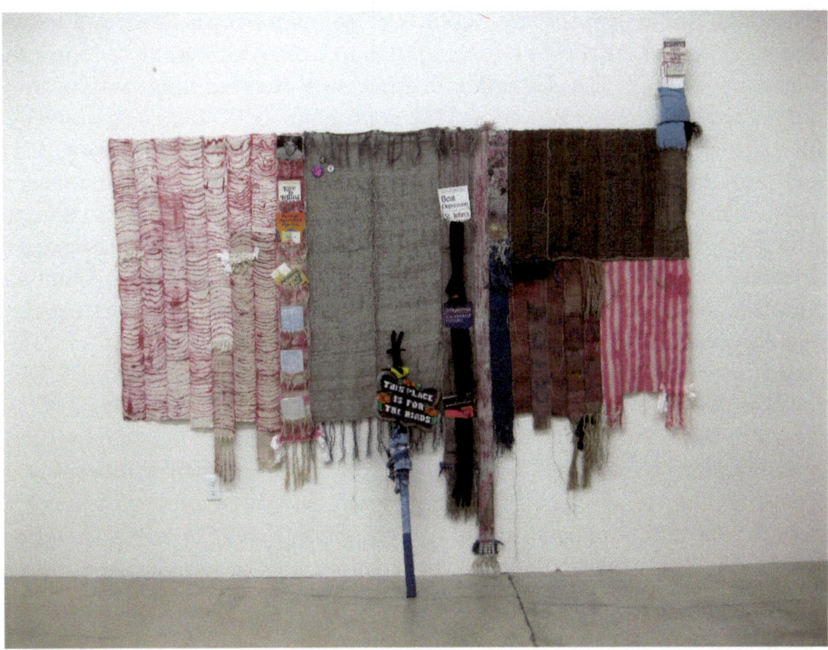

**Figure 1.6** Josh Faught, *Triage*, 2009. Hemp, nail polish, spray paint, indigo, logwood, toilet paper, pins, books, plaster, yarn, handmade wooden sign, denim, and gloves, 80 × 120 inches. Courtesy of Josh Faught.

complex relationship between amateurism and sewing from which sloppy craft emerges then, we need to consider sloppy craft, or more specifically, the act of sewing amateurishly, as a performative and distinctly queer act.[80] While sloppy crafters abandon the hallmarks of expertise that have traditionally distinguished professional from amateur craft by embracing "low," "trashy," or "abject" forms and techniques, they do so to ironically assert its variations and distinctiveness to professional craft, while also asserting their own identity in the process. Working sloppily also infers a sense of urgency, a need to make something quickly out of need and necessity. When practitioners are more concerned with personal expression rather than perfect technique, focus seems to be placed more on political and conceptual agendas. Moreover, the act of working in a deliberately sloppy way challenges the idea that craft is associated with high levels of skill or is a process of mastery over material, traditionally being understood as "something mastered in the hands."[81]

It is important to note that these discourses of "mastery" surrounding craft are firmly grounded in colonial and imperial forms of knowledge, and sloppy craft can represent an attempt to break away from this logic, calling for the fraying and unraveling of these colonial constructs.[82] It is worth recalling Lorde's well-known phrase, "the master's tools will never dismantle the master's house," which she used to describe systems of oppression from an intersectional Black and lesbian perspective.[83] With this, Lorde reminds us that we cannot solve issues of oppression by working with the tools of a system of oppression. Here, we might invoke Lorde and theorize "the master's tools" as "the craftsman's tools," tools like needles or pins that have the power to repair or to injure depending on how they are wielded, and "dismantle the master's house" as a metaphor for the need to dismantle and transcend intersecting systems of oppression rife within both society and the craft sector itself. In Roberts's own statement, they explicitly say that they aim to "reclaim the mastery of craft to create an alternative set of tools that could potentially dismantle 'the master's house.'"[84] Like Roberts, Yore encourages us to turn away from practices of material domination or mastery over material and instead turn towards a new orientation.[85] During this process, they may craft new houses and worlds where mastery ceases to maintain its colonial and imperialist power. In summary, Yore's works "play up" to the grandiose historicism of European and colonial landscape painting traditions while undercutting their authoritative or supposedly "heroic" claims by appealing to a camp, playful, sloppy approach to materials—positing ambiguity and indeterminacy as generative sites of queerness.

## Conclusion

Through their processes of queer handmaking, textile practitioners such as Roberts and Yore seem to emphasize that those who have previously been denied a world and communities of support can, quite literally, craft one into being. Together, their work highlights the DIY nature of queer worldmaking and how craft, or more broadly, the process of *crafting*, is an essential strategy for survival in an often hostile world. Roberts's work reminds us of the poetics and politics of queer community building beyond cis-heteronormative understandings of "home" and "family," celebrating its transitory and untethered positionalities, past and present. Ultimately, Yore's work offers up future glimpses into the possibility of new queer worlds, bringing the warm and inviting horizon that Muñoz describes ever closer to the foreground, one sequin and sloppy stitch at a time. Their engagement with textiles becomes a way of making political commitments, well, material.

## Chapter 2

## CERAMIC

### CERAMICS IN TRANSITION: CENTERING THE TRANSGENDER EXPERIENCE

*Introduction*

The process of making ceramics relies on a process of transition. The term "transition" broadly refers to a process of change from one state to another. Ceramicists often use it to describe the physical changes during the firing process, where malleable raw clay is fired at high temperatures in a kiln and *transitions* into hard but brittle ceramic, emerging as a new entity, reborn in flames. The term transition, or process of transitioning, also refers to the series of changes (such as social, legal, or medical) that a trans person may undertake to affirm their chosen gender identity. The ability of clay to resist change and adapt to extreme and hostile conditions under firing, its material resilience, can be seen as analogous to how many trans people are forced to resist enduring pressure from external forces, connecting to the material experiences of being trans.

Working with clay is also an intense bodily process that requires care and collaboration between maker and material. Clay is carefully caressed and usually molded by hand through pinching, coiling, cutting, shaping, and extruding processes. It receives the fingerprints and marks of its maker, becoming an archive of touch. Especially in pottery, objects are described in anthropomorphic ways, such as the "lip," "shoulder," "neck," or "bottom" of a vase, and these objects are often called "bodies" or "vessels." Allegories of the plasticity of clay and the crafting of the human body have generally existed for millennia, and people have long related ceramic objects to human bodies and have used clay as a metaphor for life, birth, or resurrection. One only needs to look at the use of clay in various creation myths in multiple cultures worldwide to see how the shaping of clay is a powerful tool for the human condition and the metaphorical crafting of bodies. This includes sacred texts such as the Bible ("O Lord, thou art our father; we are the clay, and thou art our potter; and we the work of thy hand…") and the Quran ("I am going to create a human being out of clay. When I have formed him and breathed My Spirit into him…").[1] There are also religious figures such as the Sumerian Mother

Goddess Ninhursag[2] who is said to have fashioned humankind from clay, as well as Jewish tales about Golem,[3] anthropomorphic beings said to be made from earth and animated through ritual, to name but a few examples. In short, the qualities of the material "has led to the metaphoric uses of clay and ceramics that permeate culture."[4] Because a person working with clay can transform it into almost any form they desire (at least within the limits of the material), the process of making ceramics has been seen by several trans practitioners as a metaphor for crafting the trans body—just as bodily feeling and sensation transform clay, bodily feeling and sensation transform flesh.

The exceedingly long lifespan of fired clay also renders ceramics an ideal medium to record events, express opinions, and establish conversations that have the potential to play out over generations; they can become living archives that tell our stories even when we are long gone. Moreover, as historians and archaeologists have attested, it is largely thanks to the longevity of ceramics that we know LGBTQ+ people have always existed. Examples might include ancient Greek amphoras depicting gay male sex scenes,[5] pre-Columbian Moche "sex pots" (several of which are said to represent queer, trans, and intersex subjects),[6] and the ceramics of We'wha (c.1849–1896),[7] a renowned lhamana from New Mexico. Despite these clear links between gender, sexuality, and ceramics, scholarly attention to this intersection remains limited.

However, recent exhibitions and publications suggest a growing awareness of these practices within contemporary practices. For example, the 2015 exhibition *SEXUAL POLITICS: Gender, Sexuality and Queerness in Contemporary Ceramics* at the Northern Clay Center in Minneapolis, featuring six American practitioners, offered a valuable platform for exploring these themes.[8] In the catalog, curator Kelly Connole highlighted the influence of publications like Paul Mathieu's *Sex Pots* (2003) and Judith Schwartz's *Confrontational Ceramics* (2008) which, she argued, have provided a new generation with a "who's who of LGBTQ" working with clay.[9] These contributions have been important in establishing queer ceramics as a distinctive area of creative exploration. However, representation of the full LGBTQ+ spectrum, particularly the inclusion of transgender practitioners in publications and exhibitions, has been limited. A more recent exhibition, *Making in Between: Queer Clay,* held at the American Museum of Ceramic Art in 2023, sought to address this by explicitly foregrounding "queerness as an unapologetic presence" in the work of numerous LGBTQ+ practitioners working with ceramics, including trans practitioner Nicki Green, whose work is discussed in this chapter.[10] In the catalog that accompanied *Making in Between*, art historian Matthew Limb notes that "[t]here is something inherently queer about clay. It is changeable, malleable, a material in a constant state of transformation that becomes both delicate and durable. Clay is an apt medium for queer artists to take up the exploration of the self, their embodied experience, and use it as a building block for the construction of queer worlds."[11] While embodied experience and clay's malleable potential are central themes across the field of ceramics, many trans ceramicists take this exploration a step further. Their work explores the body as a malleable form, using clay to challenge and reshape ideas of identity.

As Limb notes, embodiment is often a key consideration in queer craft practices, and this is especially felt across the work of trans practitioners. Embodiment encompasses the body as "lived" and the body *as* the context of knowledge and experience. French philosopher Maurice Merleau-Ponty popularized the understanding of embodiment premised on the notion that our bodies are simultaneously material *and* experiential entities—"I am not in front of my body, I am in my body, or rather I *am* my body."[12] Many scholars in trans studies have also taken up these ideas of embodiment, particularly arguing for the need to acknowledge both the materiality of the trans body and the "material world" of being trans, including structures of personal or state violence that often lead trans bodies to feel "brittle," akin to the ceramic itself.[13] As a result, this chapter draws upon trans theory to articulate how the crafting of ceramic from clay can be used as a metaphor for crafting the trans body, illustrating and archiving how embodiment and the handmade "generates new evidence of what a body and its difference might be."[14] Building on Vaccaro's call to explore "the ordinary feelings and textures of crafting transgender life" in textile crafts, I argue that ceramics offer another powerful avenue for such exploration.[15] In a climate that is increasingly hostile towards transgender individuals, the chapter argues that craft, particularly ceramics, serves as a potent form of creative resistance while also celebrating the resilience of trans communities. However, it also foregrounds narratives of refusal, resistance, and resilience, cautiously examining the material conditions that force trans bodies to be resilient and resistant in the first place.

Clay, which comes from the earth, is often seen as a material that can cultivate a sense of being "grounded," feeling present in one's body, and connected to the surrounding world. Centering refers to the process of centering clay in wheel-thrown practices, but working with clay can be a way of "centering" the self.[16] This chapter explores the work of Rose Schmits and Nicki Green, who both use clay and ceramics to put trans bodies and politics center stage, establishing tangible archives of trans experiences. For these practitioners, it is not just about finding "lost" histories or inserting contemporary narratives. Their work critiques the systems facilitating this erasure, encompassing exclusionary political structures, ideological agendas, and digital cultures. Many craft scholars posit that the ubiquity of technology has ignited a desire to seek something more "human," a yearning for the handmade and the authentic. Ceramics, a relatively slow and physical process, might seem in stark contrast to the fast-paced nature of the digital world. However, the work of Schmits and Green shows that craft can preserve identities, experiences, and communities in ways that the digital cannot. Hence, the chapter has a nascent focus on the relationship between digital and handmade, exploring how Schmits and Green use ceramics as an offline method to archive online cultures.

### *Rose Schmits (b.1998, the Netherlands)*

Rose Schmits talks openly about how she finds the process of making ceramics to be a "metaphor for the transgender experience."[17] This metaphor is perhaps most explicitly explored in the ongoing *TransForms* (2019) series, a collection of 281 hand coiled and wheel-thrown ceramic vessels that stand in for bodies and comment on how they can grow, change, and be sculpted at will (Figure 2.1). Each vessel is unique and distinctive, just as our bodies are unique and distinctive. Most of the forms are phallic and tendril-like, they are relatively long and narrow in shape with an "erect" point. Some are twisted and seem to curl around themselves. Others droop and are "bent." Some have long vulva-like gashes or gaping holes carved into their center, revealing fleshy innards of unglazed earthenware. Many are tall and have wide-lipped openings at the top like traditional ceramic vases, rendering them both decorative and functional; they are objects ready to receive, hold, or release fluids, much like a functioning human body. The earlier thrown vessels from 2019 are complete with fingerprints and natural indentations from Schmits' hand, resulting from the hand coiled process. Although each is different, one uniting characteristic is that all the ceramic forms are decorated with white and blue glazing. At first glance, the blue patterns painted onto the white surface seemingly bear innocent words associated with making ceramics, including "shape" or "fold." Yet, on closer inspection, words with more overt associations with medical procedures become visible, including "stitch" and "tuck." Likewise, viewers will first notice that many of the objects carry simple horizontal and vertical lines, as well as dots, which instinctively seem like abstract surface patterns that might be used to decorate any ceramic object. However, these seemingly innocent decorations are evocative of incision marks or "cut" lines, and the dots might resemble healing wounds, ghostly residues of the surgeon's hand, the piercing needle, and the sutures. More explicitly medical, a few even have scientific diagrams of the structures of various hormones, including testosterone and estrogen. There is no denying that these ceramic bodies are metaphors for human bodies that, like the clay, can be shaped, folded, and tucked at will.

When discussing ceramics, there is often a tendency to focus solely on the aesthetic experience. This often manifests in superficial descriptions, such as a vase's glossy luster or ornate surface decoration. However, these crafted objects embody a far more extensive process rooted in the haptic. As Sorkin notes, "ceramics is a fascinating and entirely confounding medium, in that its resultant object is a work that entirely conceals the performativity of its process and instead extols the virtues of its materiality."[18] In the case of *TransForms*, the process behind crafting ceramics and crafting the body are made visible. Notions of the body's "constructedness," its crafted nature, take on a distinctively literal edge here, which emphasizes how trans bodies can be crafted within a wider community of people and often in collaboration with the medical establishment.[19] Although the ceramics have been fired and are arguably in a "fixed" state compared to the more malleable pre-fired clay, Schmits suggests that the pieces are a reminder of the wider process of transition and that

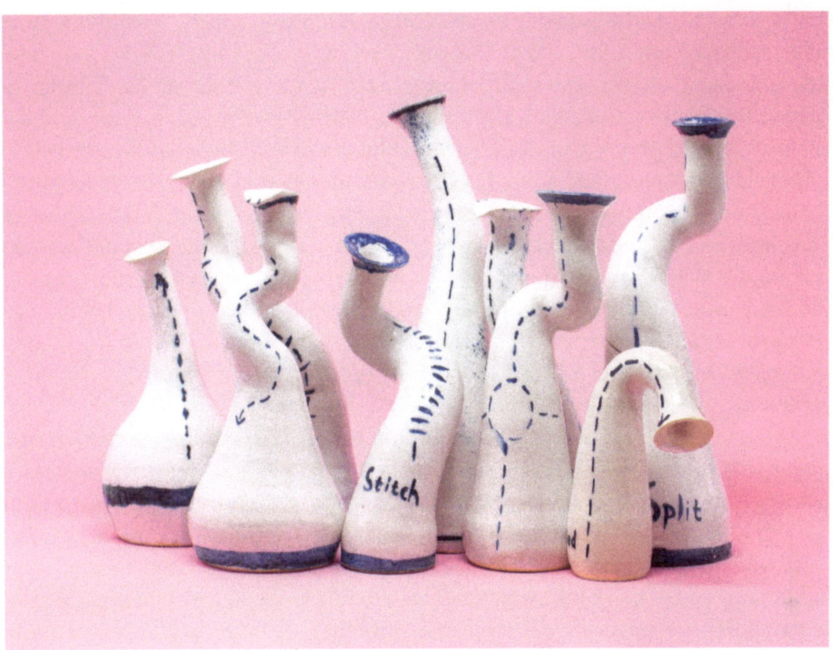


**Figure 2.1** Rose Schmits, *TransForms*, 2019. Collection of 281 ceramic vessels. Courtesy of Rose Schmits.

their decorative markings suggest further possibilities for change.[20] Both the crafting of ceramics and the crafting of the trans body are ongoing processes; "unfinished yet enough (process, *not* progress)."[21] In many ways, these objects echo what Vaccaro calls "a process of assembly and disassembly in which bodies auto-engineer shape and form, building and remaking connections between the soft and pliable material forms of emotional and material life."[22] Specifically writing about crochet and textile crafts, Vaccaro calls the handmade a "methodology—a call to value the aesthetic and performative of making an identity."[23] Although ceramic as opposed to textile, the crafted nature of the objects discussed here are also physical traces of crafting an identity, and often the crafting of the body, that defines many aspects associated with trans experiences. Like the malleability of fabric, the plasticity of the unfired clay can be seen as analogous to the "soft and pliable forms of emotional life, skin elasticity, scar tissue, cellular organization," and so on.[24] The use of craft tools and techniques in relation to specific trans constructions of the self "orients our thinking to the labour and materiality [. . .] of crafting identity."[25] One of the unique aspects of trans ceramics is its emphasis on tactile and sensory experiences. These tactile experiences invite the viewer to engage with the work on a deeper level, encouraging them to consider their relationship to gender and the making of the self.

Just as ceramics are often only discussed in aesthetic terms, the trans experience is often only discussed in medical terms. It is essential to note that many trans people choose not to undergo surgery or medical intervention, which certainly does not make someone any "less" trans. The emotional and social processes of transition have also been explored by many writers, such as the gender studies scholar Jay Prosser, who has argued that transitioning is conceived of multiple facets and that different meanings of transition exist, including (although by no means limited to) "conceptual, somatic, narrative, historico-discursive, and political" transitions.[26] Rather than becoming wholly preoccupied with emphasizing the crafting of the trans body via the medical establishment, which many may not wish to access (or may not be able to gain access to as a result of long wait times, extortionate costs, and increased state regulation of trans healthcare), we might also think about how "trans identities are often created communally, in the context of defining identity in a group and in relation to others."[27] After all, crafting identity and crafting community often exist in tandem.

While objects in the *TransForms* series certainly speak to acts of physical creation, they also speak to emotional, psychological, and experiential ways of creating the self, particularly to the crafting of community. Whenever objects from the *TransForms* series have been shown in public, they are often exhibited together as a collective, not as isolated or alone. Much like a play on the idiom "taking up space," meaning to be unapologetically yourself and asserting physical or psychological territory, these objects quite literally take up a large portion of the room, as if celebrating their distinctive forms and identities, or as if they are gathered at a march or protest. They are a testament to how trans identities are often crafted collectively just as much as individually. When I interviewed Schmits about *TransForms*, I questioned why she created a series that included such a specific number of vessels. She stated there was no significance to the number she had created, but it was simply because she wanted to make as many as possible to create "as large of a community as possible."[28] She stated that some of the original 281 vessels have since been sold to support her practice, often in small batches of three or four—"never alone, always part of a community"—and that the fact that these vessels can be collected and given homes across the world adds further layers of meaning.[29]

These objects, some of which might "pass" as traditional ceramic vessels, and others which are more "out" and proudly wear symbols or messages that overtly reference the trans experience, might become sites of discussion for those visiting the domestic space in which the vessels inhabit. A pot or a vase is ultimately an ornament; its purpose is often to be displayed and admired within a room. It can be a status object that tells a visitor something about their host. In this sense, these objects which express trans identity in subtle ways may operate as a form of quiet activism within the domestic space. The work consciously appropriates banality, allowing it to infiltrate the most traditional of heteronormative and cisnormative domestic spheres. The place for "coming-outs" and awkward conversations, the "private" space of the home can be a lonely and intensely "public" space for queer people. The presence of Schmits's ceramics within the home not only offers a quiet protest then but a quiet allyship. More recently, Schmits has made ceramic medicine jars with phrases such as "Good ol' Vitamin T," "The Gender Juice," and "The Notorious H.R.T" (a play on the name of the rapper, "The Notorious B.I.G") inscribed upon their surface, in her signature dark blue text. These jars are designed for both aesthetic pleasure and practical use, potentially being purchased by a trans person to store medications such as "T" (testosterone) and forms of HRT (hormone replacement therapy). These objects reference the broader historical traditions of Delftware "drug jars," which were usually used by apothecaries for the storage of powders, ointments, syrups, and oils, which were especially common in forms of English Delftware from the late sixteenth century through to the late eighteenth century.[30] Rather than secreted away in a bedside drawer or stashed in a bathroom cabinet, these medications can be displayed loudly and proudly within the home in Schmits's jar, perhaps leading to a sense of gender euphoria, a state of comfort or joy that can occur when gender expression is aligned with chosen gender identity rather than the one assigned at birth.

Aside from the surface pattern designs and their function within the home, Schmits's color choices are central to constructing meaning. Their blue and white vessels have always been displayed against a pink background in public, such as when they were shown as part of the British Ceramics Biennial in 2019. The pink backdrop, in combination with the blue surface patterns, evokes the colors associated with the gender binary in contemporary culture, blue often being seen as "masculine," and pink as "feminine."[31] Yet, the stark whiteness of the porcelain provides an intervention, a counterpoint, and a third possibility beyond the gender binary. Taken together, the three colors that Schmits uses make up those of the transgender pride flag. Designed by pioneering American transwoman Monica Helms in 1999, the flag's design—itself an important aspect of queer craft history—represents the transgender community and consists of five horizontal stripes: two light blue, two pink, and one white in the center. Helms describes the meaning of the transgender pride flag as follows: "[t]he stripes at the top and bottom are light blue, the traditional color for baby boys. The stripes next to them are pink, the traditional color for baby girls. The stripe in the middle is white, for those who are transitioning or consider themselves having a neutral or undefined gender."[32]

The color choices are not just a reflection of Schmits's identity as a proud trans woman who reflects her identity through the ceramics she creates, but they also represent another facet of her identity; her Dutch heritage and experience of growing up in Delft, a city in the Netherlands famous for its blue and white ceramics, or "Delftware." "Delf" was used to describe the blue and white ceramics made at the factories in Delft, which, within the early eighteenth century, had become the pre-eminent center in northern Europe for producing tin-glazed earthenware. Before long, however, "Delft" or "Delft Ware" (sometimes spelled "Delf" or "Delph" in more historical records) came to be used as a term for tin-glazed earthenware produced in Europe more broadly, reflecting the dominance of the Dutch factories.[33] Delftware is most closely associated with functional tableware, including objects such as plates, jugs, sugar casters, candlesticks, flower vases, and more. Schmits notes, "using the Delftware pottery technique to create pieces that reflect my experiences as a trans person having altered my body and identity allows me to gain ownership of the struggles of transitioning as well as remember where I came from."[34] In more recent works, a pink glaze is applied to the bottom of the Delftware-inspired pots where a maker's mark usually appears. When displayed on a shelf or a table, these objects may "pass" as traditional Delftware ceramics, but with the *crafty* addition of pink on their bases, Schmits offers up a further subversion, a "queering" or perhaps more accurately, a "transing" of traditional Delftware techniques. The idea of "transing" is often discussed in trans studies as a conceptual and philosophical means to cross or contravene boundaries, analogous to the idea of "queering" something. As Susan Stryker, Paisley Currah, and Lisa Jean Moore note, transing "is a practice that assembles gender into contingent structures of association with other attributes of bodily being, and that allows for their reassembly."[35]

Recently, Schmits has become well-known among many craft communities, especially in the United Kingdom, and her practice received increased visibility after being appointed as the technician on Channel 4's popular television show and pottery competition, *The Great Pottery Throw Down* (2015–), in 2021. While Rose's increased visibility across TV and media provided important representation for many in the trans community, it also gave way to a wave of transphobic attacks, especially across social media platforms such as Twitter. Sadly, Schmits also began to face heightened discrimination from scholars, practitioners, and curators of craft—a vital reminder that within the study, practice, and preservation of crafting, there are still major underlying systematic issues. These questions of visibility are often at the forefront of writing in trans studies and discussions among trans practitioners. Most notably, the paradoxical relationship between trans visibility and anti-trans violence is central to the critical anthology *Trap Door: Trans Cultural Production and the Politics of Visibility* (2017). The editors Johanna Burton, Reina Gossett, and Eric A. Stanley explain that while trans people are frequently offered "doors"—entrances to visibility, recognition, and opportunity—these are almost always "traps," accommodating trans bodies and communities only insofar as they cooperate with dominant norms.[36] Essentially, they warn that providing positive representations, images, and objects relating to trans bodies is not necessarily a solution to trans liberation. Visibility might seem, then, at best, a thin promise of representation as a substitute for actual political power or, at worse, further exposure to violence and discrimination.

In 2022, Schmits began an extensive series reflecting on her lived experiences and responding to the online transphobia she began to receive. *We Live in A Society* (2022) is a simple, vessel-like form reminiscent of traditional Delftware vases. Again, they feature the signature blue and white surface decoration, but most have phrases such as "Trans people always existed always will" and "Trans women are women" applied to their surface. The collection title refers to the phrase "we live in a society," which began to be used across the internet in 2015. It was initially intended to be an enlightened statement denouncing society's many flaws and contradictions. Later, coinciding with the release of films such as *Justice League* (2017) and *Joker* (2019), it was turned into a piece of satire primarily associated with Joker. Like the supposed "antagonist" from the Batman franchise, many felt ignored by society, and the phrase began to be used more broadly to call out the ridiculousness of society and its numerous injustices. Here, Joker was not seen as a pathetic anti-hero or villain but was re-cast into a figure of anarchism, emblematic of those who felt their identities marginalized and representative of misunderstood or exploited peoples. Yet, the meme was also appropriated by more conservative and right-wing groups who began using it to talk about the so-called "wokeness" of society, re-casting the likes of Donald Trump and Elon Musk as the anti-hero, encouraging people to rally behind them in support of their politics. Schmits's series was created directly when these circulated across social media. With the work, she wanted to point to the ridiculousness of these online cultures and the dangers of appropriation that comes with the digital—unlike the seemingly "fixed" and permanent nature of ceramic that she uses, which cannot be overwritten as easily. Schmits's process is cyclical; she responds to online discourse through her ceramics but also returns her ceramics to the digital space they were inspired by. She shares photos of all her work on social media, particularly Twitter and Instagram, returning the works to the site of inspiration. This online space, ordinarily a site of hostility, equally becomes a platform for shared joy, healing, and connection among other trans people, which she sees as part of the process.

Countless online memes are referenced in the series, including a personal favorite, "gangster crab with knife." In February of 2016, a video of a crab wielding a kitchen knife went viral, as if attempting to defend itself from impending death.[37] A year later, a Twitter user posted a screenshot of the knife-wielding crab with the caption "you mess with crabo, you get a stabo," which was retweeted and shared widely.[38] Schmits enshrined this rather humorous meme in ceramics to highlight a grave and darker issue: how trans people constantly have to defend themselves, both online and offline, articulating that if you attack the trans community, then you will face the consequences. The internet itself has long been an important space of connectivity for trans people, especially those who may be geographically isolated from other trans people. As researchers such as Amery Dame-Griff have explored at length, the internet has shaped transgender identity and activism from the 1980s to the present and has helped trans people leverage visibility into substantial policy gains, playing a pivotal role in "the transgender movement" or the "transgender revolution."[39] However, as they note, this increased connectivity has somewhat been a double-edged sword. While the early internet of the 2000s established a way for trans people to connect easily, quickly, and over long distances, a "second wave" of digital advancement—particularly an increase in the use of social media—has resulted in conservative backlash and a campaign to reverse many of the gains that trans people have made. Schmits's *We Live in a Society* series directly responds to the rise in transphobia and specifically reacts to the forms of hatred and abuse that she received from trans-exclusionary radical feminists across various online platforms—using ceramics as an offline technique to archive online content.[40] Schmits notes about the series: "as a trans woman in a time that seems to become [an] increasingly hostile environment for trans people here in the United Kingdom as well as the United States, at a time when most communications happen online, I want to be able to directly respond with my work…[b]ringing online memes, discourse and slogans onto pottery reveals the ephemerality of digital infrastructure. A digital post will become obsolete within our lifetime, but a pot will stay for hundreds if not thousands of years. I want to raise questions about the value of images, words, and how we relate to them."[41]

One object from the *We Live in a Society* series that directly reacts to much of this online discrimination is a wide, shallow vessel that has "Emergency Trans Toilet" written on it in a blue Comic Sans font (Figure 2.2). The font and form of the chamber pot are humorous and playful, but there is a darker, much more serious undertone at play here. This porcelain vessel, which takes the form and size of a chamber pot, speaks to the fact that the public toilet—a ceramic-built environment—has become a prominent site of conflict and a focal point for trans-exclusionary radical feminism. For many of these "gender-critical" feminists, the walls of women-only facilities such as changing rooms and bathrooms "have come to symbolise the boundaries of womanhood: a "safe" space where the terms of inclusion are vehemently regulated and protected."[42] Clearly, epistemologies and ontologies of sex and gender are not confined to the public toilet, nor has the public toilet been the only space for gatekeeping and discrimination, but at the time of writing this book, it has been particularly central to many discussions on the transgender experience and somewhat of a battleground for trans people's participation in society; a particularly gendered architecture of exclusion. Although some would argue that there has been incredible progress in securing trans rights in Britain, where Schmits is currently living and working after immigrating from the Netherlands, a wave of abhorrent anti-trans sentiment is emerging from within self-proclaimed "LGB communities". Recent data from the Home Office further evidence that anti-LGBT+ hate crime in England and Wales has grown at twice the rate of other forms of hate crime for the last two years and transphobic hate crimes are at a record high having increased by 186 percent in the last five years.[43] The government also continues to consider amending laws that would make it more complicated for trans people to transition and access facilities such as gender-neutral bathrooms and changing rooms "on the pretext of protecting cisgender (non-trans) people from a non-existent peril."[44] With this in mind, Schmits experiments with the traditional form of the chamber pot, a portable toilet often used in a domestic space where there is an absence of plumbing or flushing toilets, as a satirical commentary on the policing of public toilets, the lack of access to gender-neutral spaces, and to raise awareness of the violence and aggression that often ensues when trans people are misunderstood as attempting to "pass" as an alternate gender identity than that which they may present. Although Schmits's work is sometimes exhibited in museums, galleries, or craft and design fairs as beautifully decorative (and thus aesthetic) objects, these ceramic objects are still vessels that can at least nominally perform the function of holding urine—even if they have never done so. Even unused, there is a performative capacity for these vessels, made by hand, to interact with other human bodies, a sense of imbued potentiality. Unfortunately, "we live in a society" where *Emergency Trans Toilet* may have to be used as a functional object, not just an acerbic comment.

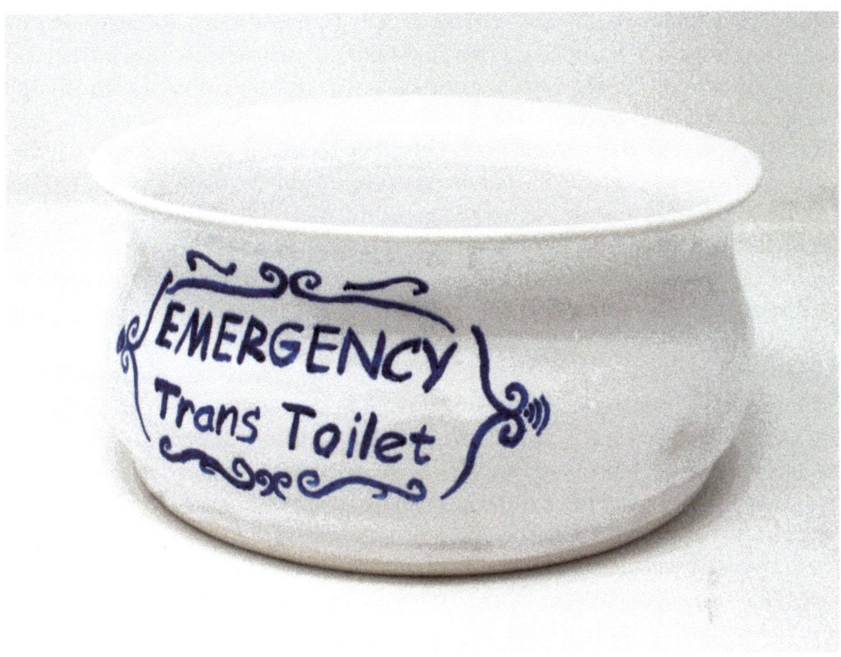


**Figure 2.2** Rose Schmits, *We Live in a Society (Emergency Trans Toilet)*, 2023. Ceramic vessel. Courtesy of Rose Schmits.

### *Nicki Green (b. 1986, USA)*

Nicki Green uses ceramic objects to explore "history perseveration, conceptual ornamentation and aesthetics of otherness" in reference to queer and trans identity formations.[45] Often constructing large-scale objects using experimental and organic hand-building techniques, Green approaches the malleability of clay as a site of discursive possibility and uses clay to "explore material and object integrity by utilizing transness as a lens with which to look at the world."[46] "Clay is a trans material to my mind…[i]t does this sort of transformation from liquid slip to plastic, moldable clay to porous but hard to vitreous, super dense, strong stone. It has this fluidity to it," she claims.[47] Green's work shares formal and conceptual similarities with Schmits's, and both practitioners develop a new visual language that simultaneously draws on a traditional past and looks towards an inclusive future. However, because each practitioner explores their distinct experiences of transness, it is important to avoid conflating their work.

Like Schmits, Green also works with traditional Delftware techniques and iconography. Although Green is American, her partner is Dutch. They recall spending a lot of time surrounded by Dutch Delftware, including in the countless museums and galleries that house Delftware across the Netherlands. The traditional white surface of Delftware continues to be appealing for Green because it is an ideal space to illustrate various scenes or narratives associated with the human condition, a blank canvas for storytelling. Traditionally, Dutch Delftware was highly decorative, and objects would often depict scenes of rural life, including windmills, hunting, farming, and fishing—iconography that is thought to have been appropriated and modeled on traditional blue and white painted Chinese porcelain that was often stolen and brought back to the Netherlands by the Dutch East India Company as part of its colonizing missions.[48] Instead of the traditional Delft blue, Green uses dark purple. Purple is a color that has been associated with the LGBTQ+ community for decades, especially lesbian culture: from the poetry of Sappho about beautiful women adorned with violets,[49] to the 1970s' activist group called the Lavender Menace,[50] and more recently with purple being used in the background of the lesbian labrys pride flag.[51] These associations are furthered by the fact that in many works, Green actively paints decorations of specific flowers, such as violets, pansies, and carnations, which have historically been used to signal queerness.[52] These decorative patterns are visible in editions such as *Pansy Bricks* (2015), which reference the industrial traditions of clay brick making as well as the queer histories of the 1969 Stonewall riots, an uprising that was said to have been started when a patron of the Stonewall Inn in New York (primarily debated to be Black trans activist Marsha P. Johnson) threw a brick at a police officer in reaction to continued police brutality and discrimination. The work serves as a reminder of the subversive potential of clay; it can be used to produce bricks, which can either be used to build worlds or tear them down, depending on how they are wielded.

Traditional Delftware designs and forms are central to Green's practice, especially vessels such as the tulipiere, or "tulip-holder," an ornate vessel typically used to grow tulips. These vases were usually constructed to accommodate one tulip bulb per spout with a larger common water reservoir base, but later, multi-spout designs were standard, often constructed in a wide fan-like shape or a tall multi-tiered shape. Before the nineteenth century, these were more commonly known simply as "flower vases," used to display any form of cut flower, but were often referred to as "tulip vases" in the nineteenth century to re-assert the significance of supposed "Dutch" heritage and culture, but also likely for the commercial benefit given their role in tourism as typical souvenirs.[53] In several of Green's works, such as *Splitting/Unifying (toilet tanks, slip spigots, and medical sink laver with faucets)* (2019), sprigs of dried lavender are often inserted into the phallic spigots instead of the traditional tulip. As lavender has often been a sapphic code, the insertion of lavender as part of the work contributes to a further queering of the Delftware and becomes a subtle way of signaling how queerness has historically existed in fleeting codes, signals, and symbols.

The traditional Delftware flower vases are intensely phallic, and their spouts feature heavily in Green's work, particularly in *It's Almost as if We've Existed (Tres in Una)* (2015), where these are reimagined as six phalluses, decorated with flowers and pansies (Figure 2.3). Similar to Schmits's explorations of digital media through the series titled *We Live In A Society*, Green's *It's Almost as if We've Existed (Tres in Una)* references one of a series of images that went

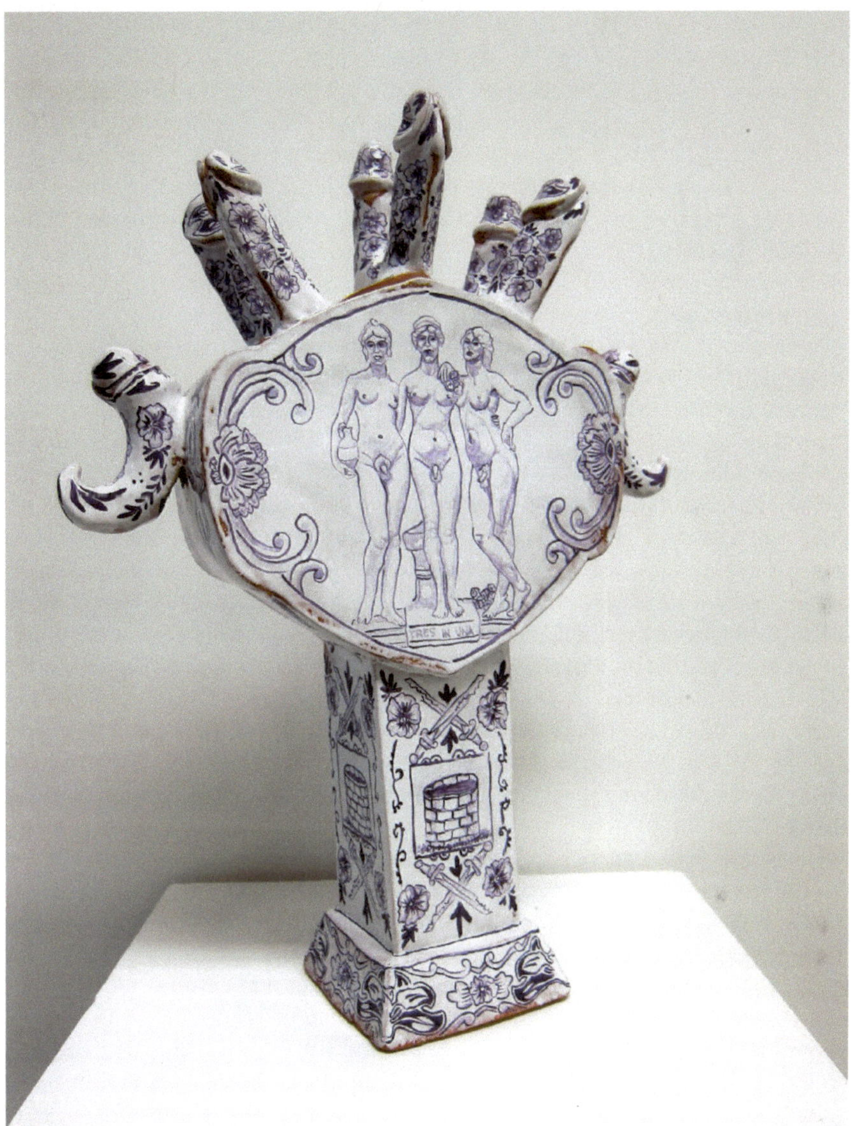



**Figure 2.3** Nicki Green, *It's Almost as if We've Existed (Tres in Una)*, 2015. Glazed earthenware, 15.5 × 12 × 3.5 inches. Courtesy of Nicki Green.

viral on the internet around 2014 via Tumblr, an American microblogging and social networking website. One of the images was of *Sleeping Hermaphroditus* (1620), a sculpture by Gian Lorenzo Bernini depicting a reclining nude intersex figure in the collection of Musée du Louvre in Paris. A second image was of *Les Trois Grâces* (The Three Graces) (1831) by Jean-Jacques Pradier (1970–1852), also in the Louvre.[54] *Les Trois Grâces* is an iconic neoclassical marble sculpture that depicts the three graces, the three daughters of Zeus in Greek mythology. The three daughters—identified as, from left to right, Euphrosyne, Aglaea, and Thalia—were said to represent mirth (Euphrosyne), elegance (Aglaea), and youth/beauty (Thalia).[55] They were believed to bring goodwill to both gods and mortals and to endow artists and poets with the ability to create beautiful works of art. However, while the image of the *Sleeping Hermaphroditus* was left intact, the one of *Les Trois Grâces* was digitally manipulated so that it looked as if each of the daughters of Zeus now had penises. Although the original creator of the digitally manipulated image is not known, the editing was so seamless that many people were not aware of the digital fabrication, and many trans people began to celebrate it as evidence that trans and intersex people have existed throughout history, tapping into broader conversations and debates about the ongoing search for trans ancestry, or "trancestry."[56]

The digitally manipulated image of the three graces garnered further attention in 2019 on Reddit. On this similar American discussion website, the manipulation eventually became known but was still nonetheless an important point of discussion for queer and trans communities, especially discussions around archives and (lack of) trans visibility. At the time, many bloggers began to write about how it highlighted that there is a serious lack of reference points in art history and visual culture that celebrate the trans body in the same ways in which cisgender bodies are celebrated—as one blogger noted, "I hope to find real pieces like this in the future!"[57] The post received many transphobic claims from "gender critical" people saying that people were stupid for believing the image was real because these identities could never have existed throughout history because gender-affirming surgery and HRT, they suggested, didn't exist back then. Yet, it also became an educational tool—one blogger responded, rightly pointing out that you do not have to have surgery to be trans and that HRT has been made from the estrogen-rich urine of pregnant horses for thousands of years. Drawing upon this digital image—and specifically borrowing the composition of Paul Richer's (1849–1933) later version of the three graces, *Tres in Una* (1913)—Green's work reflects these debates and celebrates diverse and fluid gender identities. By enshrining these forms in ceramic, Green is creating work that gives visibility and legibility to a trans history that has previously been erased and preserves the experiences of trans people in the present. The digitally manipulated image of the three graces has also since been rendered into a 3D printable model by community designers, allowing anyone with the technology or access to a maker space to download it and print it, enabling further sharing of it.[58]

One striking thing about the work of both Schmits and Green is how both practitioners see their vessels as a form of archiving the trans experience, as previously alluded to. They provide an act of preservation and record the maker's lived experiences within a society that designates them as "other." It is important to note that our contemporary understandings of craft practices are primarily built through collecting and display practices in galleries, museums, and archives, supported and propelled by the symbiotics of the field known as craft history. People often say that there is no queer or trans craft history. Or, more accurately, there is, but we do not often know about it. This is primarily because of the systematic issues within society and institutions that have played a key role in gatekeeping, omitting, and erasing these histories. If, as KJ Rawson (Director of the Digital Transgender Archive) states, "'transgender' becomes legitimated as an identity through the rich historical lineage that the archive evidences," then what happens when this historical lineage is erased and obscured?[59]

Current generations of queer and trans practitioners, Schmits and Green included, who are finding themselves without legacies or representation, are now turning to create their own archive of objects in search of this desire for visibility and the need "to be seen." The artist and founder of the Museum of Transgender Hirstory and Art (MOTHA), Chris E Vargas, writes: "[t]ransgender people are a creative and hardy folk–we've endured invisibility and hypervisibility; we've been demonized and pathologized, ridiculed and melodramatized. We have been the subjects of metaphor, suspicion, academic theorizing, medical and anthropological research and in the worst cases, violence and murder. But we've survived in creative and ingenious ways."[60] Vargas' idea that trans people are inherently creative and hardy, a result of having to become inventive and survive in a hostile world, is reflected in these works. The interest in the creation of archives of trans experience is not just a practice of reflecting upon the past, but the creation of an archive that focuses on the experiences of trans people also looks to form, or craft, a future. What better way to do this than through the handmade, a method that allows for the literal *centering* of the trans experience? As Schmits notes, "[w]hat does it mean to create and document queer and trans history in ceramics knowing that the clay body might break, the ceramic might break, but the image or the history will live on indefinitely?"[61] Ceramics is well positioned for this because of its ability to document history and create a legacy. As a haptic, affective theorization of the transgender body, this process becomes a mode of animating material, evoking the transformational qualities of bodies, images, and affects, and preserving these identities, experiences, and communities for future generations.

Similar to Schmits's pointed critique through *Emergency Trans Toilet*, Green also examines the role of ceramic objects such as toilets, sinks, and bidets as recipients of our bodily waste. More specifically, her practice explores the role of these objects in both religious and everyday cleansing rituals and how this relates to Green's work. It also provides a direct critique of the gendered policing of public toilets, specifically in the United States, where transphobic and exclusionary policies regarding bathroom discrimination meant that trans people were not initially permitted to utilize the facilities that matched their gender identity in state buildings. This was especially true during Donald Trump's administration, which introduced these policies. It was mainly a "hot" issue in North Carolina, where it became informally known as the "Bathroom Bill." In 2019, coinciding with the Bathroom Bill and this backdrop of anti-trans sentiment, Green was offered a residency at the Arts/Industry program hosted by Kohler Center for the Arts in Sheboygan, Wisconsin. Kohler is a company particularly renowned across

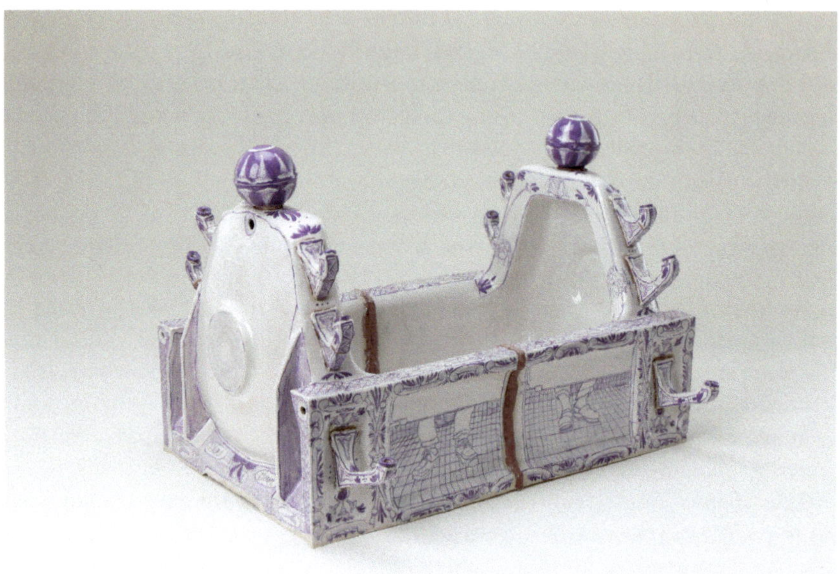

**Figure 2.4** Nicki Green, *A Discrete History of Intimacy and Violence (Double Urinal Basin With Faucets)*, 2019. Glazed vitreous china and epoxy, 27 × 36 × 34 inches. Courtesy of Nicki Green.

the United States for its kitchen and bathroom plumbing fixtures. This program allows practitioners to expand the scale of their practice, working within a factory setting and providing access to machinery and mass-manufactured ceramic objects. Concurrently angered by these attacks on trans rights and inspired by the domestic objects within the factory, Green began working with objects such as bidets and urinals, playfully making hybrid works that explored the gendered politics of the bathroom. In *A Discrete History of Intimacy and Violence* (2019), she fused two urinal basins and utilized the stark white surface of the ceramic to illustrate a scene about partitioned bathroom stalls (Figure 2.4). Painted on the surface are tableaus of feet under bathroom stalls in which the gender of the inhabitants may only be indicated by the style or size of the shoe. It reflects the absurdity of policing gender within bathrooms and implicates the viewer within this voyeuristic dynamic, as the composition is cropped in such a way that only the bottom of the door, feet, and floor are visible. The paradoxical title highlights how these supposedly intimate spaces can become sites of violence for so many trans people.

Of course, objects like sinks, toilets, tiles, and bathtubs are usually made of porcelain for practical purposes; porcelain vessels hold hot water without cracking or corroding and are easy to clean. However, these valuable and functional objects sold to commercial and residential clientele have become functionless in Green's scavenging practice. The faucets mentioned in the work's title have been upturned and attached as decorative appendages on the exterior of the basin. Because of this, there are no basin holes for "dirty" water to drain away. Devoid of instruments of drainage and cleansing, Green seems to construct a commentary around waste, cleansing, and the abjection of queer and trans bodies. These associations are significantly furthered by the fact that Green is using the factory's discards—its waste products—the broken, rejected, discarded ceramic "bodies." Yet, Green breathes new life into them, seeing their value and beauty. Of course, disasters are inevitable in ceramic practice, but for factories like Kohler, these "damaged goods" are no longer suited to commercial benefit and gain. Green's use of the factory's rejects and discards becomes a neat metaphor for discussing the identities of those frequently designated as society's rejects and discards. If dirt is "matter out of place," as Mary Douglas infamously proclaimed, then people who are marked as dirt and disposable are also "out of place."[62] More specifically, Green's reappropriation of these factory discards seems to comment on purity politics, precisely how toilets have long been a political battleground and space for segregation.

As writer and journalist Eleanor Penny observes, panics around trans people using public bathrooms are "just the latest salvo in an ongoing battle over whose bodies are worthy of dignity, whose lives should be protected, whose existence the arbiters of public morality can bring themselves to tolerate."[63] In fact, these spaces filled with seemingly mundane ceramic objects can be used to reflect upon the ideological and political leanings of Western powers throughout modern history, as sociologists such as Tara Atluri have also attested.[64] Or, to put it simply, our lives and our identities have long been governed by the ideologies of places in which we piss and shit. Historically, this has included various social groups including women who were originally denied access to toilets in US workplaces, then gay men who were attacked and criminalized for cruising or "cottaging" in public toilets in the United Kingdom, and racial segregation across most of the Global North.[65] These examples are all analogous to arguments in favor of trans-exclusion as they all encourage similar absurd fears about the need to protect one social group against another social group who are perceived as a threat to the dominant order, as corrupting or "polluting" vessels. In short, these ceramic objects, which ordinarily belong in bathrooms, are inextricable from classification systems and discourses of purity that frame racial, gender, and class hygiene—especially notions of purity and cleansing.[66]

The politics of discrimination, segregation, and racial purity are even inextricable from modern ceramic history, more broadly, and this is reflected at the very material level of ceramics and its use among specific communities. As European potters attempted to imitate the refined porcelain of China in the mid-eighteenth century, dishes became whiter by varying degrees until whiteware was eventually developed between 1820 and 1830. Coarser, more "earthy" (and therefore darker) ceramics remained in circulation during the nineteenth century but mainly for use among the working classes, especially Black laborers. This played a central role in what anthropologist James Deetz terms a "whitening of America," where white porcelain tableware became a symbol of White superiority and upper-class society.[67] Craft is not neutral; it never has been. More accurately, craft is not inherently political but takes form and is embedded within broader social, political, economic, and aesthetic systems. As with most crafts, discussions of ceramics cannot be separated from the history of colonization and the subjugation of bodies.

These issues around the historical complicities of the human and non-human in narratives of colonization, race, and gender are not only reflected in Green's material choices and forms but also in their highly ornate designs, which frequently reference mushrooms and fungi. In a short entry on the popular ceramics blog *CFile*, Sorkin observes these seemingly innocent decorative forms in Green's ceramics, noting how they reflect a metaphoric rendering of the trans body. In her analysis, Sorkin notes how "Green's mushrooms are carefully androgynous: rendered as sensuous, multipartite organisms, wholly reflective of the simultaneous means of sexual and asexual reproduction possible in spores, which have web-like networks below the surface, their root systems akin to the idea of a communal support system that often goes unseen in the lives of queer people."[68] They also relate to racial, ethnic, and religious cleansing, following Green's discovery of a book from 1938 titled *Der Giftpilz* (*The Poisonous Mushroom*), a piece of Nazi-era propaganda about hidden poisonous "Jewish" mushrooms lying in wait among the "harmless" edible mushrooms of the forest. The cover shows an anti-Semitic caricature of a bearded Jewish face under a mushroom cap. "So much about the development of queer cultural iconography is about reclaiming derogatory concepts and images…[s]o the idea of reclaiming the mushroom feels like this super empowering thing," Green said in a studio visit.[69] To Green, mushrooms are not slimy, deadly fungi, they are things of beauty and inherently related to queer and trans identity, as many ecological scholars have attested.[70] As Sorkin alludes to, their mycelial networks spread underground, helping forests receive nutrients. They form a network of kin, disparate but connected, and highly resilient.

The themes of spirituality and cleansing in Green's work extend beyond mere decoration alone and are reflected in the forms her large hand-built ceramics take. These often reference the space of the mikveh, a large (and usually public) bath used for ritual purification in Judaism wherein the body is immersed and emerges transformed. The mikveh is fundamentally a site of transition, too. Those converting to Judaism are submerged entirely under the water and emerge as Jews. Many immerse themselves in the water to mark other transitions: graduations, b'nai mitzvahs, healing from a long illness, and orthodox women cleanse their bodies at the end of their menstrual cycle. Today, some gender-inclusive mikvehs invite trans Jews to use the space to celebrate their transition to a new embodiment of gender.[71] However, much like the space of public bathrooms and changing rooms, the mikveh can be subjected to a policing of the gender binary, reinforcing traditional gender norms and ways of being whole, excluding queer bodies. Green's work reimagines the religious ritual as an active space of inclusion for trans bodies, as reflected in works such as *The Porous Sea (Tub)* (2019). This piece takes the form of a sizeable hand-built tub. Although it is too small for most people to submerge themselves in, it references the mikveh's tiled spaces and watery ecologies. The inside of the "tub" is glazed and decorated with images of fungi and alchemical symbols. Due to the hand-built nature of the clay, the surface is even, and the surface patterns become distorted by the fingerprints and marks in the clay. Because of this, the images painted onto the glazed ceramic become slightly warped, as if distorted by gentle waves of water, despite the empty tub. White glaze drips down the brown earthenware exterior as if it splashed out. Green fungi also surround the base of the tub, as if providing a support structure and holding it up. When queer and trans bodies have frequently been the targets of violence and marginalization under the guise of religion, this embracing of one's faith, a connection to a power greater than oneself, seems crucial to many.

## Conclusion

Ceramics are clearly well positioned to document and archive trans experiences. As handmade objects that are uniquely individual, they uniquely embody the marks of their maker, acting as an indexical trace of the body. In the work of Schmits and Green, a connection emerges between resistance, resilience, and the inherent fragility of material, the body, and the body *as* a material. Schmits's *TransForms* series exemplifies how crafting objects mirrors the process of crafting the self. These ceramics not only carry the physical mark of their creator but also, through narrative forms, offer a lasting record of the injustices faced by the trans community. Unlike fleeting digital trends, ceramics ensure these stories are passed on for generations and demonstrate the creative spaces of resistance that flourish in the wake of hostility. Both Schmits's *We Live in a Society* series and Green's *Tres in Una* showcase a symbiotic relationship between the digital and the handmade. Ceramics, as an offline method for these practitioners, becomes an invaluable tool to preserve online cultures. These creations are then reintroduced to the world, online and offline, sparking conversation and enriching meaning. Despite ongoing discrimination and violence towards trans people, Schmits and Green's work ultimately celebrates the enduring spirit of trans bodies, mirroring the enduring nature of ceramics itself.

# Chapter 3

## WOOD

### AGAINST THE GRAIN: QUEER FURNITURE AND THE POLITICS OF DISCOMFORT

*Introduction*

Are you sitting comfortably? If you're a fellow queer, then perhaps not! Joked about between those within the LGBTQ+ community and reflected in countless memes circulated online, many queer people refuse to sit "properly," "correctly," "normally," or, well, "straight."[1] This discourse gained further attention in July 2019 when a drawing by Brazilian illustrator Má Matiazi went viral on Instagram. Matiazi's design for a wooden chair, dubbed the "bi-chair," "[d]esigned for people who can't sit straight."[2] Posted with the caption "Have you heard about bi-sitting?," the drawing was intended as satire, commenting on stereotypes of how LGBTQ+ people sit.[3] Inspired by the drawing, Iowa-based carpenter Israel Walker contacted Matiazi for permission to build the chair for his genderqueer and bisexual child, who often joked about their own sitting habits. The resulting chair featured various elements to facilitate different postures: a small shelf built into one leg for resting a foot, crossing a leg, or even crouching instead of sitting. Matiazi's design and Walker's realization of it (several versions of which were sold on Etsy) garnered international press coverage, sparking discussions about "queer sitting" and the "queer use" of furniture.[4]

While generally discussed in light-hearted terms, notions of queer sitting engage with a real and lengthy history of bodily regulation and expression, especially for queer disabled and neurodivergent bodies who may not sit "differently" out of choice but out of necessity. Of course, the "politics of posture" is well documented—from historical expectations that women would sit with their knees together to symbolize modesty and piety, to more contemporary debates about "manspreading," countless examples illustrate the control and defiance surrounding gendered politics and the occupation of space.[5] Furniture can become an extension of our bodies, facilitating behavior, enabling movement, and generating comfort. Conversely, it can also control behavior, restrict or deny access, and limit comfort for certain bodies. To use furniture queerly is to disrupt normative modes of sitting, being, and existing. This nonconformity encourages alternative orientations and relationships with objects in space—perhaps sitting cross-legged in a chair, standing on a table, or using furniture in unintended ways. Queer sitting challenges dominant culture's compartmentalized, strictly defined, and socially prescribed rules about how bodies interact with space and objects, resisting assimilation. After all, "to make things queer is certainly to disturb the order of things."[6] Many queer woodworkers creating furniture (or sculptural objects that at least nominally *perform* as furniture) may experiment with non-traditional forms and techniques to facilitate these queer uses, or to encourage new orientations by playfully blurring the lines between form and function.

Although the field of woodworking is incredibly expansive—encompassing a range of specific practices such as cabinetry, carving, carpentry, furniture making, joinery, turning, and more—it is perhaps no surprise that many conversations about queer woodworking have specifically revolved around furniture. This is likely because, as the writer, curator, and woodworker Dierdre Visser argues, "[m]ore than any other single material we use, for most communities around the world wood is the literal foundation of home, both its structure and its furnishings."[7] Furniture can especially "invite and constrain, blur boundaries, suggest intimacies, or determine and reinforce relations of power . . . [w]e cleave, carve, and join wood to make the world habitable, to create the objects that make it possible."[8] Furniture is highly personal, reflecting our very identities and personalities. Despite this, discussions on queer woodworking practices are only just beginning to "come out of the woodwork," to invoke both a queer and wood-related pun simultaneously. In her influential publication *Joinery, Joists and Gender: A History of Woodworking for the 21st Century* (2022), Visser articulates an enduring gender imbalance within the field, suggesting that this has caused a significant barrier to access and a reason for the dearth in scholarship. Visser's book is the first to adequately explore the relationship between various forms of woodworking and gender, providing a critical catalog of contemporary woodworkers who challenge these stereotypes and continue to expand the field. While it primarily focuses on women woodworkers who have not been given "commensurate attention" as male woodworkers, she acknowledges that this disparity also extends to queer and gender nonconforming woodworkers who, comparatively, are "invisible on bookshelves and in woodworking magazines."[9]

Conscious of a continued lack of visibility for LGBTQ+ makers working with wood, the Museum for Art in Wood, based in Philadelphia, initiated a series of roundtable discussions titled "Queering Wood Craft." These roundtables provided a space for LGBTQ+ woodworkers to connect, collectively advocate for greater representation within the field, and to "share the ways their lived experience impacts their craft, process, and aesthetic."[10] At the time of writing, the series is still ongoing. I have had the privilege of chairing one of the sessions and attending many others, learning with and from other practitioners, curators, writers, and researchers.[11] While hailing from different backgrounds and areas of woodworking, most attendees and participants in the discussions continue to report that a very hetero-masculine archetype still dominates the field of woodwork. Many have attested that they have experienced mistreatment and even violence within spaces such as the hardware store or lumber yard. What emerged from most of the sessions was a clear need for greater visibility within the field, but also the need to develop a critical framework from which to articulate and conceptualize queerness within a range of wood crafts, which I hope to contribute to in the pages that follow.

This chapter aims to continue carving out an important space for queer woodworking practices, specifically those oriented around furniture. It first outlines a brief theoretical framework surrounding the queer capacities of furniture and domestic objects. Then, it focuses on the handcrafted sculptures and wooden furniture by Raul De Lara and Nifemi Ogunro as a particular site for analysis. Both De Lara and Ogunro use a range of pre-industrial techniques associated with furniture making (including carving, joinery, carpentry, and woodturning) to create queer objects that relate to the politics of (dis)comfort. The title of the chapter is drawn from the expression "going against the grain," a woodworking term that means hitting snags or splinters in a piece of wood, preventing a smooth finish and surface. It is also an idiom that means contrary to the natural inclination. This parallels queerness, which can be felt as a rejection of the supposed natural order of cis-heteronormitivty. The practices of De Lara and Ogunro reflect this sense of going against the grain, encouraging new relationalities and orientations that are far from the norm.

### *Queer furniture ...?*

But what is so queer about furniture? Can we argue that furniture is, by design, rather queer? Furniture offers an entry into discussions about identity and the capacity of furniture to function as orientation devices—objects that structure our lives and which may help us to "find our way" through life. For want of a better example, one might think of how the personified domestic objects and furniture in *Beauty and the Beast* (1991) form a network of queer kinship, helping to orient Belle to the unfamiliar space of the Beast's castle. These objects—including the excitable wooden wardrobe "Madame Armoire" and a pendulum clock "Cogsworth," whose stiff and strict manner is as distinctly "wooden" as the material he is made from— invite Belle to be their "guest," supporting her through hardships and ultimately helping her to feel comfortable within an environment that was initially hostile and unfamiliar. These ideas reoccur in various methods of "low" cultural representation and appear across a range of "high" theoretical literature.[12]

Often, to engage with queer theory is to engage with a theory of furniture. Although it may seem like a curious preoccupation, queer theorists have long written about objects such as closets, tables, chairs, and beds because of their ability to tell us about their function as orientation devices. Our bodies, identities, and experiences are often oriented around furniture, be it physical or metaphorical, and they can be associated with personalities, memories, and experiences. For instance, Sedgwick orients us towards the closet in her book *Epistemology of the Closet* (1990). She turns to several definitions of the closet as a "room for privacy," and a space associated with phrases such as "skeleton in the closet," meaning that someone is concealing a truth.[13] She argues that the symbolic space of the "closet" is a feature of most people's lives, but especially for queer lives who may find themselves *in* or *out* of the closet, concealing or revealing one's sexuality.

Bisexual activist and author of *Sexual Politics* (1970), Kate Millett, received critical acclaim for her scholarship which denounced heteronormativity, masculine authority, and patriarchal divisions of labor within the domestic sphere.[14] Yet, unfamiliar to many people, her writing was preceded by an extensive period of making where she produced a series of "fantasy furniture" from hand-carved wood. These were first exhibited as a solo show in 1967 at the Judson Gallery in New York and were "re-discovered" in 2022 when they were posthumously displayed at Salon 94 in New York (Figure 3.1). Like her writing that would eventually follow the creation of the series, these objects critiqued the couple form. Her anthropomorphic furniture provided a pointed but humorous mediation on how the division of labor is reflected in home furnishings and how these objects reflect gender politics. Re-made in Millet's image, seemingly mundane domestic objects, including a bed, a cabinet, a piano, a stool, and several chairs, are ascribed some degree of agency as opposed to performing their expected passivity. They become "alive," with arms, hands, legs, feet, heads, and eyes, and become somewhat of a physical realization of the unheimlich. In *Bed* (1965), two figures seem to lay upright, their feet stiffly facing the ceiling rather than intermingled in passion. They seem engulfed or confined by the form, and a clear dividing line separates them. In *Love Seat* (1965), two more figures carved from wood sit next to each other but face opposite directions, using the visual language of a traditional Victorian-style courting chair but suggesting a lover's tiff instead of a lover's flirtation. Millet explained that making these sculptures allowed her to hone her ideas, and "made its own meaning, stronger and better than words could say it."[15] Yet, these works were belittled by critics at the time who said that they evidenced she was an "overwrought and undersexed woman" and her academic colleagues saw them as a "frivolous distraction" to her writing and activism. Not only did the discourse at the time serve to delegitimize practice as a valid form of knowledge, but it also reflected the sexual politics of the division between art and craft, especially given that objects created by her then-husband, Japanese sculptor Fumio Yoshimura, were praised for showcasing the "artistic" potentials of wood.[16] Given that Millet married Yoshimura and moved in with him in 1965, the same year most of the objects in this series were created, her "fantasy furniture" might speak less to a fantasy of domestic bliss and more of a nightmare of domestic misery. The works reflect how furniture and the spaces it inhabits can be constraining, just as much as it can be hospitable, and unhomely just as much as homely.

Similar ideas are also explored in Ahmed's book *Queer Phenomenology: Orientations, Objects, Others* (2006). Here, Ahmed refers to the English-language idiom "you treat me like furniture," which is an expression that means "you treat me like I am not here," or more accurately, "you treat me like I am part of the background."[17] Queer theory's considerations of queer furnishing might not be such a surprising formulation after all, given that the word "furnish" is related to the word "perform," thus inherently tied to concepts of visibility and appearance.[18]

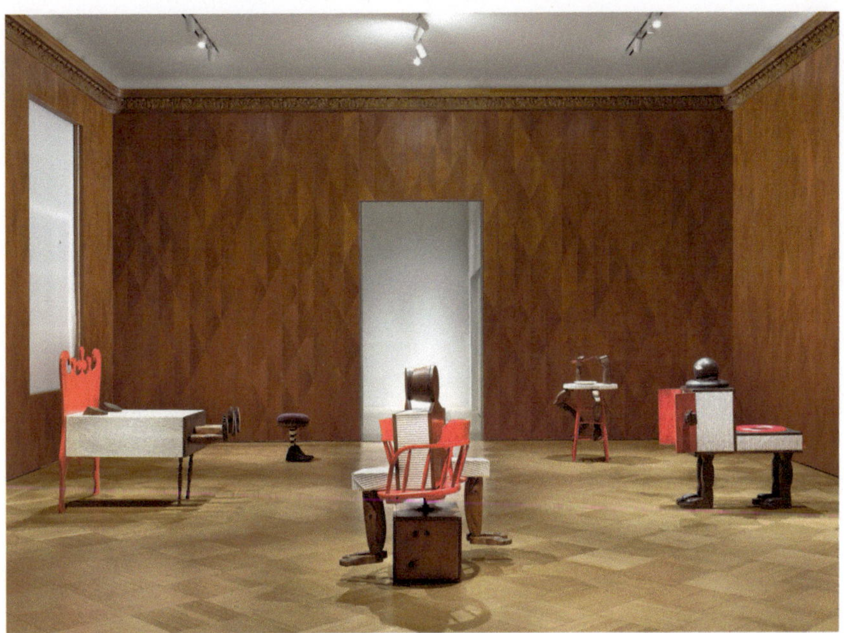

**Figure 3.1** Installation view, Kate Millett, *Fantasy Furniture*, 1967, 2022. Image courtesy of Kate Millett Trust and Salon 94 Design. © Kate Millett Trust. Photo: Dan Bradica.

Yet, if "[q]ueer becomes a matter of how things appear, how they gather, how they perform," Ahmed argues, then the opposite is true of furniture. In a conventional sense, furniture often "disappears" as we become accustomed to it, becoming an unnoticed everyday essential. A queer furnishing might therefore be about making what is in the background, what is behind us, more visible: "[a]s soon as we notice the background, then objects come to life, which already makes things rather queer."[19] This is certainly true of the work of Millett and other practitioners working with furniture who may exaggerate or experiment with its forms so that they "appear."

Ahmed also examines dual approaches to the concept of "orientation": both in terms of sexual orientation and how we orient or position ourselves in the world. She uses furniture as a metaphor to explain how particular objects and spaces shape our movements and attractions, especially focusing on the queer capacities of tables and chairs. She observes:

Stories of queer kinship will be full of tables. This does not necessarily mean that the table itself becomes a queer object, or that the table necessarily has a different "function" in queer gatherings. And yet, the table might still be the site upon which queer points can be made. To make such a point would be to suggest that there is something rather queer about furniture.[20]

Tables are sites of queer gatherings, where community is built, and activism is born.[21] Ahmed claims that furniture is not necessarily inherently queer because one object might have multiple uses, including non-queer uses, but that we can certainly suggest there is something queer about furniture. Ahmed also articulates how space and objects depend on bodily inhabitance: "orientation is not so much about the relation between objects that extend into space (say, the relation between the chair and the table); rather, orientation depends on the bodily inhabitance of that space."[22] While discussing how queer bodies, and especially queer bodies of color, navigate and understand space, Ahmed stated that to be oriented is "to be turned toward certain objects, those that help us find our way. These are the objects we recognize, so that when we face them we know which way we are facing . . . [t]hey gather on the ground, and create the ground upon which we can gather."[23]

Ahmed also uses the analogy of a chair, reminding us that a chair that feels comfortable to one person might feel awkward to another. Heteronormativity, she suggests, functions similarly—it is a form of public comfort that allows bodies to extend into spaces that have already taken their shape, to assimilate and attempt to "pass" or "fit in." For Ahmed, these orientations, or potential disorientations, can be gendered, sexualized, and racialized, reflective of how queer people, and especially queer People of Color, can often feel like they either "fit" or "do not fit" within certain spaces. In some cases, this might be comfortable, leading to feelings of warmth, satisfaction, and a sense of "easiness"—like that "sinking feeling" we get when we sit in a comfortable chair that may have molded to the shape of our body over time. Yet, on the other hand, this pressure to follow the rules of heteronormativity can produce feelings of discomfort, and we may "lose ourselves" or feel disoriented and uncomfortable with unfamiliar objects and spaces, like sitting in a chair accustomed to someone else's body.

Many of the objects featured in this book act as orientational devices. The objects provide an essential source of identification and support, sharing a language of belonging and a desire for acceptance while ensuring that an archive of the complexities and nuances of the queer experience endures. The interconnections between queerness, identity, and furniture that have been briefly outlined here are clearly of relevance when considering furniture making and woodworking through a queer lens, especially allowing us to consider the relationship between crafted objects and bodily inhabitance as these objects and bodies "work together." With this framework in mind, I now turn to the work of De Lara and Ogunro.


### Raul De Lara (b.1991, Mexico)


Raul De Lara's hand-carved furniture and sculptures explore cultural identity, language barriers, and body language—a language that transcends borders and state lines. His work is narrative-driven, ruminating on his personal experiences of immigrating to the United States from Culiacán, Sinaloa, Mexico, aged twelve, and growing up in Texas, USA, as a non-English speaker. De Lara recalls a captivation with wood (especially its use in furniture) from a young age, as his father worked for an architectural firm, and he regularly visited woodshops and furniture factories with him. Later in life, De Lara also spent several years working in a furniture shop in Chicago and was also an assistant to the queer African-American artist Nick Cave (b.1959, USA), where they "bonded over attention to detail, histories that are embedded within materials, and seemingly mundane objects that can become symbols of race, racism and power."[24] His work is highly conceptual and process-oriented, demonstrating a skilled knowledge of his chosen material, wood.

After an early career as a sponsored freestyle BMX rider, De Lara began taking art classes at a community college before enrolling at the University of Texas at Austin in 2012 to study a BFA in Art. While there, he also took a wood design course in the School of Architecture, sparking a deeper interest in material and form which he then explored through an MFA in Sculpture. With a foundation that spans architecture, studio art, and sculpture, De Lara initially focused on experimental and sculptural practices—crafting wooden plants, cacti, talismans, and masks that explored organic form and symbolic meaning. He became well-known for his series of "tired tools"—carved interpretations of mops, brooms, and shovels that twist, droop, and sag—anthropomorphically evoking exhausted immigrant laborers and emerging as abstract "portraits of invisible labor."[25] Still, he recently desired to utilize his woodworking skills in making functional objects. De Lara explained that the multifaceted nature of his practice is deliberate and informed through his multiple experiences across art, craft, design, and architecture environments. In our conversations, De Lara revealed a sense of never really "fitting in," both in terms of his national or cultural identity and a sense of disciplinary identity, but that his practice enables him to embrace this sense of awkwardness. "I used to think I had to choose—do I want to be a designer? Do I want to be an artist? Do I want to make furniture? Do I want to make things that *look* like furniture? I realized I don't have to choose; it can be its own thing, I can be my own thing. I started thinking about queering ideas of tradition, function, and personhood."[26] "People often describe me as an artist, but I do not really identify with that; I usually refer to myself as a sculptor. Anyway, I'm not huge on labels," he added.[27] De Lara said: "I see my work as a way of honoring craft traditions, respecting generational knowledge, and keeping them alive. But also combing this with new developments in woodworking and making space for the creation of new or often unheard narratives," sentiments that reverberate through the words of many of the featured practitioners.[28] Operating within a fluid and broad spectrum but still firmly grounded in the materiality and histories of wood, De Lara's works are invested in queering categories while also deliberately blurring the line between form and function.

Since then, De Lara has produced hand-carved, functional chairs, employing both reductive and additive techniques. He explains, "I've been perfecting my tufted carving technique for eight years now, and I finally feel ready to start expanding my practice into furniture and functional objects."[29] *Soft Chair* (2022) exemplifies this shift, though its title is somewhat misleading. Carved from a single block of mesquite wood, the chair uses *trompe l'oeil* to mimic the soft textile cushioning of a chintz armchair. Carved lines and buttons on the back and seat recreate the folds of upholstery and the fabric tension of button tufting. In contrast to the smooth, oiled, and seemingly "soft" wood of the chair's "fabric," the legs are rough and rustic, with visible live edges that hint at the chair's origins and inherent rigidity. De Lara's first chair, a variation of this design, was created during the wood design class he took during his BFA. Chair-making is often a rite of passage for woodworkers, teaching fundamental tools and techniques while testing the ability to create something functional, ergonomic, and aesthetically pleasing. Rather than crafting a simple chair, De Lara experimented with the tufting technique, which confused his peers. "They asked if it could actually be sat on and were very confused by the form of it," he recalled.[30] De Lara found this ambivalence especially interesting, "it became this *other* thing . . . whatever visual language that chairs are supposed to have, I just took a left. I wanted to create something that lures you in."[31] He explores these different associations in the work, playing on forms of comfort and discomfort. The chair masquerades as inviting, promising a soft seat, only to reveal a hard, solid surface that denies the expected "sinking feeling." This denial resonates with Ahmed's work on the queer and racialized politics of "fitting in" and the "public comfort" of heteronormativity, which is often not extended to queer bodies, especially queer bodies of color.

While often associated with hardness, solidity, and weight, wood can be a light, versatile, and malleable medium—a duality De Lara frequently explores. But this is no easy task, especially given that mesquite is a tough and dense wood due to its interlocking grain. While prized for stability, this characteristic makes it notoriously difficult to carve intricate shapes, especially compared to softer woods. Consequently, mesquite is often used in industrial processes, where machinery can easily cut through it, or in woodturning, where high-speed rotation aids shaping. De Lara's intricate carving of an entire chair from a single mesquite slab is a testament to his skill. Mesquite, a shrub native to the southwestern United States and Mexico, connects him to his geographical roots and also holds further symbolic weight for De Lara. This resilient deciduous plant thrives in extreme desert conditions, establishing deep roots and forming extensive thickets—a powerful allegory for the growth and resilience of the queer community, its ability to withstand hostile environments, and its deep ties to ancestry.

De Lara has made many iterations of these "plush" seats, including earlier works such as *Thinking Chair* (2015) and *A Korean Affair* (2016).[32] He continues making multiple versions of the same work to perfect his craft and recently made different variations of the *Soft Chair* (Figure 3.2) from different woods, animating the material and imbuing it with a sense of character. As De Lara attests, "I don't think of wood as a flat piece of material; I think of it as form, line, rhythm, energy"—sentiments which are echoed by Ogunro later in the chapter.[33] In addition to the one made from mesquite, he also made one from walnut sourced from Pennsylvania and one from Siberian elm sourced from Massachusetts. There is a sense of humor and playfulness in De Lara's approach to his chosen material, and the resulting objects are somewhat whimsical. While the mesquite and walnut chairs feature four carved "buttons," the elm chairs have only two, suggestive of

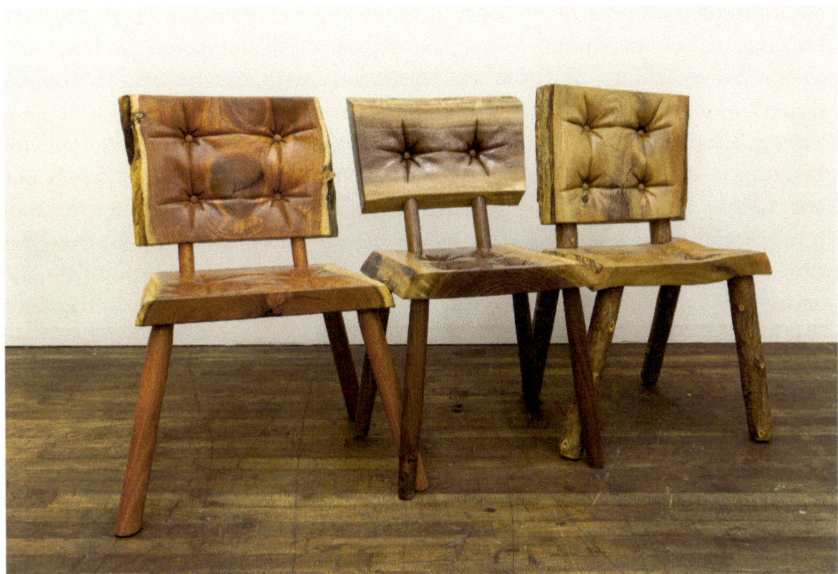

**Figure 3.2** Raul De Lara, *Soft Chair*, 2022. Series of three functional chairs, hand-carved wood (California Mesquite, Siberian Elm, Walnut), dimensions variable. Courtesy of Raul De Lara.

a pair of beady eyes or a pair of inverted nipples. Furniture readily lends itself to anthropomorphism and even our language reflects this, such as referring to the "legs," "backs," "arms," and "feet" of a chair. Photographed together, the three chairs resemble a community, each with its own distinct personality, mirroring the individuality of the wood itself. Furniture is designed in relation to the human body, echoing and supporting its forms. It is fundamentally a bodily experience. We can even feel attraction to furniture, finding it desirable and experiencing sensations of touch as our bodies merge with its surface—inviting habitation and engaging the senses. In his extensive critical analysis of work by American performance artist Scott Burton (1939–1989), queer theorist David Getsy discusses "furniture's solicitation of bodily engagement" at length, particularly regarding Burton's sculptures and public furniture made in the 1980s.[34] Getsy points out that furniture can also perform; it can provide conjugations, offer bodily rest, facilitate queer behaviors such as cruising, and solicit intimacy through touch. In reference to Burton, who saw furniture not as a series of static objects but as a series of "different poses" that can "suggest different genders," Getsy theorizes bodies and chairs as performing agents that can be more than they might first appear and exceed the presumptions that others brought to them. In this view, by enabling or pursuing the queer experience, furniture can encourage new, more inclusive possibilities that challenge the idea of "normal" furniture.

This bodily and sensual quality also characterizes De Lara's work, which acts as a stand-in for the (queer) body even before physical contact. He frequently explores these qualities in his work, particularly with smaller offcuts from his carvings, often transfiguring them into body parts, as seen in *Torso No. 2* (2022). In this piece, De Lara carves a single button into a small square of Siberian elm, suggesting a section of an abdomen with a navel. "Or maybe it's just a butt," De Lara explains, "the ambiguity is fun."[35] In *Torso* (2022), De Lara renders a variation on a classical nude torso statue or headless bust carved in mesquite from San Antonio, Texas (Figure 3.3). Here, the "buttons" carved into the wood function as breasts with pressed, indented nipples. The knots, burls, and cracks in the wood are reminiscent of birthmarks, moles, and wrinkles. De Lara leaves another intact at the bottom of the work, appearing rather vulva-like, and above it, he roughly carves a muscled stomach into the hunk of wood. In these works, the curved lines mimic the folds of upholstery and the folds of the skin. Here, natural aspects of the wood, its knots, and cracks are not concealed but embraced. In a technical sense, he is perhaps more accurately working with, rather than necessarily against, the grain. By highlighting the natural beauty of the wood itself, strategically leaving certain qualities intact as opposed to carving or cutting them off, De Lara seems to celebrate how both the skin of our bodies and the skin of trees have the power to show the passing of time, encouraging us to be comfortable in our own skin and embrace our own materiality.

Unlike those in the *Soft Chair* series, which invite habitation and can physically support a body, other chairs are less welcoming and only give the illusion of function. Many of them comprise thousands of nude sharpened spines that resemble cacti, symbolic of his Mexican roots and a recurring trope in his work to encourage conversations around "nationality, self-hood and identity."[36] These spines are set against the chair's main body, dyed green by mixing green and yellow pigments with a matt binder and applying a light wash to the surface, enabling the wood's natural grain to shine through. Carved over several years, his cacti chairs include *Tornado* (2020), *Lectica* (2021), *Sugar* (2021), *The Wait* (2021), and *The Wait (Again)* (2022), which are more sculptural in form and conceptual in approach—if the viewer were to ever sit on the chair, they would be sure to feel a good "prick." The delicate appearance of the cactus spines, which look like they would snap under a person's weight (despite being made of strong, stable wood), rouses a feeling of vulnerability and precarity. "With the cactus chairs, I was thinking about the space between furniture and design and blurring form and function," De Lara explained.[37] One chair, *For Being Left-Handed* (2020), is designed to look like a small school seat with a writing desk that even has chewing gum stuck underneath, but the chair's use is only implied (Figure 3.4). The work consists of over two thousand individual hand-carved spikes that run over the entire surface of the chair and even raise it from the ground. These are made from wooden dowels that were sanded and left naked to emulate the pale color of cacti spines. These are slotted into holes that were bored into the main body of the chair, and they are held in place by natural pressure. De Lara's close friend, the writer and poet Kevin Fitchett, helped him to place all the spikes within the work. "To

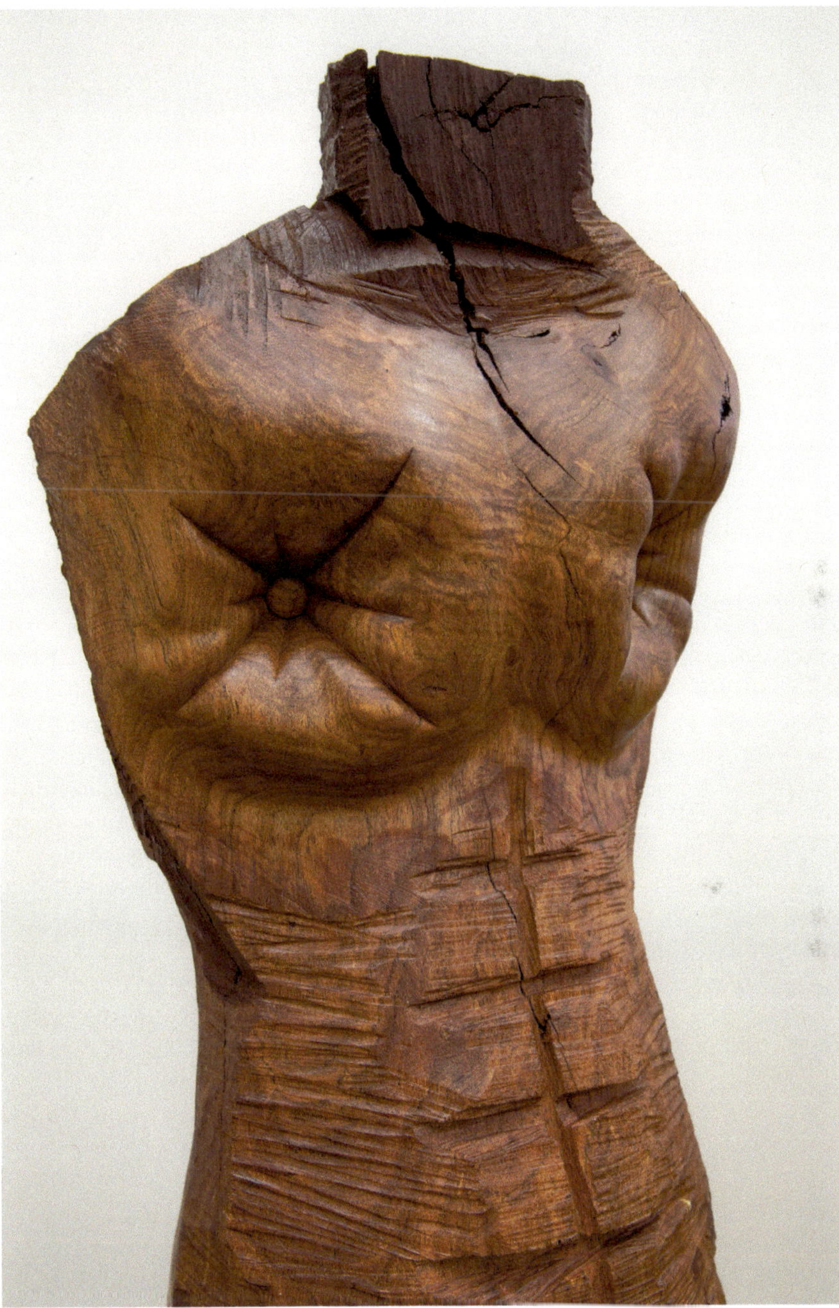

**Figure 3.3** Raul De Lara, *Torso* (detail), 2022. Hand-carved Mesquite from the Carnes Ranch in San Antonio, TX, 28.5 × 10 × 14.5 inches. Courtesy of Raul De Lara.

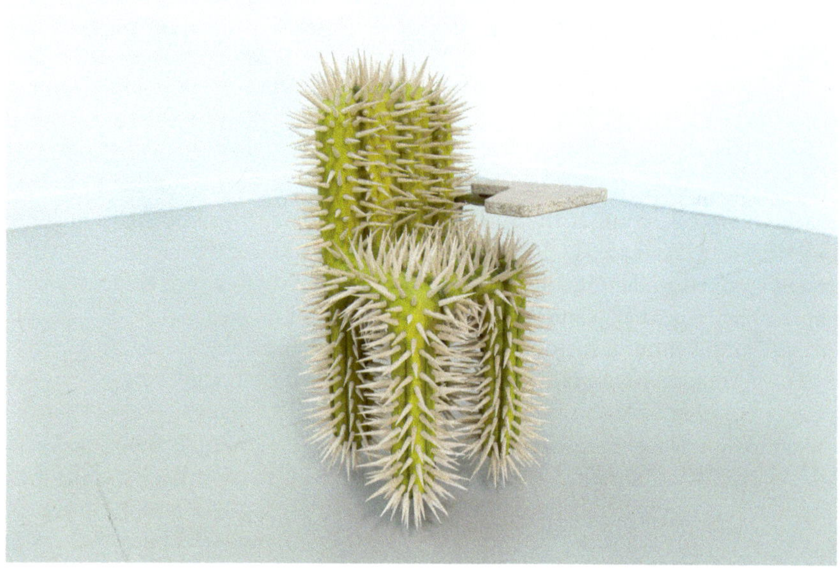

**Figure 3.4** Raul De Lara, *For Being Left-Handed*, 2020. Self-Portrait. Pine, Chiclets Gum, Acrylic, Brass, Steel, Particle Board, 24 × 13 × 13 inches. Courtesy of Raul De Lara.

ensure all the spikes were even and secured, we had to stand face to face, cradle the chair between us, and press our bodies against it. We were both chewing gum, and then a lightbulb moment went off. I asked Kevin to hand me his gum, spat mine out, and stuck both under the desk – then I knew the work was finished," De Lara said.[38]

De Lara's exquisite craftsmanship and attention to detail are key, and he feels it is "a way to infiltrate a message."[39] At first glance, you cannot possibly believe the works are made entirely of wood. The sheer beauty of the work and its material trickery captures the viewer's attention and then demands that you fully engage with the serious topics it addresses. Far from a gimmicky illusion, De Lara describes the work as an exploration of the *uncomfortable* experiences of growing up queer and closeted in school, even calling the chair a sentimental self-portrait. He explains:

"With all the spikes, I wanted to portray hardship, difficulty, and discomfort – that is what the piece [*For Being Left Handed*] is really about. Growing up being a left-handed person, being a Mexican person, being a Spanish speaker, being Dyslexic, having a stutter, being queer . . . it was the whole package of things to get bullied for. I use cacti because it's a poetic way of discussing painful situations. But it's also about beauty and growth as well. Cacti and toxic plants are often beautiful and alluring but also dangerous and painful – you want to touch them even though you know you shouldn't. The work also speaks to this kind of temptation – we shouldn't do a lot of things, but there's always a temptation . . . ."[40]

As De Lara indicates, these works are inherently personal and not just about queerness. After all, queerness does not exist in a vacuum and can be compounded by other facets or intersections of our identity and lived experience. Here, he mentions the intersections of race, ethnicity, migration, queerness, neurodiversity, and disability, all of which informed his childhood experiences, and which are channeled through his work today to explore both the beauty and pain of not "fitting in." In *The Cultural Politics of Emotion* (2004), Ahmed notes that "queer feelings may embrace a sense of discomfort, a lack of ease with the available scripts for living and loving, along with an excitement in the face of the uncertainty of where the discomfort may take us."[41] Ahmed particularly argues that norms are a matter of impressions and describes how bodies are "impressed upon" by the world. After all, she argues, "[n]ormativity is comfortable for those who can inhabit it," but not so much for others who fail to follow normative scripts.[42] In this sense, discomfort is not about assimilation or resistance but about inhabiting norms differently. It is about embracing or re-directing those feelings as positive energy, as De Lara does through this work, approaching wood with excitement and a sense of playfulness.

De Lara's exploration of discomfort extends to other cactus chairs, including *The Wait* and *The Wait (Again)*, which take the form of oversized bucket chairs with functional rocking mechanisms made from walnut and cedar. Here, De Lara experiments with the form of the rocking chair, which is often associated with nosy elders sitting on porches, and imbues it with a kind of adolescent wonder, experimenting with different sizes and forms. On the back of one of the chairs titled *The Wait (Again)*, he soldered an image of a heart pierced by an arrow, and its center is colored with pink pencil.[43] This references the practice of carving initials into trees, often within hearts, as a symbol of the perceived permanence of a young couple's love. More accurately, it references the fact that there is a tradition of carving messages to loved ones into cacti in Mexico. This practice can be seen along the border between the United States and Mexico, where refugees and immigrants leave notes to friends, family, and kin who may follow in their footsteps, often including advice, warnings of danger, messages of love, and symbols of hope. The heart on the back of the chair in this work speaks to heartache and pain and simultaneously to love and hope, including the spiritual and ancestral ties that remain even when physical connectivity is impossible.

De Lara and his family originally entered the United States on a tourist visa, but once that expired, they lived there undocumented, and he revealed that this experience is important in understanding the work and his position within the art and design world today. While studying for his degree programs, De Lara became eligible to apply for the Deferred Action for Childhood Arrivals (DACA) scheme via the United States Citizenship and Immigration Services, which was eventually awarded. While this has enabled him to continue living and working in the United States since 2012, he still cannot leave the country and has to reapply to the scheme every two years, "it is a bit of a trap because you can't stop reapplying, and you can't take a step further to become a citizen – it's this weird limbo," De Lara said.[44] The first exhibition he was invited to participate in was in Mexico. He was the only Mexican practitioner featured in the show but could not travel to deliver work or attend the opening. This prompted a new way for De Lara to think about his practice: "What do I want to say? What do I stand for? How can the work and material speak for me when I cannot?".[45] De Lara sent Fitchett on his behalf: "I gave him the spiritual powers to be me and go as me. I even trained him on Spanish and what to say," De Lara joked with me.[46] In today's increasingly global woodworking industry, modularity in design (a principle of subdividing an object into smaller parts or "modules") has become an essential principle for many practitioners in recent years. It enables flexibility and means that objects can be sold internationally and shipped across the world quickly while offering other practical benefits such as reduced shipping costs and environmental impact. All of De Lara's works are modular, apart from those in the *Soft Chair* series, which are built to be solid. However, modularity is necessary for him and is not just a conscious design choice. The bitter reality of US immigration policies is that his materials and objects have greater freedom of movement than he does as the maker. As a DACA recipient, he cannot deliver or install work himself. Hence, it must fit into a crate to transport via airplane and be easy enough to fit together so that a client or curator can assemble an object themselves. He states: "I find craft to be an act of self-empowerment and liberation because these skills are something that can't be taken away from me even in the case of being deported."[47] In her writing, Ahmed also writes how she is "struck by how movability is a condition of meaning for furniture," and how we "furnish space with "moveable objects.""[48] The movability and portability of objects for practitioners such as De Lara is not only a necessity but also becomes part of its story and narrative.

In navigating multiple countries, states, and cultures, "home" becomes less about the physical space and more about the objects surrounding us, sentiments which De Lara echoed. Designer and scholar Yénika Castillo Muñoz notes, "[i]n the experience of migrating and becoming part of a diaspora, our identities shift, as we enter a state of tension between total assimilation and resistance, questioning our national hegemonic values and ways of being."[49] Research across fields such as design theory, material culture, and the nascent field of queer migration studies, shows that marginalized and displaced groups, despite limited access to resources, continue to customize their homes and cleave their own objects to reflect their memories and traditions through an "aesthetics of the everyday."[50] The interaction with the domestic space and material objects that furnish them hold personal significance and contribute to a deep sense of belonging, as De Lara has attested. Arts and culture editor Debika Ray argues, "[i]n these circumstances, home becomes less about spaces than the objects you can take with you—objects that are not just reminders of specific moments but carriers of meaning and ancestral ties. These things are bound up with who we are, where we've come from and what we want to be and, by placing them in new contexts . . . we make ourselves at home again."[51]

Unable to visit his homeland of Mexico and feeling heartache for "home," mementos surround De Lara in the studio—mostly made from wood—including folkloric sculptures and traditional wooden masks posted to him by family members and friends. Such narratives offer De Lara what he calls "energies," from which his work draws its force and inspiration.[52] He even thinks about his craft as a form of storytelling through making. "Exploring the visual language of mask making, furniture design, architecture, and nature, I practice traditional hand-carving and power-carving techniques to imbue social, cultural and spiritual qualities into wood—as I see it, storytelling via wood," De Lara explains.[53] Further, it is essential to note that wood holds an important spiritual and cultural referent in Mexican culture, and even more so in forms of Catholicism. Growing up, De Lara was "fascinated with the idea of being able to capture certain kinds of energy into chunks of wood."[54] He recalls: "I was exposed to religious wooden figurines placed inside these wooden shrine frames that symbolized either a saint, an event, or a deity . . . once we moved to the USA, my family only brought a few of these shrines with them. I found two empty wooden shrine frames in my parents' garage, and that gave me the idea of placing materials, objects, and reminders of important ideas inside them."[55] Integrating his growing knowledge of furniture with his roots in sculptural building, De Lara's objects act as talismans and symbols of empowerment for Mexican and Latinx LGBTQ+ people that can become positive beacons of energy within the home, not unlike the carved material culture of Mexican Catholicism.

Woodworking is ultimately a "gateway to habitation and domesticity," but De Lara highlights the instability of these associations among queer people, especially for queer migrants, immigrants, and refugees to whom the notion of "home" is so contested. As mentioned in Chapter 1 concerning forms of queer worldmaking, home is not necessarily a "fixed" location. Having a place to call "home" and owning handcrafted furniture to adorn the space with is ultimately a luxury. De Lara talks openly about his experience of migration and how it forms a central focus of his work, which also considers ideas of national identity and "rootedness" through materials that are inextricably linked to a sense of place. In 2015, he was invited to partake in a residency at Ox-bow School of Art in Michigan, and one of the other residents was a writer and scientist who delivered a lecture about invasive species. De Lara asked the scientist, "How long does it take to no longer be considered invasive?".[56] He responded, explaining that it is often not about time or event about the plant species and its qualities, but about who has the power to name something as invasive or native. De Lara became invested in how this narrative extends to naming people and communities: "Who is getting to call us the citizens, or the natives of America?", he rationalized. The categorization of plant species as "invasive aliens" has been characterized as an extension of xenophobia, tied to much longer histories of colonialism, imperialism, and violence against both lands and bodies.[57]

De Lara demonstrates great care and respect for the land from which his materials originate. Working with a natural resource can reveal a "narrative rooted in geography, climate, and migration, or provide an entryway into ideas about agency and the agent"—wood is engrained with countless stories and histories.[58] When asked where De Lara sources his material, he states, "[w]ood is generally my first choice to work with. Some pieces of wood I use are from historical sites, some are from Home Depot, some pieces are cursed, while others are rescued, and others are smuggled into the country."[59] Some of the woods De Lara works with must be sourced and harvested directly as they are not commercially available. He often works with every part of the tree at every stage of its life cycle, including seeds like Tz'ite—a bright red, bean-like seed from the coral tree often used in Mayan divination—which he sometimes incorporates as decorative details. To cleave wood is to engage with layers of history, connecting to a lineage of hands responsible for planting, nurturing, cutting, and distributing the tree. De Lara honors these labor patterns through his practice. Before his father's passing, they connected with a friend in Mexico who farmed Zompantle wood, a material De Lara desired to use, forging a link to his homeland. "To bring it into the country [the United States], we effectively had to drag it up. We cut the wood into a shippable-sized rectangle, wrote 'live, love, laugh' and shipped it as art. Art has less issues traveling between countries than raw wood does, so we wrote that on the paperwork instead. While we made sure to comply with all regulations, I was effectively playing with the law just as the law plays with us. When it arrived in my studio, I just sanded off the lettering and started carving."[60] "Live, laugh, love," a clichéd slogan frequently found on home décor, has become a symbol of kitsch heteronormativity and homemaking. By appropriating this phrase and inscribing it on the piece of wood, De Lara knew that the (presumed heterosexual) customs officials would readily classify it as "art." When De Lara had an exhibition at the Honor Fraser Gallery in 2023, he took the opportunity to display one of the pieces.[61] He decided to mount it straight on the wall, surrounded by the cardboard packaging that carried it into the country, complete with all the shipping documents and import paperwork attached. "A lot of people were confused because usually there's lots of refinement in my work, but this piece tells an important story, it's perhaps one of the most narrative-driven works I have made and speaks to much of my personal experiences."[62] De Lara treats wood with the utmost care and respect, whether reusing it, rescuing it, or transporting it into the country This agency isn't often afforded to immigrants entering the United States. There is a careful consideration of "rootedness" and attentiveness to the stories or histories embedded into the wood before De Lara breathes new life into the material.

### *Nifemi Ogunro (b.1995, France)*

Nifemi Ogunro is a Nigerian-American practitioner who makes "functional sculptures" that "reimagine the design language we associate with everyday furniture."[63] The term "functional sculptures" frees her from the limited definitions of any specific disciplinary terms of reference. Ogurno's work has included a range of objects, including stools, bookshelves, tables, and chairs, and those that simultaneously encourage multiple functions—"a coffee table? A stool? Who knows," Ogunro writes about one piece.[64] The works are inherently personal, and deeply connected to a sense of self. "The only narrative I feel confident in telling is my own. The root of my work is to reimagine the way we traditionally engage with objects, question what spaces deserve beauty, and challenge the assumptions we place around functionality," she summarizes.[65]

Ogunro embraces a sense of fluidity by design, allowing the objects to be used *queerly*—when things are used for purposes other than the ones for which they were intended; an "improper use" or "perversion" of material, in Ahmed's view.[66] This is a concept particularly relevant here as many of the works by Ogunro, and many of those featured in this book, are "queer" insofar as they are created by queer-identifying individuals and often about the queer community, but they are also queer in the broader sense of this "improper affiliation"—of failing to abide by social norms and preconceptions of how these objects *should* be made or used, effectively queering them and encouraging queer uses that extend far beyond the identity of its maker. This taps into the history of the word "queer" itself, which has been reclaimed and reappropriated—queer as reused, reuse as queer use.[67] Ogunro stated: "When buying furniture, it is dictated and sold as a specific object – as a side table, or as a stool. I don't like defining how someone will see something in their space, my work can be multiple things with multiple uses."[68] "It's interesting to me that there are norms of how to use furniture, but they're only upheld in specific contexts or such as social etiquette which me and most of my friends don't care about. I enjoy playing with perception," Ogunro added.[69] As Ogunro hints, there is a power, and even enjoyment, in the subversive nature of queer craft which fundamentally delights in fluidity, slipperiness, and play.

When she set out to study industrial and product design at North Carolina's Appalachian State University, a mandatory course in furniture led Ogunro to experiment with queering its typical forms, such as placing the chair frame to the top of the work rather than the bottom. "It was really liberating," she said. "I was able to not only have an idea, but three days before it was due, I flipped the frame upside down because I wanted the piece to look different. I just *reoriented* what I'd drawn and went with it."[70] "Furniture, something that interacts with the body, is just a surface . . . these objects are just planes; you have the floor, the ceiling, and walls. When you think in that way, you can really make anything," she describes.[71] "We see a chair the way that we've been told a chair needs to look, but the second you strip it of four legs and a back, all of a sudden you have different lines and curves . . . everything can be a source of inspiration."[72] This idea of refusing to follow the "rules" demonstrates how re-orientation and forms of "failure" can be productive, and even a site of resistance, encourage different relations to objects and ways of living and being. In this sense, it can represent a performance of dissent and refusal while also emerging as a productive force. Ogunro's objects push us to actively build new connections by accepting, rather than disavowing, different orientations or feelings of unease.

Shaped by her experience navigating various cultures, Ogunro's approach to woodworking is deeply informed by the way her body moves through and interacts with the world. Born in Lyon, France, to a Nigerian family, Ogunro moved to Colorado, where she worked for sculptor Michael Beitz (b.1966, USA), known for his artistic but functional contorted furniture. She grew her portfolio during downtime at Beitz's studio, eventually receiving several commissions and exhibition opportunities. Ogunro then lived in North Carolina to study at Appalachian. After graduating in 2017, she moved to Brooklyn, New York, for graduate school, where she still lives and works. Putting down roots and forming connections without a permanent or stable home is often difficult. Throughout all these moves, Ogunro has had to bring her family with her in spirit, and in her first collection, she produced a series of functional objects inspired by them. *Mrs. Sola* (2020) and *Tob(i)* (2020) are a pair of bent-plywood stools named after Ogunro's mother and father (Figure 3.5). Both designs share the use of arches, a form Ogunro frequently employs for its evocative duality of "openness and enclosure."[73] It is also a testament to her skill given that bending solid wood is highly technical and time-consuming, including the use of many jigs and clamps to "set" the wood in its desired form. Similarly, a coffee table titled *Tope* (2020) honors her brother. This piece blends modern and rustic elements, featuring a curved, bent-wood base that supports a natural log top with a chainsaw-cut edge and exposed bark. "The 'Mrs Sola' stool is an inside joke," says Ogunro. "When I was growing up, my mother was always like, 'I'm not your friend. Put a Mrs in front of my name.'"[74] "The "Tob(i)" stool was based on my father," she continues. "He's an engineer, and people would always misspell his name as Toby."[75] As for the table, Ogunro felt that only her brother would appreciate its true abstract beauty.[76] When discussing furniture, we often do so as a collective. For example, we may refer to a "family" of stools, which would indicate a group of stools of the same type, a "nest" of tables where different-sized tables can slot under one another, or a "coterie" of tableware where all the pieces are identical. These ideas are realized quite literally in Ogunro's work, which draws inspiration from her own closest relations.

In addition to previously drawing inspiration from her family, Ogunro's immediate environment and interactions within the world more directly inform her work. She creates novel furniture forms by observing how the human body moves and interacts with different surfaces. In recent years, Ogunro has focused on rethinking the design of chairs, particularly the contrast between their formal structure and the body's natural desire for movement and freedom. Living in Brooklyn, she is inspired by tight apartment corridors, sprawling plazas, and claustrophobic subways. Her process involves spending a vast amount of time visualizing her body's movements and reflecting on its feelings before even reaching for a hammer and chisel. She often makes sketches comprising fluid lines and organic shapes that reflect the natural curves and movement of the body as it navigates through space, as well as sharper lines and geometric forms

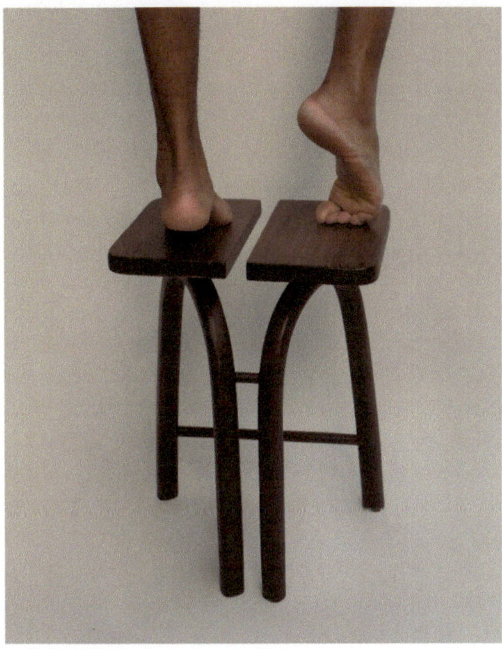

**Figure 3.5** Nifemi Ogunro, *Mrs. Sola*, 2020. Courtesy of Nifemi Ogunro. Photography by Lucy Gale.

to convey its aches, pains, and tightening. Gradually, these responsive gestures are then translated into formal designs. Sometimes, these are visualized digitally using 3D modeling software, but often, Ogunro goes straight to working with the material, making a direct haptic engagement with the wood—responding to it and designing *through* it and *with it*, as opposed to *for* it. Her process is highly intuitive: "the work always looks a specific way when I model, but when I start building it, I always tweak something. It either feels right or it doesn't. It's up to the piece; it does what it wants."[77] When working with wood, the log may split where you do not expect it to, joints might not be tight enough, and the varnish might look different from what you expect, but this is all part of the story and reflective of how we move through life embracing the unexpected. Experiments with unusual textures and engaging with the natural and urban world also permeate Ogunro's work. For instance, her *Untitled* plant stand started in wood before she poured on a gritty concrete slip coating by hand, a technique that has now become a signature of her work. "Textures are an interesting way to play with this dystopian time," she says.[78]

As with many featured practitioners (especially Affect Metals featured in Chapter 5), Ogunro takes creative control over the documentation and display of the objects to claim ownership over the complexities of representation, and the "trap" of visibility, especially for queer practitioners of color. She often stacks or places her functional sculptures askew in the landscape, whether piled up outside a New York brownstone or stacked in a grassy field, frequently returning the works to the sites of their material origin. In a series of videos that she created as part of an online residency with Shelter in Place, which she participated in during the Covid-19 pandemic, Ogunro stands, dances, and interacts with the objects in ways we might not expect, performing their multiple queer uses.[79] She sits on a table, crouches on a bench, and cradles a stool. Further, Ogunro places herself in front of the camera as the model, documenting and videoing her body alongside her work which she feels can promote a challenge to Eurocentric design narratives, in which many craftspeople of color who played a key role in the labor of making are frequently left unseen and uncredited. Recording and documenting her body in conversation and collaboration with her designs means that Ogunro's labor and presence within the work cannot be overwritten, denied, or made invisible. It is a declaration: I am here; I made these objects. For Ogunro, what is equally as significant as the creation of the objects themselves is the creation of a space within a field that has been a locus of privilege and anti-Blackness. This includes uplifting other Black, queer, and femme designers: *we* are here, *we* made these objects. For her, this process is not only crucial to forms of visibility and legibility, but it is also used as an extension of the practice itself to demonstrate the queer uses of the objects she creates. "When creating, I consider my Blackness, my Nigerian-ness, my queerness, my femininity," she states, "and what it means to take up space in an environment that traditionally uses people that look like me for labor, rather than as people whose stories are worth sharing," she summarizes.[80]

Like De Lara's "tired tools," Ogunro draws attention to forms of invisible labor and laborers who are not often acknowledged in the craft world, particularly highlighting the lack of racial and gender diversity in the design industry. "There's disparity between the people who get credited for a product and the people whose hands actually built the product . . . I use my skin to assert my presence, that Black and Brown people do exist in this world," she adds.[81] Debates about decoloniality in design, as well as its connections with intersectional issues around gender imbalance and lack of queer representation, certainly remain primary concerns for those within the field. Decoloniality in design is a process of shifting power and making space, facilitating dialogue with unheard voices across material practices. It becomes a useful way "to re-learn the knowledge that has been pushed aside, forgotten, buried or discredited by the forces of modernity, settler-colonialism, and racial capitalism."[82] As echoed in multiple sections of this book, this is perhaps not only a reclaiming of knowledge or a process of making but also a re-orientation or unmaking, shifting the center of focus and changing cultural attitudes through sensory and affective engagement with materials and materiality. It argues for a fundamental shift in how we view design, encouraging the deconstruction of traditional design narratives and often using sensory knowledge or storytelling, as in De Lara's and Ogunro's work, to imagine new and more inclusive design practices. In this way, their work is not just a practice of making objects but also of care—attending to the histories, the tools, and materiality of wood while holding space for others in the industry.

Despite ongoing conversations and an increased visibility for queer designers of color, when I talked with Ogunro, she revealed that she is becoming increasingly concerned, or at least skeptical, about hypervisibility. This extends beyond just Ogunro's experience and is keenly felt by many practitioners featured in this book, including De Lara and Antonius-Tín Bui (see Chapter 4), who share that strategies of "queering" and/or "decolonising" are simply being used by the cultural sector as buzzwords rather than opportunities for sustained engagement to address systemic inequality and cultural imbalance. Ogunro lamented how curators or writers who are not queer continue to frame her work purely through the lens of identity politics—using her Blackness, her Nigerian-ness, her queerness, and her femininity (as she previously notes) as an exercise in the name of "diversity." Certainly, she states, her work is inspired by all these intersecting experiences and her own body, but this should not be at the detriment of recognizing the actual *craft* of making. Each object demands a minimum of four weeks, assuming Ogunro devotes her full attention to it. "In other interviews, I have been talking about my identities less because I don't get to discuss the process as much. For the work to be valid, it feels like you must have a story, but for cis, straight, white men, the work is just valid," she said.[83] Ogunro adds: "anyone who is othered in any way, existing in a space is already a very radical act. If you don't fit a certain mold, your identities become something of a commodity to justify why the work is important. The pragmatic processes seem to be neglected. I recently made three jigs just to simply bend a piece of wood. I hand-carved all the joins. There are technical things that are also going on."[84] Ogunro's caution about the co-opting of minoritarian voices resonates with the ongoing struggle for queer visibility and legitimacy, especially within the cultural sphere. There is a crucial need to "carve out space" for self-narrated queer experiences and opportunities for authentic recognition. However, to do so, there also needs to be a strategy for resisting the tendency of mainstream culture to extract or reinterpret these experiences in the articulation of so-called "difference" or "otherness." In contrast to Ogunro's earlier very personal series, in which she positioned herself alongside the works, recent pieces shroud the body rather than reveal it, moving more to a language of abstraction as both creative choice and survival strategy. Even in documentation, the objects are now presented against plain backdrops, devoid of people, landscape, or any suggestion of use. This concealment becomes a powerful strategy, cultivating tension through a palpable sense of absence. The only discernible traces of the designer are the subtle imprints left by her hand on the objects themselves. The act of rendering the creator's identity ambiguous constitutes a captivating facet of the work in itself.

Her latest series of chairs prioritizes pure experimentation with form and technique. This shift showcases her mastery in crafting furniture and perhaps a conscious decision to avoid its objectification. These were created for Side Gallery's *Global Tools* exhibition, which featured "ten international designers from five different continents focusing on everyday life and aiming to rediscover a direct relationship between craft and design product."[85] The exhibition title is borrowed from The Global Tools movement, a multidisciplinary experimental program of design education founded in 1973 in Italy by the members of Radical Architecture.

The group aimed to promote the "study and use of natural materials and their behavioural characteristics" and to encourage individuals to develop their creativity freely, outside of the constraints of any identity or disciplinary categorization.[86] Side Gallery aimed to re-invoke these mantras, recognizing the shifting parameters of design in an increasingly globalized world, along with a "return" to the handmade in an age permeated by soulless mass-manufactured IKEA furniture. Ogunro created three works for the exhibition, *Object 1 "Pew," Object 2 "Aside,"* and *Object 3 "Vate,"* which were "grounded in craft and making do with materials."[87] The cohesive series of three chairs, constructed from poplar and birch offcuts, exemplify Ogunro's obsession with the interplay between angular forms and fluid contours. *Vate* (2023), characterized by its open and unadorned design, eschews a traditional backrest in favor of a minimalist form with a fluid arch that forms both the seat and armrests. *Pew* (2023), conversely, presents a study in solidity and strength, referencing the sturdiness of historic church pews and contrasting with *Vate*'s openness. *Aside* (2023) introduces a touch of intrigue with its sculpted seat with two buttock-like indentations, hinting at a long history of use. An application of a dark polystain results in a classic matte black finish and imbues the pieces with timeless quality. As Ogunro reveals, these chairs engage in a deliberate exploration of tension between opposing forces. The series juxtaposes the concepts of old and new, imperfection and perfection, weight and lightness, and openness and enclosure. She said: "I was curious what it would mean to play with both softness and boxiness while designing for this show. That tension excited me. Tension excites me. I wanted my objects to feel like they held weight visually but also soft enough to be inviting. I wanted to make a series of pieces that made sense apart but could create something special together."[88] This sense of existing independently but with the potential for coming together is central to furniture, which encourages the coming together of objects and body or bodies. Furniture certainly encourages gatherings, but it is often a form of gathering, made in a series.

Ogunro's practice has taken yet another turn, mirroring the inherent fluidity of material exploration. She has recently pivoted from designing personal furniture for private spaces to thinking about collaborative pieces for public use. "The practice feels more abstract or conceptual than ever, very uncertain, but intentionally so," she told me in one of our recent conversations.[89] "Sometimes the work is very personal and has to do with my family, but now I am interested in developing works about play and rest as something shared," she added.[90] In June 2024, Ogunro ran a community movement/building workshop in Socrates Sculpture Park in New York, collaborating with movement artist and close friend, Coco Villa. At the public workshop, Nifemi shared her process of building objects, and Villa led the movement portion of the workshop, using one of Ogunro's chairs to perform with, interacting with its surface and forms (Figure 3.6). After the performance, they encouraged participants to move around and pay attention to their bodies' forms and gestures. Participants then made drawings and extrapolated these into designs, eventually building objects that captured the spirit of these movements and reflecting Ogunro's intuitive and empathic process that is attuned to the body. "Stories in craft and design have largely become about consumers and markets.

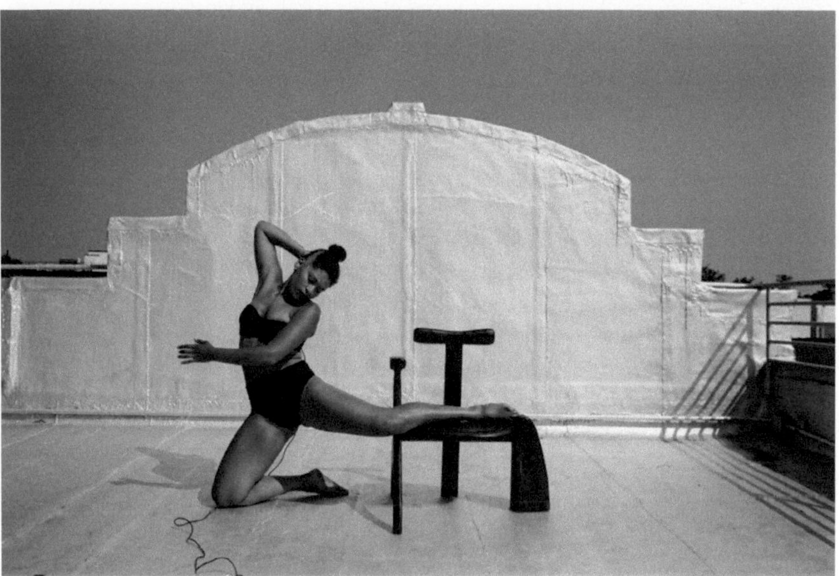

**Figure 3.6** Nifemi Ogunro, *Tumi*, 2023. Courtesy of Nifemi Ogunro and Coco Villa. Self Portrait and Movement by Coco Villa.

Mass-production is necessary and gives everyone access to design, but everything has become homogenized. There is no fun, no play. I want to bring us back to that," Ogunro noted.[91] Building on this experience of sharing design within the community, she is currently aiming to "reimagine what a playground can look like, who it is for, what it means to create a public space for both play and rest" and explore if that space can also feel like its own work.[92] "Much of my practice revolves around feeling and questioning. Why does a chair have to look like a chair? Why do objects for children have to signal that they're for children? Why do tools for healing have to expose an injury rather than add beauty to it?", Ogunro questions.[93] Working towards her first solo show, the designer draws inspiration from the domain of public furniture and recreational equipment, particularly focusing on the seesaw. This fulcrum-based apparatus necessitates the participation of two individuals, each contingent upon the other for ascension. It functions as a metaphor for the reciprocal exchange of queerness within the community, illuminating the structures of support holding queer bodies "up." Individually, we remain grounded. Together, we *rise*.

## Conclusion

Drawing upon a range of theoretical approaches from queer theory and queer phenomenology, this chapter investigates the dynamic interplay between queerness and furniture. Through an analysis of handcrafted wooden furniture and sculptures by De Lara and Ogunro, it explores how they utilize tools and techniques associated with furniture making and woodworking to create objects that relate to the politics of (dis)comfort. Both De Lara and Ogunro push the boundaries of form and function in their designs, which transcend conventional furniture forms and encourage unconventional or indeed "queer" orientations. Wood is often perceived as a solid and inert material devoid of agency—a hard, solid material that is dead once felled. De Lara and Ogunro, however, actively challenge this perception, subverting established associations with wood and exploring its "aliveness." Both De Lara and Ogunro reference the stories and histories associated with wood and woodworking, acknowledging genealogies, ancestries, and absences within design narratives through their practices. Working skillfully with functional aesthetics that lure the viewer in, they offer space for representation and narratives to come to the fore, using their practice as a mode of personal and collective storytelling.

# Chapter 4

## PAPER

### PAPER TRAILS: (DE)CONSTRUCTING IDENTITY THROUGH PAPERCUTTING AND COLLAGE

### *Introduction*

Although we are supposedly living in a "digital age" and a "paperless" society, paper remains a ubiquitous material, as it has been since the invention of papermaking nearly two thousand years ago.[1] We record our lives on paper in the form of diaries, documents, letters, lists, books, articles, manuscripts, zines, manifestos, drawings, scrapbooks, magazines, notes, and more. It forms the foundation of archives, organizing identities, experiences, and even bodies. This act of documentation is inherently tied to social and political power, raising questions about whose stories are preserved and remembered, and whose are lost or erased—the "paper trails" that mark our existence, or, in their absence, hint at what was. To possess paperwork is to be documented and accounted for—birth certificates, passports, visas, and residence permits are all markers of our identity and are used as mechanisms of state control, sometimes even state violence. Its very ordinariness, however, can lead us to overlook paper's significance as a material for creative expression. While craft scholars like Adamson often define "the crafts" as "ceramics, glass making, metalsmithing, woodworking, and the various combinations of process and material that fall under the heading of the textile arts," paper crafts are increasingly recognized as a vital part of this field.[2]

New York's Museum of Arts and Design (MAD) sought to address the perceived lack of attention to paper crafts with its 2009–2010 exhibition *Slash: Paper Under the Knife*. The exhibition aimed to highlight the "international art world's renewed interest in paper as a creative medium and source of artistic inspiration" and showcased a range of paper-based practices, from paper cutting and collage to 3D sculptures, wallpapering, and various "book arts" like scrapbooking, bookbinding, printmaking, and papermaking.[3] In the exhibition catalog that accompanied it, David Revere McFadden, the Chief Curator of MAD at the time, argued that because of its mundane status, paper "carries little cultural, social, or economic baggage."[4] Although commendable in its scope and originality, the intersections between identity politics (particularly queerness) and the creative use of paper were utterly absent, and even obscured, from both the exhibition and its catalog. For example, work by Oliver Herring (b.1964, Germany) was featured. Still, descriptions of his work mentioned nothing of how Herring's creative engagements with paper during the height of the HIV/AIDS crisis reflect upon queer identity and the fragility of the body. This is reflected in works such as *Untitled (Red Coat)* (1993), which was featured in the exhibition. It is a life-size sculpture of a coat constructed entirely from knitted paper (Figure 4.1). This was part of a series from 1991 to 2001 that paid homage to Herring's close friend and drag performer, Ethyl Eichelberger, who died by suicide in 1990 after being diagnosed with HIV/AIDS.[5] Herring had never knitted before but thought that a man working in traditionally feminized craft techniques was an apt tribute to Eichelberger because of the performer's process of gender transgression. He also used the form of a coat as a particularly genderless item of clothing to represent the body in absentia. Knitting with paper is a seemingly impossible act, requiring great care to avoid rips and tears. This offered Herring a slow and meditative process that allowed him to come to terms with Eichelberger's death. Although Herring also knitted with other household materials such as tape, the use of paper served as a metaphor for the fragility of many queer bodies during this period, a material that, like the bodies themselves, would sadly degrade over time. Contrary to McFadden's claim that paper carries little cultural, social, or economic weight, it is arguably one of the most laden, versatile, and physically malleable materials, precisely why many contemporary LGBTQ+ practitioners have explored its queer potential.

One of the few exhibitions to explicitly address the intersection of paper and queerness was *Cock, Paper, Scissors* at the ONE Archives in 2016.[6] This exhibition brought together an intergenerational group of fifteen queer artists, including Jade Yumang (b. 1981, Philippines), Enrique Castrejon (b. 1972, Mexico), and Glenn Ligon (b. 1960, USA), who explored paper's materiality, primarily through collage and collaged scrapbooks. Drawing heavily from archival collections, particularly pornographic print material, the exhibition and its catalog examined how contemporary queer artists have appropriated, reused, and "queered" normative print culture to build new worlds, spanning from the gay liberation era to the present. As curator David Evans Frantz observed: "the production, accessibility, consumption, and, for collage artists, reuse of erotic material has played a powerful role in crafting queer culture."[7] A central theme was the function of the human figure in the work of queer artists using cut paper. Like Herring's work, the physical properties of paper—its flexibility, density, and fragility—become potent metaphors for the skin that covers our bodies. The creative process itself is tactile and often sensual, involving the smooth caress of paper, the fingering through ephemeral print materials (especially with erotic material), and the sticky residues left behind. Even in an age of digital sexual expression, the physical malleability, potential sensuousness, and democratizing nature of paper and erotic print culture make it particularly fertile ground for strategies of queering. As discussed in the Introduction, "queer" often describes the use of something in ways unintended

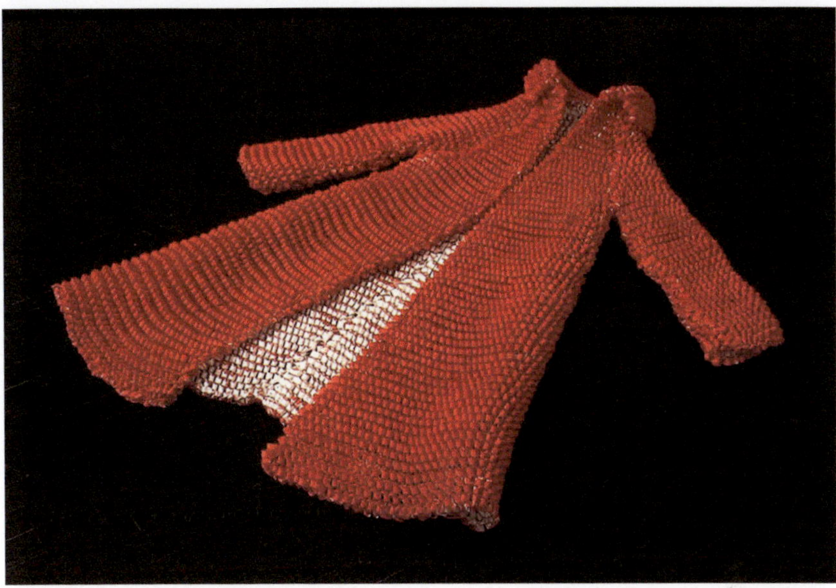

**Figure 4.1** Oliver Herring, *Untitled (Red Coat)*, 1993. Knit paper and gouache, 80 × 80 inches. Courtesy of Oliver Herring.

or by those for whom it was not intended. Cutting and manipulating paper for creative purposes can thus be considered a "queer use" of the material.[8]

While academic scholarship specifically addressing queer paper crafts remains scarce, it is striking that queer theory itself frequently employs terminology and metaphors rooted in paper-based crafts. This likely stems from queer theory's foundation in deconstruction, a concept that manifests here not only philosophically but also physically. For example, Getsy proposes that the process of *queering* offers a strategic "under*cutting* of the stability of identity and of the dispensation of power that shadows the assignment of categories and taxonomies."[9] Ahmed more explicitly theorizes "queer use" as "recover[ing] a potential from materials that have been left behind, all the things you can do with *paper* if you do not follow the instructions."[10] Using paper as an illustrative example, she describes queering as a process of things being "redeployed, twisted, queered from a prior usage," even articulating that the process of queering often involves a process of "vandalism" or "willful destruction" of an original.[11] Although the above terms used by both Getsy and Ahmed are applied within the context of queer theory, not craft studies, many of them are all hallmarks of creative engagements with paper, such as: *undercutting, reuse, recover, destruction, vandalism,* and, in Ahmed's case, overt references to *paper.* There are clear affinities between how collage deconstructs images and the conceptual use of *queer,* which, when utilized as a transitive verb, can serve to deconstruct systems of power and tear binaries apart. I use the term "deconstruct" here because, as a verb, it signals this act of dismantling and undoing at both a conceptual and a physical level. Paper's inherent malleability allows it to be transformed through numerous actions—cutting, tearing, puncturing, perforating, folding, erasing, and scoring—to create something entirely new.

This chapter explores how paper and print culture are being utilized in innovative ways to express distinct, queer worldviews. It focuses on two creative methods—paper cutting and collage—which share similar approaches but possess unique cultural histories and practices. First, the chapter examines the traditions of paper cutting, discussing the intricate hand-cut works of Antonius-Tín Bui. These works connect to broader East Asian paper cutting traditions while exploring issues of representation, documentation, and archiving marginalized bodies. Second, the chapter analyzes the queer potential of collage and appropriation as another "queer use" of cut paper, focusing on the collaged works of Troy Montes-Michie. Montes-Michie has become well-known for reconfiguring vintage pornographic materials as a method of disrupting the normative gaze, specifically collaging with erotic print culture as a way of deconstructing binaries associated with race, gender, and sexuality. While Bui and Montes-Michie have distinct practices and lived experiences, their work shares a common thread: both employ fragmentation as a generative method of challenging cis-heteronormative frameworks. They explore the inherent tension of "the cut" as an act simultaneously deconstructive and constructive—a process that relies on destroying to create. Using paper cutting and collage techniques, both practitioners draw attention to histories and bodies that have been rendered invisible, or, conversely, explore the complexities of hypervisibility, specifically using cut and collaged paper as a means of assembling and dissembling, obscuring and revealing, specific bodies and their representations.

## Paper Cutting

The origins of paper cutting, much like those of papermaking itself, are complex and subject to ongoing debate. However, it is generally accepted that paper cutting originated in China "as part of folk indigenous knowledge and ritual power in rural society," with archaeological evidence suggesting that the practice dates back to the Northern Dynasties (386 to 581 CE).[12] Over the centuries, Chinese practitioners have explored the medium in many applications—from paintings and calligraphy to printed texts, currency, and decorations. Traditionally, papercuts would be small, about the size of one's palm, and were more commonly called "window flowers."[13] They were usually cut from red paper using scissors and pasted as decoration on wood-framed windows made of rice paper. The negative shapes created from the paper cutting process would allow the light shine through, casting playful shadows. These papercuts were particularly popular during celebrations and cultural events such as weddings and to celebrate Chinese New Year, but they were also used more commonly to symbolize good luck and encourage bountiful harvests, with depictions of flora, fauna, and agricultural production.[14]

There is no denying that craft is a gendered, classed, and racialized field in Britain and much of North America, where scholarship on queer crafts has primarily been limited to. As noted by Adamson, craft's perceived inferiority in these locales stems from aspects of a "sexist, classist, racist" typecasting, as well as its tendency to be "coded as feminine or even 'ethnic.'"[15] However, this situation is diametrically different in many parts of East Asia. Art historian Yujo Kikuchi makes an essential distinction between the differences in the hierarchy of craft between Anglo-America and Asia, specifically in Japan, articulating that beyond the "West" craft is not often stereotyped as "women's work," but is often seen as "a strictly professional, male-centred world," a form of highly specialized and professional *art*.[16] This is particularly evident in the cultural history of paper cutting. Cultural anthropologist and gender scholar Ka-Ming Wu observes that while East Asian papercuts were traditionally considered a rural, domestic, and feminine practice, their associations shifted in the twentieth century. In China, particularly during the Yan'an period (c. 1937–1947), the People's Republic of China established mass-production papercut factories, leading to its association with urban, industrial, and masculine labor.[17] While many designs from this era still depicted prosperity, they also served to disseminate revolutionary ideas and state propaganda, becoming, as Wu argues, a "signifier of different desires and visions in modern China" through political appropriation.[18] Today, we see a flourishing of papercut works across East Asia, including Japan, Vietnam, and Taiwan, ranging from traditional to subversive styles. They also exist as stand-alone works, becoming more extensive and more varied in terms of size, color, and pattern, as contemporary practitioners have appropriated age-old techniques to explore queer identities.

### *Antonius-Tin Bui (b.1992, USA)*

It is to these cultural histories of paper and its uses in East Asian Indigenous craft production that Antonius-Tin Bui attends to in their work. Bui, a self-described "queer, nonbinary, Vietnamese American…shapeshifter," asserts that their "polydisciplinary" identity profoundly shapes how they "visualize hybrid identities and histories."[19] Their work explores the "transformative potential of ritual, portraiture, craft, and performance to visualize hybrid identities and marginalized histories."[20] A Vietnamese-American child of Vietnamese refugees whose parents moved to the United States in 1975, Bui frequently references their family's heritage through "allusions to the spiritual significance of Joss paper."[21] Sheets of Joss paper (more commonly known as incense paper) are used as burned offerings and for ancestral worship, such as the veneration of deceased family members and relatives on holidays and special occasions. Joss paper is traditionally made from coarse bamboo paper, although rice paper is also commonly used. It may be decorated with seals, stamps, pieces of contrasting paper, engraved designs, or other motifs, though it is rarely cut into in traditional use—a rule that Bui bends.

In their work, Bui uses Joss paper to "reclaim the Asian craft tradition of paper cutting" from a "queer, non-binary, and intersectional perspective."[22] Their pieces often begin with white paper, sometimes left untouched, while others are dyed blue or red, alluding to blue-glazed East Asian porcelain, the American flag, or the traditional Asian association of red with good fortune. This is most notable in the series *Not Sorry for the Trouble* (2019), where Bui remains true to the origins of paper cutting but queers these traditions. Carving traditional objects and motifs like Vietnamese opera masks, paper lanterns, and outlines of mythical creatures into the red and blue paper, Bui juxtaposes these seemingly innocent forms with bold phrases like "FUCK TRUMP," "YEAR OF THE QUEER," and "FIGHT SEGREGAYTION" as mantras of resistance which could easily be hung in windows just as traditional paper cuts would be. This series exposes and reappropriates racist and sexualized stereotypes targeting the Asian American and Pacific Islander (AAPI) LGBTQ+ community, including phrases such as "NOT "EXOTIC," "YES ASIANS, YES FEMMES," "NOT YOUR FETISH," and "FUCK RICE QUEENS." The term "rice queen" is used to describe people of non-Asian descent, usually white men, who are predominantly attracted to Asian men and sexualize or fetishize them based on their race or ethnicity, which is problematically deemed as "exotic." Other terms used here, such as "YES ASIANS, YES FEMMES" refer to discriminatory discourse often experienced by members of the AAPI LGBTQ+ community on dating apps such as Grindr, where users might include phrases such as "no fats, no femmes, no Asians" in their profile as a form of racism (compounded by fatphobia and fragile masculinity) disguised as "sexual preference."[23] Through the process of cutting, which has often been theorized as an aggressive, destructive, and even traumatic act, Bui seems to take out their anger and frustrations of the ongoing inequalities, racism, and microaggressions faced by AAPI LGBTQ+ individuals. Yet, there is also a *craftiness* (in both senses of the word) in how Bui reappropriates and almost embraces these terms, simultaneously subverting these sources of abjection into a source of queer strength through this meditative and somewhat therapeutic process of meticulously cutting out figures and text. These works can be interpreted as embodying "disidentification" which Muñoz used to theorize "a version of self that is *crafted* through something other than rote representational practices, produced through an actual disidentification with such practices."[24] For those who find their racial, sexual, or gender identity to be marginalized, a disidentification with mainstream culture is a mode of survival, a way of negotiating majority culture—not by aligning with or against exclusionary systems or representations but rather by transforming or (re)crafting them for their own cultural purposes, as Bui's approach to paper demonstrates.

Bui's works are quite literally an exercise in imagining a crafted version of the self. In an ongoing series of large-scale portraits titled *The Slaysian Dynasty*, Bui works exclusively with huge singular sheets of Joss paper to create and carve life-size, or larger-than-life (some are over 10 feet in height), portraits of LGBTQ+ AAPI individuals, positioning each work almost as an offering to honor queer communities. The term "slaysian" is an amalgamation of the terms "slay" and "Asian," with "slay" being a term of encouragement and affirmation in queer culture. Like traditional portraits, Bui depicts their subjects in moments of what they call "radical mundaneness," conveying a sense of tenderness and quiet power—qualities historically denied to these communities.[25] Each work in the series offers an intimate reflection on the kinship within the queer AAPI community, capturing relatable moments of shared experience that resonate with viewers regardless of their own identity.

*The Slaysian Dynasty* allows Bui to create counter-narratives to reductive histories and stereotypical representations, effectively crafting their own dynasty and documenting both their biological and chosen families. This establishes an ancestry unbound by traditional biological or familial ties, gender, or other conventional markers. Each piece begins with a photoshoot and conversation with the sitter, allowing Bui to witness how individuals have crafted themselves and their identities. "Regardless of my relationship to them, I think they provide me a possibility," Bui explains.[26] "They remind me of my identities, fluidity, expanding the contours of who I can be. Many of them have aided me in my own transition, have helped me realize how I wish to continue to evolve and express myself. They all teach me to dream bigger than I'm ever able to do individually," they add.[27] Photographs of the sitters are projected onto a single large sheet of Joss paper, where Bui creates drawings incorporating elements of their narratives and histories before meticulously hand-cutting the patterns with a scalpel—a process that can take two to four weeks, depending on the work's scale. When interviewed about their process, Bui shared:

> My intensive paper cutting process is highly meditative, providing me the time and space to confront every aspect of myself. The sheets of paper are an archive of every slice and memory, mirroring the intergenerational trauma that so many refugee communities are faced with. When I am working on these hand-cut paper sculptures, I actively carve out space for histories that are actively forgotten and erased in this white supremacist nation. The reductive process deconstructs the white canvas, revealing more and more truths with every slice.[28]

The idea of carving out space for representation is powerfully illustrated in *Vanguard* (2019), a portrait honoring Aiden Khanh Nguyen, a close friend of Bui and the founder of Vănguard, a transnational zine connecting and uplifting LGBTQ+ Vietnamese artists through art, literature, and activism—another reminder of the importance of paper in queer culture and the long history of zines as a mode of messaging, organizing, and expression.[29] Bui first traveled to Vietnam with Nguyen in 2017 to explore their cultural heritage and biological family lineage. Nguyen is represented here looking defiant and fierce, directly confronting the viewer's gaze. This is furthered by the scale of the work (198.1 × 107 × 5.4 cm), which means that it emerges as a larger-than-life incarnation of Nguyen. The symbolic and decorative border blends in with the tattoos that adorn Nguyen's body, including those of a pug, a snake, and two figures engaged in sexual activity. The ornate patterns in the background of many of Bui's works in this series are each chosen to complement the unique narratives of each sitter, their history, or Bui's relationship with them. As is the case here, Bui often pays particular attention to how these individuals adorn or "craft" their identity through fashion, tattooing, jewelry, and personal objects, all of which are intricately cut into each piece and blur with the figures they depict, suggesting their importance in the crafting of the self. The "stratified linework evokes a porous and flexible form" and the organic lines that seemingly weave in, around, and between each of the sitters are reflective of the environments in which these individuals are literally "grounded in, and formed by."[30]

This is also evident in *The limits of my language are the limits of my world* (2021), where Bui painstakingly cuts out books that frame a portrait of a queer couple (Figure 4.2). Several book titles are made visible, including *Want* (2008), an anthology of poetry from queer Filipino writer Rick Barot, *Ghost Of* (2018) by Diana Khoi Nguyen, and *Not Here* (2018) by Hieu Minh Nguyen. The Joss paper is dyed blue and often positioned in front of a white wall to highlight the intricacy of the cut out details. The colors and patterns reference the blue and white ceramics associated with East Asia, which were traditionally decorated with bold illustrations, including waves, wings, mythical creatures (namely the dragon and the phoenix), birds, flowers, and branches, just like those that are interwoven into this series. During the Covid-19 pandemic, when many museums and galleries began making their archives available online, Bui recalls: "I started rummaging through their collections in search of Asian art, specifically Vietnamese art, and was immediately confronted by their focus on our connection to porcelain vessels or ceramics in general – we are constantly denied the right to embodiment and self-determination, our own humanity and body, simply objectified."[31]

Instead of creating figurative portraits that could be co-opted into systems of prejudice and stereotyping, Bui's delicately cut works represent the body in a way that celebrates a renewed sense of identification and strength. In this sense, Bui's works not only represent a disidentity but more broadly reflect "the essential need for an understanding of queerness as collectivity," informed by cultural objects such as books, vases, and archival documents.[32] In *Queering Contemporary Asian American Art* (2017), Laura Kina and Jan Christian Bernabe suggest that this is a common trope in queer Asian American cultural production, arguing: "Asians who misbehave or practice transgressive cultural politics through their expansive practices pose a direct challenge to racial, gender, and sexual normative boundaries. While self or community representation in cultural production works to cohere notions of belonging to a racialized minority, Asian American artists who identify as LGBTQ+ may choose to disidentify with representational practices that are devoted solely to representing Asian American bodies and spaces."[33] As Grace Kyungwon Hong and Roderick A. Ferguson also echo in *Strange Affinities: The Gender and Sexual Politics of Comparative Racialization* (2011), such an approach can "profoundly question nationalist and identarian modes of political organization and *craft* alternative understandings of subjectivity, collectively, and power."[34]

This method of questioning dominant or normative modes of categorization by crafting alternative futures is reflected at the very level of Bui's material choices.

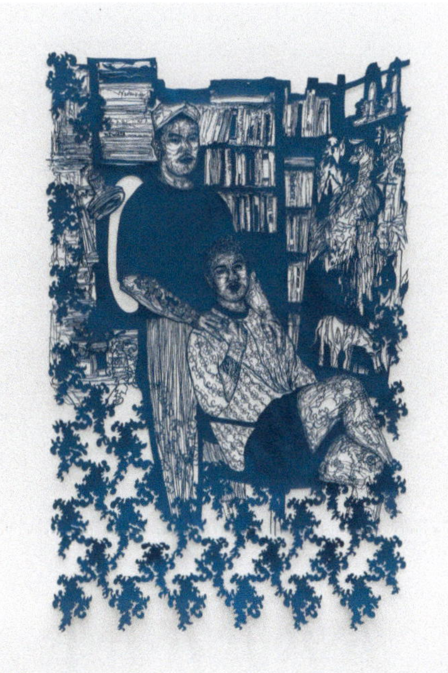

**Figure 4.2** Antonius-Tín Bui, *The limits of my language are the limits of my world*, 2021. Hand-cut paper, ink, pencil, paint, 84 × 56 inches. Courtesy of Antonius-Tín Bui and Monique Meloche Gallery. Copyright: Antonius-Tín Bui.

Their engagement with the whiteness of paper is particularly meaningful, imbued with the potential to explore race and identity formation—a deconstruction of the white canvas to dismantle white supremacy. This is evident in works such as *If I had the words to tell you we wouldn't be here now* (2020) and *for hunger is to give the body what it knows it cannot keep* (2020), where the resulting forms carved from white paper appear ghostly and spirit-like, referencing Bui's assertions around the need to craft a new ancestry and archive of AAPI LGBTQ+ communities for future generations to honor (Figure 4.3). By cutting and carving white paper, it can be argued that Bui deliberately attacks whiteness and its dominance throughout history. American feminist scholar and anti-racist activist Peggy McIntosh argues that being white "is an invisible knapsack of special provisions, assurances, tools, maps, guides, code books, passports, visas, compass, emergency gear and blank cheques."[35] The term "whiteness" is often used to refer to the historical, social, political, and cultural organization that shapes white people's lives and informs a position of power and dominance in society; how whiteness installs itself as the dominant worldview, the standard from which everything else is judged and which has infiltrated every stratum of life, aspects which Bui highlights through their creative engagements and interventions with white paper. Here, Bui envisions the cut as a ""metaphor for history," illustrating how queer AAPI people have

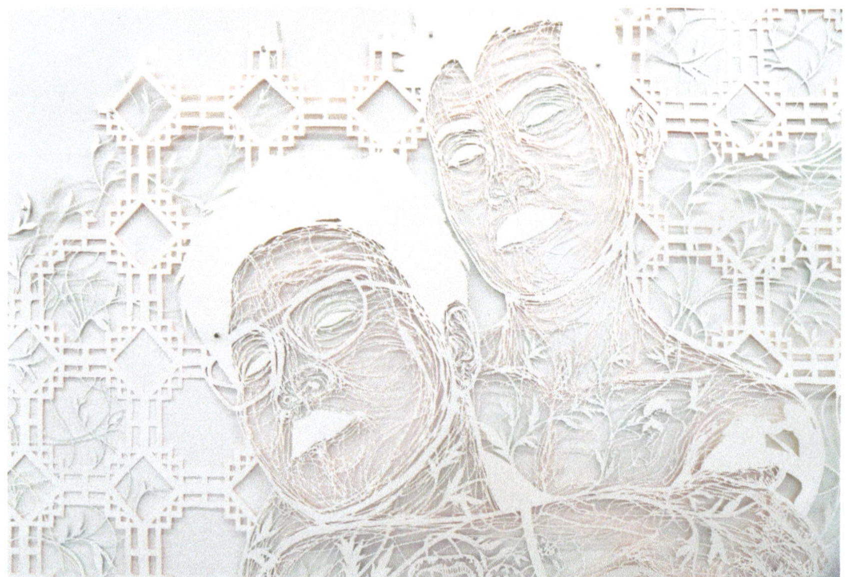

**Figure 4.3**  Antonius-Tín Bui, *for hunger is to give the body what it knows it cannot keep*, 2020 (detail). Hand-cut paper, ink, pencil, paint, 122 x 65 inches.

constantly been erased from existence, largely at the hands of white colonizers and dominant powers.[36] The reductive process of paper cutting deconstructs the traditional *whiteness* of paper to metaphorically and physically carve out space for narratives omitted from "whitewashed" histories, with each slice mirroring the intergenerational trauma of refugee and migrant communities.

While works like *Not Sorry for the Trouble* certainly express anger and aggression, Bui's meticulous paper cutting process is also deeply meditative and therapeutic. Each sheet of paper is carefully and intuitively crafted to embody an archive of memories and oral histories, particularly in *The Slaysian Dynasty*. Bui's dissections of white paper quite literally carve out a space to give form to portraits of AAPI LGBTQ+ individuals who have not been documented or recorded in such a way throughout history and visual culture. In this sense, it is perhaps inappropriate to consider cutting in Bui's work as purely aggression and deconstruction. Another strategy runs parallel to this: cutting can be reparative and constructive. As is the case here, it can "carve out space," providing representation and visibility. While cutting is often seen as a banal act, cutting has important implications, and when removing part of a material, we grant that element a new life and reconstruct it in a new worldview. A duality is at play, an act that enables both destruction and rebirth. As Bui notes: "[t]he act of cutting can be so violent, but my process is one of transcendence. Yes, we as Queer and Trans People of Color have endured a lot of scars, oppression, and injustice, and continue to, but we refuse to be solely define

[sic] by that. I'm carving away at a white canvas to reveal the beauty, divinity, and resilience of those around me."[37]

In short, through their engagements with paper, Bui utilizes the transformational properties of their material to excavate a narrative that no longer places trauma and displacement at the forefront of queer AAPI cultural production. Instead, each delicately woven work inhabits the body in a way that honors a reinvigorated sense of identification while echoing a fluid notion of interdependence and community, resulting in works that celebrate queer life and joy. Indeed, the process is reductive and deconstructs the whiteness of the page, but "the cut" here has another crucial function—providing counter-narratives to reductive histories and representations, or lack thereof, of queer AAPI communities. Bui's use of paper reflects upon its significance in Vietnamese culture but also its role in archival documentation, reclaiming authority over how previously hidden or undocumented queer AAPI histories are made visible and represented in contemporary culture. Paper cutting here functions as a visual diary for Bui to tell their life story and the life story of many other members of their community. Rather than something purely destructive and aggressive, Bui's papercuts lean more towards acts of healing and reparation, of documenting the undocumented. Crucially, this destruction is transformative; by compromising the material's integrity, paper loses its passivity, plainness, and neutrality. Bui's work demonstrates that paper is, and always has been, deeply intertwined with the social, cultural, and political.


## Collage

Like paper cutting, collage, another technique reliant on manipulating paper, has become a significant means of critically engaging with the materiality of the world. Most books on collage, however, perpetuate the myth of its exclusively Eurocentric origins, attributing its "birth" to the Modernist period and the Cubist movement, and citing the same male, pale and stale artists as the "fathers" of collage—particularly Pablo Picasso (1881–1973), Georges Braque (1882–1963), Juan Gris (1887–1927), and Kurt Schwitters (1887–1948).[38] In contrast, scholars employing queer, feminist, and decolonial approaches to art history and visual culture have challenged these patriarchal and Eurocentric narratives, demonstrating that collage, as a creative process, has existed globally for centuries in diverse forms and practiced by a wide range of individuals.[39] However, in opposition to the so-called "artistic" exploits of the likes of Picasso, Braque, Gris, and Schwitters, these practices have often been relegated to the status of "craft." Again, as with paper cutting, we now see many contemporary practitioners, particularly queer practitioners, reinventing these traditions and engaging with the tactics of collage, utilizing the transformative potentials of collage for queer uses, as exhibitions like *Cock, Paper, Scissors* have evidenced.

While paper cutting has rarely been examined through a queer lens, collage has been recognized by scholars as a key process for "queering" material—

taking existing fragments of culture and reinterpreting dominant cultural norms to produce queer associations.[40] As a form that encourages hybridity and the disruption of normative formalisms, it is closely aligned with queerness, as queer theorist Jack Halberstam suggests. Halberstam argues that collage "precisely references the spaces in between and refuses to respect the boundaries that usually delineate self from other, art object from museum, and the copy from the original. In this respect, as well as in many others, collage (from the French *coller*, to paste or glue) seems feminist and queer."[41] This "queerness" then is not necessarily based on the content of a collage (although this is sometimes the case), but the very method of collage-making which relies on queer concepts like humor and camp, inversion and reversal, excess and extremes. Halberstam illustrates this point further, arguing that the likes of German Dadaist Hannah Höch (1889–1978) have utilized such a method from a queer-feminist perspective "to bind the threat of castration to the menace of feminist violence and both to the promise for transformation, not through a positive production of the image but through a negative destruction of it that nonetheless refuses to relinquish pleasure."[42] While this deconstructive collage process might therefore be seen as one of aggression—I posit the act of reconfiguring (to stitch, to glue, to bind) as both reparative and therapeutic—it is simultaneously a form of "negative destruction" and "positive production."[43] In this way, the violent process of collage can also be generative, allowing for the creation of queer worldview. Similar to Bui's approach, this symbiotic relationship between destruction and creation is also manifested in the work of Troy Montes-Michie, whose work I now turn to.

### *Troy Montes-Michie (b.1985, USA)*

Troy Montes-Michie has become most well-known for his engagement with print culture. He specifically utilizes the deconstructive and reconstructive capabilities of collage to investigate society's understanding of race, gender, sexuality, class, as well as identity and power more broadly. Archival materials, newspapers, erotic magazines, found photographs, and vintage paper sewing patterns all become engulfed in his collage practice. These ephemeral, paper-based materials are manipulated through sewing, drawing with grease pencils or Conté crayon, painting with watercolor or acrylic, and, most notably, cutting, pasting, or weaving, further blurring the lines between art and craft. Layers are usually sanded, or acrylic paint, glue, or tape might be applied and removed, leaving ghostly textures, scars, and residues. Montes-Michie's collages relate to the broader use of paper and print media in queer culture—how gay and queer youth have often turned to materials like adult pornographic or workout magazines to understand their identities and come to terms with their sexuality. While Montes-Michie employs various materials and techniques, paper is his primary medium. Through it, he "investigates the influence of print media in mass culture, disrupting modes of consumption that historically erase and fetishize specific communities."[44] Early in his career, Montes-Michie began photocopying pages of *Physique Pictorial* magazines featuring Bob Mizer's photography. He became interested in the publication's format and its role in concealment; the magazine was designed to resemble a fitness or bodybuilding publication to disguise the homoerotic male imagery and avoid obscenity charges Montes-Michie began cutting up the photocopied pages, but while handling the images, he realized his own image and identity were not reflected, at least not in an affirming way. He observed: "[m]ost of the models in the publications were white, so I would draw luchador masks over their faces and then color their skin in various shades of brown."[45]

Vintage gay pornographic magazines often feature fetishized images of nude Black men, simultaneously exalting their physicality while silencing their identities. These images inspired some of Montes-Michie's earliest collages, highlighting how even the most romanticized visuals in queer culture can be deeply damaging. This theme recurred in his work exhibited at the New Museum in 2018–2019 as part of *Trigger: Gender as a Tool and a Weapon,* a group exhibition exploring "gender's place in contemporary art and culture at a moment of political upheaval and renewed culture wars," featuring "an intergenerational group of artists who explore gender beyond the binary to usher in more fluid and inclusive expressions of identity."[46] Unsurprisingly, many of these artists, including Montes-Michie, employed techniques like collage to embrace fragmentation and forge a queer aesthetic, proposing a world where "body-in-pieces is the body-as-whole."[47] Early works created shortly after Montes-Michie graduated from his MFA at Yale School of Art were included, such as *The Shadows are Vast* (2013), *La Bicicleta* (2015), *Nobody Knows My Name* (2015), and *Arroyo* (2015), which all featured collages made from found magazines (Figure 4.4). As with most of his collages, these images were primarily sourced from gay pornographic magazines of Black men largely from the 1970s and 1980s. However, their subjects become altered and protected through the process of layering, fracturing, and obscuring that collage affords.

Throughout these works on display at the New Museum, Montes-Michie's use of "the cut" was more than just a physical act of cutting paper but became more of a conceptual "cut" in the form of castration. "By choosing to hide or remove the phallus," Montes-Michie explains, "I am hoping for an alteration to the stereotypes placed on the Black male solely being reduced to their endowment and to notions of hypersexualization."[48] Their physical endowments—the source of the eroticization of the Black male body in these images—are either replaced by arms, fists, or skin-colored textures, including wallpaper, bedsheets, and clothing. Through this manipulation, Montes-Michie explores how marginalized bodies have been fetishized or erased throughout history, a concern shared by Bui in their explorations of paper cutting and archiving. Stereotypes have routinely functioned within media imagery and language to reinforce and maintain white power and privilege. Montes-Michie noted: "I came to realize that what drew me to these materials was the way men of color were placed in a suspended state

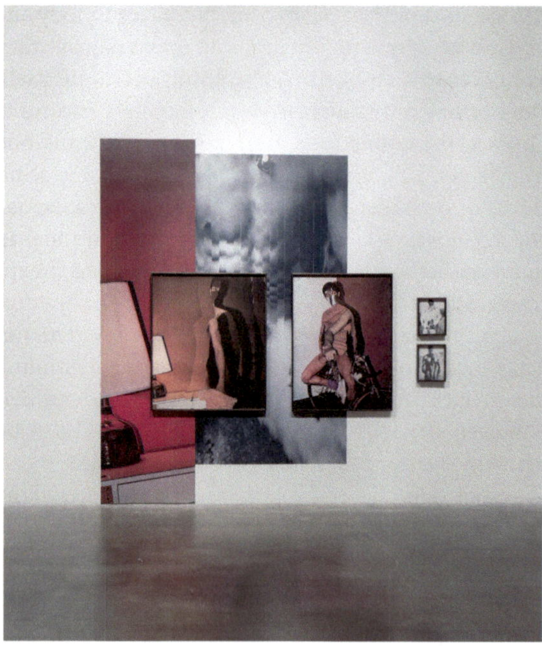

**Figure 4.4** Exhibition view, "Trigger: Gender as a Tool and a Weapon," New Museum, New York, 2017.

of objectification. It upset me. Since most of the photographers were white, the real question was about the gaze: what it meant for certain bodies to be viewed or desired by white men."[49] The resulting images reflect a complicated and often problematic relationship between the (white) photographer and the (Black) subject. By employing the very visual and discursive structures that exploit and reinscribe a dominant white view, Montes-Michie is more able to expose and usurp the operation of power, quite literally dismantling these representations through each cut and each tear of the paper, re-orienting and often disrupting or denying the gaze altogether.

A compelling tension exists in Montes-Michie's work. By using collage to both display and obscure media imagery, he simultaneously grants and denies access to the sexualized body, creating an equilibrium between hypervisibility and concealment. Like Bui, who described their paper cutting process as aggressive yet reparative, Montes-Michie notes: "[p]eople think that the cut is always a form of violence, [but] that was never how it appeared to me. When I started working with pornography, I didn't realize that a lot of these magazines were created as fetish objects for white men. Because it's very hard to find all black [sic] male or brown [sic] male magazines. Just doing research I realized, 'Oh, they're actually in the 'fetish' market.'"[50] In the curation of the exhibition further sections from the erotic magazines were blown up, enlarged, and pasted on the wall, but two framed collages, *The Shadows are Vast* (2013) and *La Bicicleta* (2015), were strategically "hung" over the top of the figure's torso and crotch, further disrupting the gaze. This challenges the act of looking itself, forcing viewers (presumably white, cis gay male audiences) to confront their expectations and complicity in that gaze. Montes-Michie's act of appropriation is an attempt to free these bodies from the context they are situated within. It is a way of pushing back against the problematic fetishization of the models, but not entirely undermining it. He retains some of the erotic charge of these images to reclaim and rebuild from the fragments.

These themes are further developed in larger-scale collages such as *Foreground As Background* (2018) and *Out of Sight, Out of Mind* (2018). In these works, Montes-Michie uses similar vintage erotic images, but cuts them into strips and weaves them together to create intricate, abstract patterns (Figure 4.5). The dissected images of Black bodies, interlaced with white paper, resemble a checkerboard, stripping identity markers and suggesting a harmonious, perpetual entanglement and intertwining of bodies. Many of Montes-Michie's works, particularly those employing the paper weaving technique, lean towards abstraction rather than strict figuration, moving beyond androgyny as a mere mediation of masculine and feminine "opposites" and refusing the hyper-sexual gaze. As Montes-Michie explains, "[s]ociety tries to simplify gender and sexuality and collage is about breaking those frameworks apart. Because they're never really binary."[51] Androgyny, then, becomes a radical means of unsettling this heteronormative binary opposition by refusing categorization within it. As Halberstam argues, "if one form of phallic queerness has been defined by the representation of the body as hybrid and assembled, then another takes as its object the disappearance of the body altogether."[52] Rejecting societal notions of fixedness and individuation, fragmentation here serves not as a method of deconstruction but as an additive process in which queer selfhood is malleable, ever-changing, tactile, and connected. Montes-Michie considers these works "portraits through the language of abstraction."[53] Their layers reflect the individuality of the models' identities and the layers of individuation, various facets of the self that make up a "whole."

Pasted over, under, and woven through the woven paper's surface are additional images cut from these magazines. As in earlier collages, many figures are castrated and overlaid with pictures or textures, their faces often concealed or excised. The addition or subtraction of material from these archival nude images means that we see these figures intimately rather than explicitly, stepping away from the fetishized Black male body that had been left on display in the magazines they originated in. The figures are disguised and veiled, holding each other, inviting you into their bedrooms, looking directly at you, and now allowed to undress *with* the viewer rather than *for* the viewer. Montes-Michie also draws attention to the role of fashion and clothing as a method of crafting an identity and concealing the body. Vintage sewing patterns (particularly suit patterns) are overlaid on many images. These yellowing and semi-transparent papers are collaged over the top of various body parts, including a person's legs, another's pubic area, and even one another that is carefully cut out in the shape of a vest and applied to a person's torso. The collar of a striped shirt is also included in the piece, echoing the "cut"

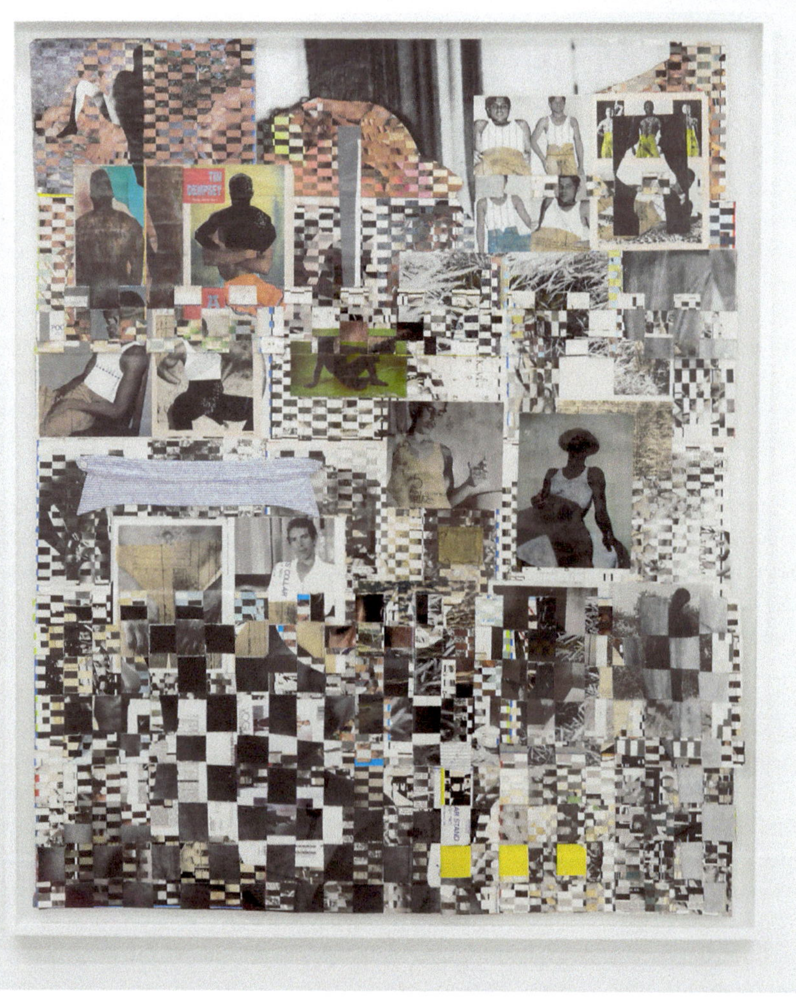

**Figure 4.5** Troy Montes-Michie, *Out of Sight, Out of Mind*, 2018. Magazine pages, inkjet prints, clothing patterns, fabric, graphite, acrylic, colored pencil, and tape, 62 × 52 inches. Courtesy of Troy Montes-Michie and Company Gallery.

and "fold" lines of the sewing patterns and the striped trousers drawn over the top of a nude figure. The prevalence of stripes and tailoring patterns references the zoot suit, popular among African American, Latinx, and working-class men in the United States during the 1940s.[54] The zoot suit was characterized by high-waisted, wide-legged, tight-cuffed trousers paired with a long, oversized jacket with padded shoulders.[55] It was often striped and traditionally worn with a matching wide-brimmed fedora, sometimes decorated with a feather. During this period, the zoot suit was celebrated in the world of jitterbug, jive, and swing, symbolizing empowerment and identity for many marginalized communities. However, due to its oversized and multi-component nature, it was condemned by government authorities as a wasteful use of fabric when trying to conserve textiles for the war effort. Central to the garment's history are the Zoot Suit Riots, a wave of racially motivated riots that began on June 3, 1943, when many white US service members attacked a group of Mexican-American men who were wearing these suits. This lasted until June 8, 1943, though, of course, the systematic inequalities and violence experienced by many of these communities would continue beyond just a matter of days. Most participants and observers of the riots did not refer to it as a race riot, and even fewer saw it as service members' vigilantism. Instead, the unrest became enshrined as the "Zoot Suit Riots," pinpointed around this specific suit, becoming the only time in American history that dress was believed to be the primary catalyst for widespread civil unrest.

More broadly, clothing patterns, striped motifs, and machine-sewn patterns often adorn Montes-Michie's dense collages and have even been featured as part of exhibition displays. For example, in *Rock of Eye* at the California African American Museum in 2022, the wooden flooring was marked with black vinyl lines and graphics, mimicking the cut lines of the paper sewing patterns he uses.[56] The lines on the floor might represent lines to cut or fold on a garment, but on this scale, they appear more like borders or thresholds, suggesting boundaries to be observed or transgressed. Beyond referencing the zoot suit pattern, some images feature nude Black men covered by vertical white stitching patterns. These patterns may be interpreted as the suturing of a wound. However, while this could be taken to symbolize care, a reparation, ultimately scars and wounds are marks on the body, a result of trauma and lasting evidence of that. The linear forms could also resemble the bars of prison cells or even topographical lines. As art critic and archivist Sharon Mizota noted about the exhibition, "dress patterns and stitching craft a kind of borderland cartography, where the figure becomes ground, and the stitch runs like the Rio Grande."[57] The stitch permeates Montes-Michie's work. As emphasized in Chapter 1, the stitch has a long, gendered social history rooted in craft, domestic work, and women's embroidery. Like collage and cutting, stitching is also both a violent and healing act—puncturing as well as uniting—and can be used both functionally and decoratively to inscribe a tactile pattern onto something. Montes-Michie uses these multiple interpretations and histories of the stitch and men's fashion and tailoring in his multimedia collages to explore masculinity, sexuality, and marginal identities (both metaphorical and geographical).

Montes-Michie's intense use of collage and various manipulations of paper can be compared to forms of camouflage; a process that relies on denying or disrupting the gaze through redirection tactics. This act of shielding desire, of arranging and rearranging the figure to conceal identity and present it anonymously, is all too familiar to the queer experience. Born in El Paso, Texas, Montes-Michie has openly discussed how his multi-layered practice reflects his experience of growing up along the United States and Mexico border, suggesting thay his camouflage and concealment tactics mirror the militarized geographies of El Paso, while the fragmentation visible in his collages reflects the cultural hybridity of identities in this border region. He has stated that his work is directly informed by a technique known as "disruptive patterning," which he relates to queerness and the camouflaging of the self within society, the safety of marginalized communities, and particularly the violence and murders against queer and trans People of Color in New York, where he currently resides. Disruptive patterning is a technique that was popularized during the Second World War by Roland Penrose, an English artist who co-founded the Institute of Contemporary Arts in London. Penrose became an influential figure in the English Surrealism movement, and his work is marked by a bold use of color, pattern, and line. As a Quaker and a pacifist, Penrose had no intention of serving in active duty when war broke out, but instead, he began teaching camouflage tactics for the Home Guard Training Centre at Osterley Park in London.[58] In 1941 Penrose wrote the *Home Guard Manual of Camouflage*, which provided accurate guidance on the use of texture, not only color, especially for protection from aerial photography, which was monochrome at that time. This concept influenced artists like Norman Wilkinson, who experimented with "dazzle camouflage" (or "razzle dazzle") for naval ships. These ships were painted with complex geometric patterns in contrasting colors to obscure their distance, speed, and heading. Found images of dazzle ships and zebras (whose stripes act as a naturally occurring form of dazzle camouflage) recur in Montes-Michie's work. He relates these tactics of camouflage to the existence of many queer people in their daily life: "As queer people, when you move around the city, there is a sense of camouflage that happens as protection. There's a moment when that begins to break down towards flamboyant and you're thinking about self-fashion as a way to talk about your identity, regardless of whether you're gonna blend in or not."[59]

Some queer practitioners may see limitations of the body and figurative representations of it. Still, there is a question of visibility and its importance, which is critical to understanding the self, community, and the construction of it. While Bui's works speak to the need to provide positive figurative representations of marginalized individuals, whose identities, communities, and histories have not been archived (at least not in an empowering or equitable way), works by Montes-Michie lean toward the abstraction of figurative representations as a mode to disrupt the normative gaze. In a brief afterword to the *Rock of Eye* exhibition at the California African American Museum, Cameron Shaw (the then Executive Director) discusses how Black artists have often wielded abstraction as a tool of resistance. This trope has also been extended to queer artists, as scholars such as Getsy and Lex Morgan Lancaster have explored in much more extensive detail.[60]

The use of collage as a form of queer abstraction in Montes-Michie's work is thus a significant tactic, not only to disrupt the gaze and comment on the fetishization and erasure of bodies, but also to illustrate how concealment becomes a mode of survival and existence in a hostile world. Montes-Michie's work shows how abstraction can be wielded as a tool for resistance—a useful mode of imagining "otherwise," of dismantling boundaries, binaries, and systems, and providing portals to new worlds.

## Conclusion

Actions of overlay, juxtaposition, and erasure are integral factors in developing queer relations to paper-based materials and processes. In works by Bui and Montes-Michie, "the cut" is used to free figures from static objectification or commodification, and they utilize the forms, mediums, and methods associated with paper queerly. Bui utilizes traditional East Asian paper cutting techniques to disrupt the dominance of whiteness and, quite literally, to carve out space for AAPI LGBTQ+ representation. Similarly, by strategically cutting, weaving, and altering these paper-based materials, Montes-Michie disrupts our seamless consumption of queer Black bodies to reflect upon how factors such as racism and homophobia have precluded a singular sense of self for these subjects. Through an analysis of works by Bui and Montes-Michie, I have demonstrated the significant potential of paper crafts, particularly for deconstructing dominant narratives around gender, sexuality, race, and other intersecting factors. Moreover, I hope to contribute to greater community awareness and, ultimately, positive social change by increasing awareness of the extent to which white biases encroach on our thinking and our lives at the very level of print culture. The materiality and tactility afforded by techniques such as paper cutting and collage continue to be alluring for many queer contemporary creatives because of the inherent tensions between destruction and creation that these material methodologies afford.

# Chapter 5

## METAL

### SHIMMERING SELVES AND EROTIC EXPRESSIONS IN ARMOR AND ADORNMENT

*Introduction*

Metalworking is perhaps one of the most expansive craft disciplines. Different kinds of ores can be mined, extracted, and made into a broad range of objects, ranging from rigid steel used in industrial infrastructure to precious metals such as gold and silver used in delicate jewelry-making practices. The term "metalworking" is often used as a broad category to signal a range of practices and professions that involve working with metal, encompassing farriers, blacksmiths, silversmiths, jewelers, fabricators, welders, sculptors, and all those working between and beyond these traditional classifications. Compared to the likes of needlework, which has historically been gendered "feminine," metalworking has traditionally been associated with a very "masculine" archetype, dominated by heterosexual and cisgender men. As a result, many queer and trans practitioners have declared that these spaces, and those that have dominated them, often reflect a very rigid, cold, and unmoving view of gender akin to the qualities of metal itself. Although the field can still be exclusionary, many queer and trans practitioners have begun thriving in metalworking environments, often *forging* their own spaces of creativity and kinship both within and external to these existing spaces. This includes groups such as Queer Metalsmiths, a network co-founded by Sol Diaz, Tracey Cardwell, and Sulo Bee (known as Sparkle Filth) to support and uplift 2SLGBTQIA+[1] voices of those working with metal, particularly jewelry. The Society of Inclusive Blacksmiths (SIB) also champions equity and diversity in blacksmithing through education, mentorship, and grants, recognizing the social and economic barriers to this work which requires access to specific materials, tools, and spaces such as a forge, hot shop, or a studio.[2]

Despite a rich field of practice, there has been a lack of writing and critical reflection on how metal has been used *queerly* across various studio-based creative practices. Yet, in recent years, a range of cultural programming has considered the relationships between queerness and metalwork. In 2022 I contributed to part of the *Queer + Metals* project. This project was the first of its kind to ruminate on the idea of queer metals within an intersectional and international community of makers. Commissioned by the UK based charity Craftspace, and led by queer metalworker Rebekah Frank, the project aimed to explore "the multiplicity of queerness in relation to metalwork and metalsmithing . . . [w]hether as identities, lived experiences, thinking, cultures, aesthetics, influences, stories, places and imagination."[3] The project was deliberately multifaceted but initially encompassed a survey and a series of interviews with 119 international LGBTQ+ practitioners working with metal and an Instagram campaign to spotlight their practices. Queer + Metals was featured as part of the 2022 Ferrous Festival in Hereford (UK) and then evolved into an exhibition and panel discussion at the Midlands Arts Centre, Birmingham (UK), the latter of which I participated in.[4] Rather than present queer metal as a monolithic field, the program highlighted a myriad of responses and creative reflections to the question "what is so queer about metal?". Our discussions highlighted how queerness is integral to the act of making with metal, encompassing the channeling of "mind, body, soul, and heart" through the material, as Frank eloquently put it. In some instances, the material was also conceptualized as explicitly queer. Some practitioners drew parallels between the fluidity of molten metal and the fluidity of gender, the decorative potential of metal and its associations with camp adornment, and the sense of connection or spirituality that comes with working with a material that comes from the earth. A whole range of objects and practices were featured in the exhibition, from the wearable metal objects created by drag performer Fei He to the hydroformed works of Roxanne Simone, which explore the parallels between the "plight of diasporic people" and the "pressurized environment" created during the hydroformed process.[5] One thing that was made clear from this wide-ranging activity was that queer practitioners especially push the boundaries of what metal looks like, what metal can do, and who creates things with metal. The exhibition and discussions revealed a surprising richness in how metalwork intersects with queer identities and experiences.

Jewelry and adornment have emerged as a particularly generative area for exploring the intersections of queerness and metal. This is perhaps unsurprising, considering jewelry's long-standing role in debates surrounding gender, cultural identity, and individual expression, especially given that it functions as an outward expression of identity and taste. One could argue that jewelry is inherently queer, aesthetically often embracing maximalism, excess, and camp—often being "over the top," "extra" or intentionally "too much." Jewelry's position within the cultural canon has also been queer, never quite fitting neatly into established categories and resisting simple classifications as fashion accessory, bespoke luxury item, mass-produced commodity, design, craft, or decorative art. Many practitioners are now pushing the boundaries of jewelry, employing terms like "art jewelry" or "jewelry-adjacent practice" to describe work that utilizes jewelry-related materials or techniques but results in objects not necessarily intended to be worn.[6] Those at the forefront of jewelry practices continue to disrupt and dismantle existing forms of categorization, with many preferring the term "adornment." This expansive term refers to an object designed to *adorn* or "enhance" the body. Queer people have long used clothing and adornment to create a sense of community of collective identity, to resist and challenge normative expectations of gender presentation, and to signal their identity to the wider world. Jewelry and adornment have often been central to this because these objects can be revealed and concealed easily or put on and taken off at will; it is fundamental to visibility and, in some circumstances, concealment. A pin badge advocating for LGBTQ+ rights, for example, can be worn openly on a sweater but easily removed or covered with a jacket when needed. After all, style can be subversive and can constitute symbolic resistance to the status quo, but in today's world of ever-increasing hostility to queer and trans subjects, this resistance may not always be writ large.

This chapter responds to the shifting nature of contemporary metalworking practices. It looks at how queer and trans practitioners have especially embraced working with metal queerly to explore ideas of the erotic, taken in its most expansive sense. I use the jewelry of Hansel Tai and the "queer armor" of LA-based company Affect Metals as particular case studies. Tai's work is invested in exploring the intersections between craft and fetish, especially the role of material fetishism. From delicate jewelry to striking chainmail garments, the "queer armor" of Affect Metals aims to imbue the wearer with spiritual protection, enabling bodies to shimmer—both physically and symbolically. These examples speak to broader themes featured throughout the book, including queer worldmaking, embodiment and empowerment, and collective joy as a site of resistance.

### *Hansel Tai (b.1994, China)*

Hansel Tai is a practitioner from rural Southern China who migrated to Tallinn, Estonia, in 2016 where he still lives and works. Tai's gender-neutral and wearable collections ruminate on queer aesthetics—potential factors that might make someone or something appear "queer." His work explores the impossibility of identifying any singular queer aesthetic, and it draws inspiration from a wide range of references, including digital porn cultures, fetish wear, militarized regalia, Chinese jewelry traditions, utopian futurism, body modification, and more. When interviewed about his work, Tai revealed that he finds terms such as "queer craft" or "queer metal" very appealing because it enables him to articulate how queerness forms a central component of both his conceptual ideas and practical approach to materials.[7] He said: "I do think my works are queer because the themes I explore are very much in my own interests and relate to my own experiences every day. It is very organic for me because I am not interested in exploring non-queer topics through my jewelry."[8] However, Tai also warned: "At the end of the day, I am just making jewelry. I am not always consciously thinking about making *queer* jewelry."[9] This reflects how, for many queer makers, their identity is inseparable from the work itself, even if the resulting objects do not overtly represent queer themes or images.

While Tai states that he doesn't intentionally create exclusively queer jewelry, many of his collections overtly reference queer cultures and his own sexuality. Tai's collection of earrings and brooches titled *Fagatopia*—a playful portmanteau of the words "fag" (an abbreviation of "faggot") and "utopia"—explores ideas of queer worldmaking and utopian aesthetics (Figure 5.1). Like the term "queer," the term "faggot" has been used as a pejorative for homosexuals (primarily gay men) since the early twentieth century.[10] Nevertheless, in more contemporary use, it can be used as a more neutral or even positive term when used in self-reference. By bringing together "faggot" with "utopia," Tai seems to hint at the possibility of crafting a desirable world in which the "faggots" reign supreme, and through this collection he imagines what systems would exist within a queer utopian society (similar to Paul Yore's vision of "Faggot Land" which was discussed in Chapter 1). This collection appropriates the military insignia systems of various nations and subverts typical patterns associated with these, such as chevrons, stripes, and stars. Given the ongoing abuse of power and unlawful killings of queer people, especially queer and trans People of Color, by police and militarized forces, Tai's use of iconography might initially seem counterintuitive. However, Tai claims: "by stripping away the meaning of a military insignia, this series of work is a visual attempt for a new alternative power system" in which this iconography is reconfigured into a new visual language, stripped of its violent and oppressive connotations, and instead intended as empowering and liberatory.[11] This also connects to a broader history of queer appropriation of uniforms and military aesthetics for resistance, most notably seen in 1970s and 1980s British Punk subcultures, post-war American BDSM communities, and the "military" category within American ballroom culture—all of which have been extensively explored in fields like fashion theory and cultural studies.[12]

Tai's *Fagatopia* pieces are primarily crafted from extruded, powder-coated brass hollow tubes, arranged in rigid, regimented patterns that mimic regimental insignias. The resulting cold, hard lines of the layered tubes are reminiscent of prison cell bars, but they are also contrasted with the use of soft pearls, which undermine the archetype of hyper-masculinity often associated with militarized regalia, thus fusing elements that might traditionally be associated with both the "masculine" and the "feminine." It is interesting to reflect upon this series concerning how queerness sometimes both aligns and diverges from systems of power. Each piece within the collection is given a different title akin to different ranks, such as *Master Sergeant*. Of course, terms like "Master" or "Sergeant" refer to respective military categories, but they also reference forms of sexual domination, sadomasochism, and uniform fetishism. It is considered that the uniforms worn by military men present an image of enhanced masculinity and authority that has often had strong sexual appeal, especially among gay male communities and subcultures. Tai's aesthetics and use of titles flirt with queer signals, perhaps only noticeable to those "in the know"—providing a "nudge nudge," or a "wink wink."

Queer people have often created visual codes over the years, with aesthetics providing opportunities for self-expression and even political resistance. Tai's

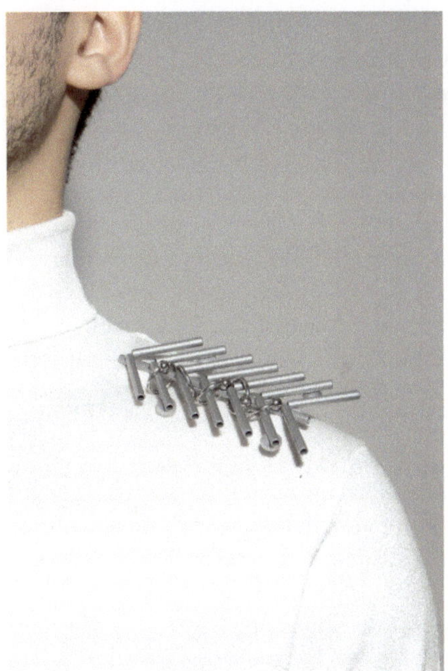

**Figure 5.1** Hansel Tai, *Fagatopia (First Sergeant)*, 2021. Powder-coated brass, surgical stainless-steel piercing, freshwater pearls. Courtesy of Hansel Tai.

work, particularly its wearable nature, can be seen as a contemporary form of "flagging," an updated and glitzy version of visual systems such as the handkerchief or "hanky" code. This covert sartorial language, primarily used by cisgender gay men in North America and Western Europe since the 1970s, allowed individuals to discreetly communicate their sexual interests and fetishes. Different sexual preferences were "flagged" by the color and placement of the handkerchief (either in the left or right rear trouser pocket).[13] While the term "flagging" originally referred specifically to the hanky code, it now encompasses a broader range of clothing and adornments used by queer people to signal their identity to others. Textiles aren't the only materials used for flagging; metal objects like keys, chains, rings, and carabiners have also played a significant role, particularly in lesbian self-fashioning.[14]

This idea that materials can "flag" messages or meaning to those "in the know" is central to much of Tai's work. In line with other forms of queer coding, camouflage, and material trickery play a central role in this collection. "I always like trickery, and I am fascinated by how I can develop the material further, beyond the material itself, beyond the metal itself," Tai summarizes.[15] For example, the pearls used in this series were selected because they appeared more metallic than pearlescent in luster, designed to mimic the surrounding metal. Additionally, although the objects in the collection look like they are made from silver, they are hollow brass tubes that have been powder-coated. Powder coating requires specialized equipment because the powder must be applied electrostatically and cured under heat or ultraviolet light. As a result, it is seen as a highly industrialized process, usually carried out on mass-produced metal objects such as car parts, bicycle frames, domestic appliances, and so on. As Tai did not have access to these forms of industrialized equipment, the hollow brass tubes he used in the collection were sent to a local factory in Tallinn. These hollow brass tubes were placed on the industrial belt alongside other objects that may have been coated in a similar color of silver to Tai's jewelry, though sometimes Tai requests specific colors to be mixed and applied to his metal objects, which means they must be treated in a separate production run. From a practical perspective, brass is also a much more affordable material to use in metalworking as it is considered far less desirable than "precious" metals such as silver, which many jewelers may not be able to afford, especially at a time where the cost of materials and energy is soaring, and the depletion of natural resources is affecting both people and the planet across many areas of the world. Tai has explained that he is not concerned with the commercial value of the material but rather the cultural value of the material and object itself: "I don't care about the commercial value of the material, for me, what is more interesting is the material itself – how the color, the finishing, and the material opens possibilities for manipulation."[16] Rather than being constrained by a limited choice of materials, Tai embraces the use of more affordable materials and delights in the aesthetics of camouflage that his chosen materials and processes offer. By using powder coating to emulate the look and feel of polished silver, he seems to establish a meaningful philosophy, reminding us of all those cliched aphorisms such as "beauty is only skin deep," "don't judge a book by its cover," or, perhaps more fittingly, "all that glitters is not gold." Nevertheless, this attempt to conceptually imagine and craft a queer utopia ultimately remains as "superficial" as the powder coating settled on the brass surface or as "hollow" as the brass tubes that make up the structure of each piece in the collection.

Other materials Tai uses are also loaded with symbolic meaning and are often erotically charged. Carefully interlinked between some of the metal structures in the *Fagatopia* series are ball closure rings made from surgical stainless steel. These are traditionally used for body piercings, namely in nasal septum piercings and penis piercings (colloquially known as the "Prince Albert"). For many people within the LGBTQ+ community, these humble metal piercings (along with other forms of body modification such as tattoos and scarification), are not only used to assert bodily autonomy but have also been used as a way of signaling one's sexuality to others. Piercing has historically been seen as a taboo or subversive practice, and it has been associated with queerness for centuries.[17] For many queer people, piercing can be a way to express their individuality, reject societal beauty "norms," and reclaim their bodies from a history of medicalization and control. Piercings still retain a central role in contemporary culture, primarily via queer SM, fetish, and kink subcultures in which a piercing may "flagrantly express nonnormative identities" and "contest the dominant fiction of heteronormativity . . . by violating bodily norms."[18] Decorating or adorning the body with a piercing, or one of Tai's pierced objects, has similar connotations, and there is now a growing body of work that acknowledges the role of craft in fetish.[19] As scholar Tom Cubbin notes in an article about the San Francisco-based fetish brand Mr. S Leather, "[t] he uses of craft are shaped by the different ways in which fetish practices sit within leather and kink communities," including the way we "relate to the feel of certain materials against the skin."[20] This is especially the case for leather but also extends to other materials commonly used among these communities, such as rubber, and especially metal, which forms a key component in fetish wear, including through rivets, rings, fastenings, belts, buckles, studs, chains, and even entire wearables—which I will turn to later concerning Affect Metals. When I asked Tai whether he views his jewelry as a form of fetish wear or fetish style, given its overt engagement with the materials and histories of fetish, he replied:

> I do, and I do not. A lot of my work is inspired by queer sexual subcultures and BDSM, which is why I use metal piercings as well as other components, such as rubber or leather, which are also highly erotic. But I also fetishize the material by making and handling it. The work doesn't necessarily need a body to function like traditional jewelry, the material is erotic and the metal is attractive on its own. In that respect, maybe I am a bad jeweler.[21]

Commonly, fetishism is still widely interpreted as something purely sexual. However, in the field of craft, there have long been discussions on forms of material fetishism—the allure and appeal of specific materials. Ultimately, the erotic can be disembodied as much as it is embodied. Jewelry itself is often fetishized in non-sexual ways—it is sometimes flaunted as a symbol of wealth and class status. However, Tai shifts this focus. The emphasis here is not on crafting a "polished" or "luxury" product, but he is interested in fetishizing the material itself, paying attention to the medium-specific qualities of metal and all its affects. It is the relationship between metal and skin that makes adornment a fascinating area of study, and a continued site of appeal for Tai, particularly considering the relationship between queer craft and fetish, given that these objects are marked by tender interactions with the body of both the maker and the wearer. Here, metal becomes something soft and close, not just hard and distant. The queering of metal seems particularly alluring for the way both the material and the practice often involve an embrace of duality, including Tai's engagement with the simultaneity of aligning and diverging from systems of power but also playing with dualisms between soft/hard, rough/tender, unyielding/malleable, disembodied/embodied.

While Tai meticulously handcrafts most of his metal components, the surgical steel rings that often pierce his jewelry are ready-made, sourced in bulk from online platforms like eBay. Tai's use of ready-made elements may be controversial to some craftspeople, especially given the traditional emphasis on "the hand" and the "handmade" within craft scholarship—a concept that, while often productive, can also be limiting. For instance, in his book *The Craftsman* (2008), sociologist Richard Sennett also takes up the German philosopher Immanuel Kant's remark "the hand is the window on to the mind" to argue that craftsmanship is not necessarily a quality but rather a way of being, a form of connection, and a way in which we can learn about ourselves through the labor of making physical things.[22] Yet, in today's digital, globalized, and capitalist world, form and meaning are often found beyond one's hand, with craft largely enacted in collaboration, or at least within a community of practice.[23] After all, for better or worse, the hand constantly finds itself in communion with the internet and industrialized modes of production. Even David Pye, writing in 1968, noted that "[t]o distinguish between the different ways of carrying out an operation by classifying them as hand- or machine-work is . . . all but meaningless."[24] Tai defends his approach, explaining: "the piercings I use are already industrial grade and I don't see the point in me imitating a piercing or making my own. It is important for me to use the same type of piercing that you could buy and insert in your own body . . . just because I sometimes use readymade materials, it doesn't make my craft any less important or relevant."[25] These metal rings, primarily manufactured in Chinese factories, are treated as carefully as any precious stone. For Tai, "they are the setting elements," they are already loaded with symbolic and conceptual potential because they already have meaning and context as ready-made pieces of jewelry used to pierce the flesh.

With his latest ongoing series titled *Nude Jade Pierced* (2019–), Tai continues to work with these themes of craft and fetish, but in addition to using metal, he also incorporates one of China's most sacred and precious materials, jade. Revered as the ultimate symbol of beauty and purity in Chinese culture, jade is prized for its ability to be polished and carved into intricate forms, including bangles, rings, pendants, and mythological or religious statuaries. Tai traveled across Southern China, which is well-known for producing jade objects, namely bangles. Creating a bangle from jade is inherently wasteful. The jeweler must carve through a solid block of jade to achieve a hollow band, meaning a large chunk of the gemstone is left over. However, this block is sometimes used to craft smaller objects like rings or pendants. The bangle itself will then be trimmed and polished to give it its near and rounded shape, leaving further misshaped offcuts that are usually considered too small to work with. Tai would not usually be able to access large quantities of jade due to the sheer expense of the material. However, he began purchasing these small offcuts relatively cheaply and gradually introduced them into this body of work. "For those jewelers, it is useless; they sell it [offcuts of jade] by the kilogram. It is very ironic because even though it is in the same category as precious jade, the price is much lower. The shape is not the point for me; I don't care if it is not perfectly round or a small chunk," he states.[26]

Tai treats these misshapen jade offcuts with the same care and techniques as traditionally valued pieces, polishing and finishing them meticulously. Sometimes, he embraces their inherent "oddities"—the rough edges, lines, and unconventional shapes—leaving them intact. Other times, he trims the jade into simple, abstract, geometric forms (like elongated rectangles) that could pass as standard jade jewelry. However, appearances can be deceiving. These seemingly innocuous shapes often take on coded meanings, employing tactics of queer abstraction.

Several pendants in the series are shaped like teabags; a coded pun on the sexual act of "teabagging" where testicles are dipped in and out of the mouth of another, akin to dunking a teabag in and out of a mug of water. This playful subversion involves using the material in an unexpected way, and playfully engages with a (presumably cisgender and heterosexual) public who might remain oblivious to the joke. These jade offcuts are transformed into pendants, strung on rubber or leather cords, further emphasizing material fetishism and play. Further, the pendants are drilled into and *penetrated* with ready-made circular barbell piercings. There is a sharp juxtaposition between the jade's pale, shimmering, and skin-like surface and the thick metal piercings that penetrate it. Just as piercing the body might be seen as a violation of bodily norms, Tai's "piercing" of the jade might also be seen as a violation of this precious material, a "wrong" way of working with these traditional materials, contrary to conventional methods and techniques. This is particularly the case as drilling into the fragile stone puts it at risk of shattering. There is a sense of pushing the material to its limits, just the body can be pushed to its limits. Some piercings appear haphazardly placed, while others are strategically positioned, referencing the human form. For example, a slender jade rectangle pierced twice near the upper middle evokes a figure with double nipple piercings (Figure 5.2). The circular rings, weighed down by the barbell, create an illusion of breasts sagging against the veined texture of the jade.

These forms of bodily abstraction play out through other works that meditate on the sexual and erotic potential of metal, but also the erotic potential of the digital. Tai explained that although he identifies as a jeweler and is firmly in touch with the languages, legacies, and materials of craft, he sometimes breaks from this tradition, often describing himself as a "cybersmith." He elaborates:

> While I do consider myself a jeweler, I sometimes call myself a cybersmith. I love this kind of stamp that I've put on myself and I want to communicate this concept. When people talk about their practice, they usually talk about the type of metal they use or the trade they are part of – blacksmith, goldsmith, silversmith, and so on. In my case, although I do work with metal, I'm from a generation where the internet has always been there. I've been surfing online much longer than I've been working with metal. In a way, the digital is the medium where I'm most experienced, and it's how I have come to terms with my sexuality and queerness. Technically, it is the most common medium I've been using and working with.[27]

This highlights how contemporary queer practitioners are constantly dismantling existing disciplinary categories and forging new ones. Tai's emphasis on the digital as a medium prompts us to consider its role *as* a form of craft. While craft and the digital might seem disparate, in *Abstracting Craft: The Practiced Digital Hand* (1996), Malcolm McCullough argues that the way expert computer users engage with screen imagery is similar to traditional forms of handicraft. McCullough argues this by suggesting that both rely on increasingly intuitive hand/eye coordination, require a certain skill level, and operate as haptic devices.[28] Further,

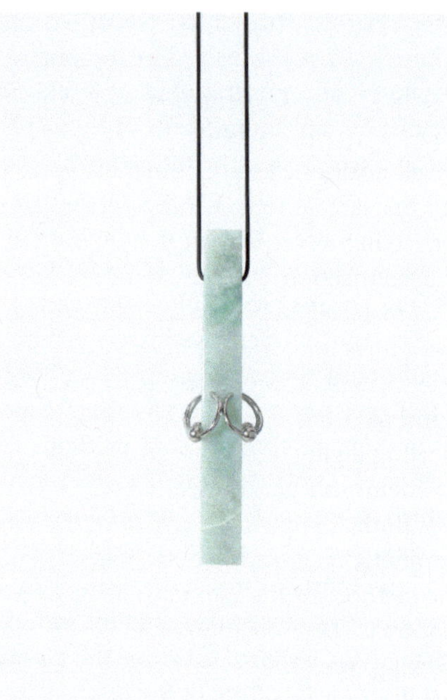

**Figure 5.2** Hansel Tai, *Nude Jade Pierced*, 2019. Jade, surgical stainless-steel piercing, rubber string. Courtesy of Hansel Tai.

Tai's description also invites us to consider the relationship between the internet and the crafting of the self. As acknowledged in Chapter 3, the internet is not only a source of inspiration for many practitioners searching for creative inspiration, but for many queer people of Tai's generation, it is a crucial place for the crafting of queer identity. Importantly, it is also a space of sexual becoming. Pornography, in particular, is a space through which many people might come to terms with their sexuality and explore new-found desires and fetishes.

Tai's series of metal brooches *BMP (Blue Milk Pierced)*, *DBMP (Diamond-Blue Milk Pierced)*, and *CMP (Cyber Milk Pierced)* most obviously reflect upon how identities are often constructed through an engagement with the internet, specifically referencing online gay pornography. Upon initial inspection, the brooches appear as abstract metallic forms embellished with numerous piercings. These objects, in cool shades of blue, resemble splatters of liquid frozen in time. They are also in keeping with the slick chrome and futuristic qualities of Tai's work, which always references a particular kind of millennial and glitchy "y2k" glamour. Like the series *Fagatopia*, where Tai relied on access to industrial powder-coating machinery, he sent these metal shapes to a local car shop specializing in bodywork to undergo a process of soft chroming so they would have a highly mirrored finish that gives them this slick, wet, and glossy look. Yet, the brooches more accurately resemble splashes of ejaculate or bodily fluid. To further these associations, Tai decided to document these works by seductively balancing them on the bodies and faces of various nude models instead of photographing them on a clothed model, which might be more common in the documentation of brooches (Figure 5.3). Staged in this way, Tai makes a commentary on the "cum shot" or "money shot" as it is colloquially known, which are part of the popular lexicon used to talk about pornography in today's digital era.

Tai's earlier collections of brooches, such as *Dirt Container* and *Not important and Not urgent,* also reflected on queer sexual cultures and how identities are crafted, both online and offline. These brooches incorporated pornographic imagery taken from the internet and were adorned with LED lights, which were soldered to the back of the metal.[29] Tai refers to them informally as the "clubbing works" and emphasizes that the concept behind them is that "you are your own light force" and carry this with you as you move through the world as an outward extension of inner queer joy.[30] However, the work also "becomes alive from being in the context of a queer space" such as a club or dark room where the LED lights on the brooch would be most visible, articulating how queerness and a sense of self is often crafted collaboratively in community.[31] Each brooch is a different color, creating a sense of community and acceptance of difference when worn by multiple people in a space, establishing a radiating spectrum that transforms fleshy bodies into ethereal visions. These objects echo how queer joy can stem from within us, a form of self-love and appreciation, but also from being around the energies of others, how we may feel more "alive" when surrounded by queer kin. The objects can ultimately mean different things in different contexts, establishing a palimpsest of queerness from within the materiality itself, its making, its adorning, through to the social contexts in which it means different things. Again, these works are inherently playful, in both senses of the word— they are light-hearted and humorous but also support sexual play. The quest for bodily pleasure can certainly characterize play, but playfulness generally indicates a drive towards improvisation, experimentation, and creativity—something that sparks joy. Queer joy is a sense of deep warmth and happiness that can bring purpose to queer lives. In a world that is so hostile to LGBTQ+ people, feelings and expressions of queer joy can feel like a frivolous luxury. These expressions are vital sustenance: they provide momentary respite and energize us, affirming our vibrant inner worlds so that we might make our surrounding world into one where we thrive, grow, and *shine* rather than struggle to survive. It is a refusal to dwell on the pain and weight of queer life and a reminder to live life to the fullest. It is not only about imagining or crafting queer futures but about the happiness we can find in ourselves and among our community in the *queer* and now. All of Tai's objects invite their owners to wear their sexuality and identity loudly and proudly on their chests, albeit in coded ways. Although they are not just about sexual pleasure, this raises interesting questions about the relationships between craft and sexual intimacy. These associations are embodied most clearly by the wearable chainmail objects of Affect Metals.

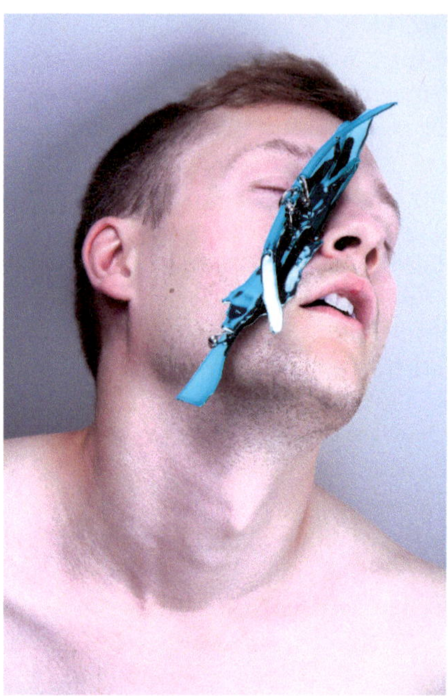

**Figure 5.3** Hansel Tai, *BMP (Blue Milk Pierced)*, 2018. Chromed silver and brass, surgical stainless-steel piercing.

### *Affect Metals (Abe Heath, b.1992, USA)*

Affect Metals is run by Abe Heath, a self-taught practitioner based in Los Angeles. They started the project in 2017 while studying for a graduate degree in gender studies and information studies. While working part-time as an archivist (a job they continue to sustain their practice), they recalled wanting to find a creative outlet to express themselves. They began creating "embodied wearable pieces" that they could wear to raves.[32] This ultimately turned into "an exploration of metal as a craft" and the project as it stands today.[33] Affect Metals aims to create contemporary wearable chainmail "queer armor" and "divine objects" that empower the wearer.[34] To date, Affect Metals has sold earrings, necklaces, chokers, collars, cuffs, leashes, belts, bras, tops, harnesses, thongs, corsets, ball gags, and more. They have even designed a metal flogger "perfect for the metal fetishist" because, as steel is a conductive material, the toy can be used for forms of electrical stimulation to create "intense partnered play."[35]

Like Tai's jewelry, the objects created by Affect Metals deftly defy neat categorization. They are, first and foremost, a form of armor—specifically conceptualized by Heath as *queer* armor. Yet, some of the chainmail objects are designed as supportive tools for sexual pleasure, such as a strap-on harness that can hold a dildo to enable penetrative sex (Figure 5.4). Others are jewelry, while still others are fully wearable metal garments—a form of clothing or fetish wear. Heath explains that they delight in how these objects refuse to conform to any one thing: "there is a queerness in all this, not fitting into a category is queer," they explain.[36] The myriad of objects sold by Affect Metals are made solely by Heath and hand-woven, link by link. Talking about the making process, Heath explains, "each chain is meant to be a positively charged and protective object for the wearer, a type of armor. It is all meant to be powerful, protective, and healing, a safe barrier between you and the world."[37] All the chainmail objects are made from 100% stainless steel due to its durability. The anti-rust, anti-allergenic, and waterproof properties of stainless steel make it better suited to sensitive skin and means that these objects will likely outlive the bodies that inhabit them. Freshwater pearls are used for decoration in some designs, and more recently, sterling silver or gold options have been available upon request—customization is key. Items can take anywhere between one and six weeks to complete and, for Heath, the time-consuming nature of crafting the chainmail "adds an element of the deeply personal."[38] At the time of writing, the works vary in price and range from around $30 for earrings to $440 for larger wearable pieces like chainmail tops, reflecting the scale of the work. While these pieces, like Tai's jewelry, may be inaccessible to some, the higher price point acknowledges the labor, materials, studio space, rising energy and resource costs, and bespoke design process.

When asked why they specifically chose to work with metal, Heath said: "I think I have always been attracted to metal and chains – some Joan of Arc obsession intersected with my great-grandfather as a miner that makes me feel a deep connection to metal."[39] As a military leader transcending gender roles, Joan of Arc is often heralded as a "trans icon."[40] Claimed to be acting under divine guidance, she was a military leader who defended France in the siege of Orléans. Forms of cross-dressing, which included wearing "masculine" chainmail and styling her hair in a cropped fashion, were supposedly used as examples of her heresy. Although chainmail is still heavily associated with masculinity and military activity, Heath and many other practitioners have been inspired by Joan of Arc's gender nonconformity and have continued to use chainmail to disrupt social and gendered norms of dress. Today, chainmail is more widely used in forms of adornment, typically in jewelry making, where individual coils are either riveted, butted, or sometimes welded together. The simple elegance of interwoven rings and the myriad of patterns that can be created via the metal weaving process make chainmail very versatile and appealing to contemporary practitioners. Historically, chainmail (sometimes spelled chainmaille) was a prominent piece of armor in the Middle Ages, traditionally made from drawing and coiling iron wire into individual links that were flattened and woven together to create a mesh-like "fabric." This contrasts with forms of plate armor, where large sheets of metal are designed to encompass the body, and the wearer must conform to the rigid shape of the armor itself, which is largely uncomfortable and burdensome to wear. In contrast, chainmail has quite the opposite effect; its shape comes from the wearer,

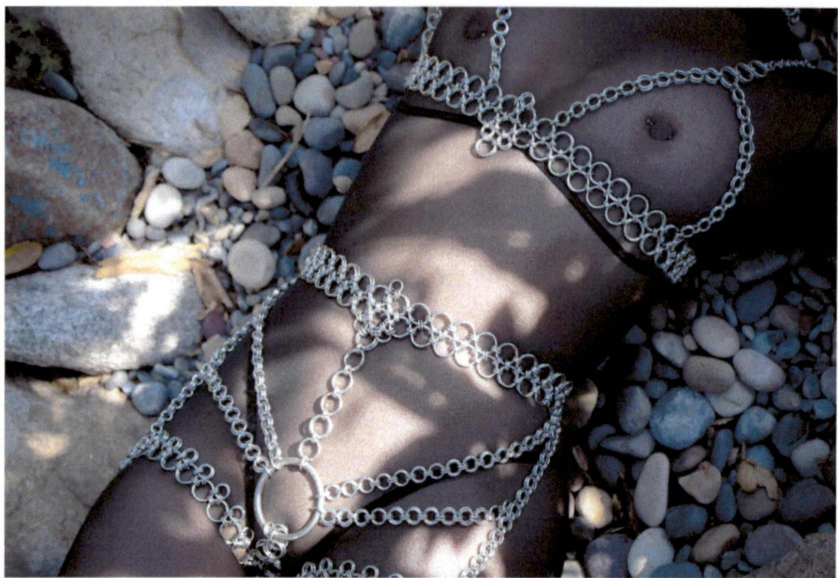

**Figure 5.4** Affect Metals, *Strap on Harness and Circe Bra Harness*, 14 and 16 gauge stainless steel, dimensions variable (custom made to measure). Courtesy of Abe Heath.

and its contours are dictated by the wearer's own, meaning it is relatively freeing and enables fluid movement. Heath sees this as a metaphor for the fluidity of queer and trans identities, and these works are ultimately "a celebration of transformation, a reminder of queer becoming."[41]

Heath's practice is dedicated to granting bodily and sexual autonomy to queer and trans communities who have often found themselves without these kinds of affirming objects. They recognize that just as queer and trans bodies are often crafted, there is a need for crafted objects to fit them and support them. As a queer non-binary business owner, Heath can understand the needs of their clientele and craft objects suitable for members of their community. Each piece is made by hand, and all collections are genderless. Working made to order and made to measure actively gives authority over to the wearer; a client can submit their design to fit their own body regardless of gender, sexuality, shape, size, or ability, all with their own pleasures and desires in mind. In this sense, the wearer can craft whatever they need and desire, not rely on mass-manufactured objects that are not often suited to a diverse range of bodies. For instance, all objects that are made to be worn across the chest are designed to accommodate people with or without breasts, mainly accounting for trans people who may have had "top surgery" (a double mastectomy), or those who may choose to bind their chests to give the appearance of a flat chest. Tailoring each object to fit each body means that Affect Metals highlights and celebrates the uniqueness of queer and trans bodies. Thus, wearing these objects can promote a sense of affirmation, and prompt a range of different affects. This is why Heath chose to name the brand "Affect Metals"; "affect" meaning to subjectively or emotionally effect, and "metals" to designate their material of choice and the affective capabilities of the metal itself.

As with Tai's practice, the metal itself here is loaded with fetishistic potential. The coolness and smoothness of the polished steel can shock and titillate when initially placed on the body, only for it to transform and warm with use from the body's natural heat. Unlike plate armor, which forms a metal shell around the body, chainmail strays between fabric, metal, and a second skin, creating a protective barrier of glistening scales that can be shed at will. "Chains respond to you, change with you, fuse with you," Heath reminds us.[42] Affect Metals, then, is about how the body and the metal interact, change, and affect one another. In the case of tighter-fitting objects such as chokers, the metal clings and caresses the flesh. The metal might impress the skin, leaving small indentations marking its use. Aside from their sensual feel on the skin, the objects in these collections are also practical and versatile. Harnesses can often be worn either backward or forward. They can be layered over clothing or worn against bare skin. Heath pays great attention to both form and function; not only are links woven to create decorative metal patterns, but they are often made to be adjustable and inclusive for every body. The addition of metal closures in specific areas, such as the thigh and waist, means that they can be adapted or can be put on or taken off quickly and easily—essential for use in sexual play. Heath notes that this is especially important for disabled people, whose bodies are often valorized by the media as supposedly "unsexy," and who are not usually granted the opportunity for sexual independence.

The objects produced by Affect Metals highlight the multifaceted use of craft in queer culture, especially the inventiveness of queer sexual cultures. Here, we can consider the sexual prosthetics of queer and trans sexuality and the intense, intimate relationship between materials and queer bodies. Objects such as strap-on harnesses, cock rings, and fetish wear are all part of what Berlant and Warner would describe as the "inventiveness of queer world making," affirming the importance that craft(ing) has for surviving in a world "inimical to one's own survival."[43] As discussed in Chapter 1, craft and DIY culture play an important role in forms of queer worldmaking. However, for Berlant and Warner, worldmaking is more than just finding kinship and crafting community—it is equally tied to creating forms of intimacy. They suggest:

> Heteronormative forms of intimacy are supported, as we have argued, not only by overt referential discourse such as love plots and sentimentality but materially, in marriage and family law, in the architecture of the domestic, in the zoning of work and politics. Queer culture, by contrast, has almost no institutional matrix for its counterintimacies. In the absence of marriage and the rituals that organize life around matrimony, improvisation is always necessary.[44]

To build a queer world, they argue, is to also "support forms of affective, erotic, and personal living that are public in the sense of accessible, available to memory, and sustained through collective activity."[45] In short, often "what brings us together is sexual culture."[46] The objects made by Affect Metals are often crafted to enhance pleasure, offer improvisation, and allow for the expression of one's sexuality and identity—recognizing that in making a new queer world, we need also need to make objects that support us in this venture. In a brief description about queer handmaking in *Fray*, Bryan-Wilson also observes that even though sex objects were mass-manufactured and available to purchase via mail order since the 1970s, many of them were crafted by hand, a mode of improvising and crafting something from what was to hand. She explains: "[t]hough the 1970s were awash in an abundance of fabricated commodities, hand making remained a creative and necessary act for some subcultural groups, a key part of forging queer identities and the enabling of queer sexual practices [. . .] crafting was a resource to physically bring objects, and new forms of representation and self-expression, into the world."[47] Bryan-Wilson explores explicit invocations of queer craft within lesbian communities, drawing on examples from American writer Dorothy Allison's memoir *Skin: Talking about Sex, Class and Literature* (1994). Here, Allison recalls the crafted toys of her butch lover, Marty, including a "large-sized glove stuffed with cotton" which formed a plushy phallus, and a harness crafted by another lover, Carey, which was made "out of a couple of old belts and carpet threads."[48] Queer communities have a rich history of crafting their own sexual tools and attire, a rejection of the narrow and often exclusionary offerings of late capitalism that fail to consider the full spectrum of bodies and desires.

Although there are clear relationships between craft and queer sexual practices here in relation to the objects that Affect Metals produces, there is often a danger of relegating the queer experience purely to sex and sexual culture. Conversely, what is often read as erotic does not have to be linked to sex. After all, many of the objects by Affect Metals, such as the chainmail tops or body harnesses, may not even be used as part of physical sex acts. This is especially important to acknowledge for customers of Affect Metals who may identify as part of the aromantic and/or asexual spectrum. Even the chainmail strap-on harness "has been tested to ensure its comfort and compatibility for use in play but works beyond the function of a strap-on harness alone."[49] The object description on the online shop encourages wearers to "[u]nbuckle the thigh straps and wear this harness as a chain skirt" or "hang it on your wall and make a statement!"[50] Although some of the objects are designed with sexual pleasure in mind, these objects are not reliant on sex at all (you can hang them on your wall after all!). These objects can also be erotic in the sense that they are affirming, empowering, and affective, which can provide a source of pleasure. In the context of their wearable objects, Heath notes, "[i]t's this beautiful cycle of the wearer feeling empowered and protected by the chain, and the chain then taking on the energy and characteristics of the person wearing it."[51]

In her 1978 paper *Uses of the Erotic: The Erotic as Power* (1978), Audre Lorde famously expanded the concept of the erotic far beyond sexual pleasure. In it, she states: "[t]he erotic functions [. . .] in providing the power which comes from sharing deeply any pursuit with another person. The sharing of joy, whether physical, emotional, psychic, or intellectual, forms a bridge between the sharers which can be the basis for understanding much of what is not shared between them and lessens the threat of their difference."[52] For Lorde, then, the erotic is not just about physical connection or even sexual intercourse but about embracing our feelings and sharing them with others, the joy we find in community. This fosters a sense of belonging that extends beyond the self; it is a "bridge" that allows for the sharing of pleasure, which can be felt in a collective. Lorde connects the erotic to social justice, arguing that when we are fully connected to ourselves and feel a sense of wholeness, we are better equipped to fight against oppression, embrace our creative potential, and build a more socially just world. This notion of sharing and mutual understanding as part of the erotic is especially relevant for communities whose experiences have been marked by trauma. If craft is enacted within a community, it invites sharing experiences and a connection with each other, generating feelings of belonging and safety. Healing is ultimately possible through the magic of community, and craft becomes a vital tool in that journey. If we can embrace who we truly are, then we can refract new possibilities for life, love, and joy around us. Heath echoes this, explaining: "[m]y queerness and my practice has largely been based on bonding over trauma with other people and us navigating our shared rejection. I've been thinking about what it would mean for a future generation of queer people not to have queerness associated with pain and trauma, and my brain cannot even comprehend it. I think joy is a complex, radical, beautiful thing that I hope is channeled into the chain and then shared through its use in the world."[53]

When Heath packages and ships each object, they even place a card in the box that reads "may this chain empower and protect you," highlighting how they see armor as a form of spiritual empowerment, more than just a sexy object. Heath explains that their process is a "deeply intimate and intentional way of weaving magic into something wearable, sensuous, and protective."[54] This relates to Lorde's concept that the erotic can be emotional, psychic, or intellectual and something that is often dually shared—for both maker and wearer in this context. Beyond mere sexual prostheses, the crafted objects of Affect Metals are also about self-love, affirmation, and empowerment, allowing opportunities to share in our pain and joy. Therefore, for Heath and many other practitioners who craft fetish objects, the exercise of making these objects, as well as the exercise of sharing them with the community, can enable forms of the erotic that move beyond sex. After all, phrases like "putting on my armor" or "putting on my war paint" are often used to describe the process of wearing objects or applying makeup, which supports us in self-fashioning. This speaks to how forms of adornment and accessorizing can make us feel strong, empowered, and fierce. To ensure these objects' affirming potential, Heath controls the entire creative process. They had previously flirted with the idea of scaling the project up and perhaps hiring others to help produce the work, but they ultimately decided against the norms of capitalistic growth, seeing it as an antithesis to the project's ethos. "I deeply identify as an animist—it would take the magic out of what I am doing," they explain.[55] "It is a long-suffering process that I am a part of every step of the way. If someone else's hands got on it, it doesn't mean that it wouldn't be special or have a different energy that isn't significant, but it would distort the work and the devotion that I am trying to put into it . . . I would worry about how the context might change or how it would be presented," they add.[56]

Conceptualizing clothing as a form of "soft armor" due to its empowering potential, and writing about gender nonconforming clothing and accessories brand Rebirth Garments, the scholar Erin J. Rand writes that "dressing the stigmatized body in "fabulous" queer style might be a means of agency and opposition, a way to rework the terms of visibility by which bodies are surveilled, and a source of joy, pleasure, and community."[57] But what about when the "armor" *is* armor, not a "soft" textile but a "hard" metal? How does that change the politics of visibility? On the one hand, these queer armored objects are equally intended to empower the wearer and encourage them to embody themselves fully, like other forms of queer style and expression. Yet, Heath recognizes that wearing a full chainmail top in public through the streets of LA (or anywhere else these objects may end up) may be seen as "strange, and thus queer," potentially leading to further stigmatization, unsolicited attention, and in worse cases, violence. To some extent, these fraught consequences of visibility are counteracted by the form of chainmail itself, which would ultimately offer some practical protection even if it is only designed with aesthetics in mind. Of course, many would also attest that queer and trans bodies are subjected to surveillance and unsolicited scrutiny regardless of what a person might choose to adorn their body with, nor should people have to self-censor based on the opinions of small-minded individuals.

Crucial to the regulation of queer and trans visibility, Heath controls all the documentation of their work. As transgender activist Tourmaline argues, in an age where images of queer and trans people "are misused, sanitized, and extracted" daily, it is hardly surprising that many practitioners, including Heath, would be concerned about the consequences of relinquishing control. Tourmaline adds that it is this kind of "violent extraction—of black life, trans life, queer life, disabled life, poor life—that leads so many of us to hold our ideas close to our chests; to never let the world see how brightly we shine."[58] Heath ensures that the objects they design for a diverse range of bodies can be actively seen on a diverse range of bodies, including trans, non-binary, gender nonconforming, fat, and disabled models who are not given visibility in contemporary media in affirming and positive ways as cis, slim, and able-bodied models often are. Affect Metals does not attempt to normalize the queerness, gender nonconformity, race, ethnicity, ability, or size of the wearer but instead puts them on display in creative, affirming, and sexy ways. Most of Heath's models are people they have "found through life," usually close friends, chosen family, or people they know within their local community of queer makers.[59] Sometimes, the works are even designed for models based on their personalities and energies and then named after them or given a mythological pseudonym. In all the photographs of the objects, the models appear at ease. This is primarily due to Heath's relationship with their subjects. Still, it is also a testament to how their queer armor is empowering and how queer style, more broadly, becomes an embodied practice of survival, invention, and transformation for marginalized bodies. Heath highlights the uniqueness of a wide range of bodies, enhancing their uniqueness rather than concealing the features that render them supposedly undesirable or deviant. These designs are not about hiding; they are about celebrating the complexities and beauty of queer and trans bodies, and this is reflected in their documentation. An open-mesh harness is photographed on a trans model who reclines on a rock, basks in the sunlight, and shows off their top surgery scars (Figure 5.6). Detailed macro shots of the wearables not only celebrate the intricate metalwork but also celebrate blemishes, stretch marks, and cellulite. Models are photographed in streets, clubs, bedrooms, and sex dungeons alike. Many gaze directly into the camera with a subtle smirk, a certain sparkle in their eye. One of the models is photographed outdoors wearing a chainmail crop top paired with a pair of sequin flares; the light bounces off both, causing light to radiate from the model as if they are reflecting their inner joy outwardly for all the world to see like a walking, talking disco ball (Figure 5.5). Heath's armored creations, which literally and metaphorically protect queer and trans bodies and make them visible in affirming ways, enable them to shine after all.

In recent years, there has been a vast amount of interest in the role of shininess in visual culture, especially within the role of fetish and material fetishism. Writing in *Shiny Things: Reflective Surfaces and Their Mixed Meanings* (2021), modernist literature scholar Leonard Diepeveen and artist Timothy van Laar articulate that "'[s]hininess' excesses lead to more than just disembodiment. Its overcharge, in certain circumstances, leads to fetishism—for example, the fetishism of the early 1970s glam rock acts like David Bowie's Ziggy Stardust."[60] Although the book does not address the role of shininess in queer culture, they do acknowledge that "the body is an object of obsessive and strange attention, and shininess in its allure and defamiliarization over-charges, redirects, and queers the body as sign."[61] They go on to add: "[w]hile shininess is often used to elicit desire, as a tool of seduction, the shiny body also has less charged versions of allure, such as playful adornment, or to heighten an occasion . . . [it] isn't always about seducing another person; bodily shininess is not inevitably goal-oriented."[62] Heath explicitly refers to these ideas of shining, describing their objects as "a kind of glamour armor – something that is transforming you into this fantasy you want to be that helps you to embody your gender or sexuality in a way that makes you feel like you're *shining*, that you're empowered."[63] While these assertions of shininess and glamour are relevant to reflect on in relation to Affect Metals, the term shininess describes the visual properties of something that shines with direct reflective light, such as polished plate armor with a smooth surface. However, as chainmail is made from individual links of thinly rolled metal, which has much more fluidity and movement, the light is not directly reflective. Instead, it bounces off each link in a soft, wavering, or dappled light. Due to the rippled surface and depth created by the woven technique, these objects, and by extension the bodies that inhabit them, more accurately *shimmer.*

Cultural analyst Eliza Steinbock has explored the concept of shimmering in relation to forms of trans embodiment. They use this idea to describe how trans bodies, and images of trans bodies, are ever-changing and evolving. Steinbock's writing is informed by Roland Barthes's idea of "the shimmer" and Michel Foucault's notion of sex as a "shimmering mirage," as well as work by trans theorists such as Stryker who have also employed ideas of shimmering in their

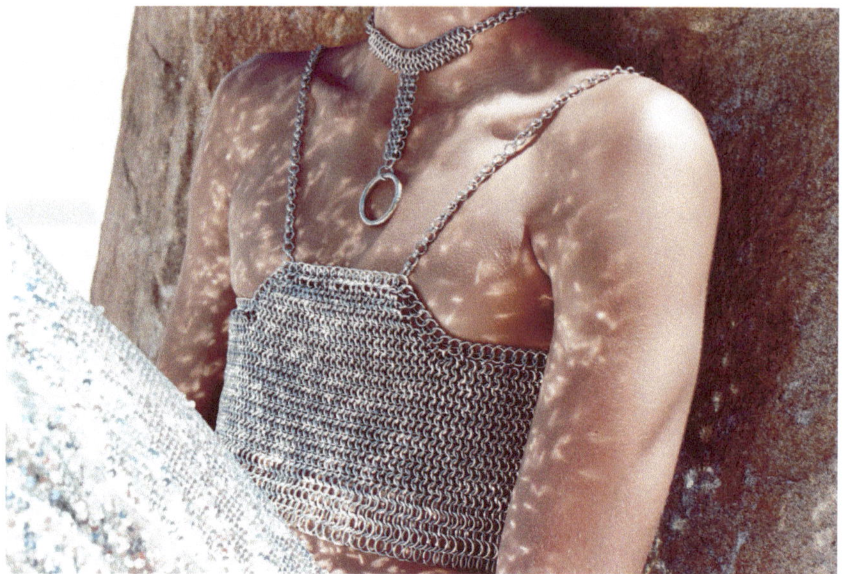

**Figure 5.5** Affect Metals, *Francesca Crop Top*, 16 gauge stainless steel, dimensions variable (custom made to measure). Courtesy of Abe Heath.

work.[64] Interweaving these theoretical approaches to notions of the "shimmer," Steinbock forges a new conception of trans bodies as "shimmering images," which they argue can be used to "describe the persistent vision of trans as change."[65] For Steinbock, the notion of shimmering recognizes that this process of trans as change is seemingly endless because "[t]rans ontologies are process-oriented rather than object-oriented" and trans people especially disrupt the fixed (or object-oriented) notion of gender.[66] According to Steinbock, shimmering embodies this "change in its alluring, twinkling, flickering form" and, as such, shimmering can be aligned with the radical, liberatory, anti-normative possibilities that are often attributed to trans liminality.[67] Although Steinbock primarily writes about representations of trans bodies in film and their shimmery or "glitchy" nature, their conceptual theorization of trans bodies as "shimmering" is pertinent here when considering both the visibility and documentation of trans bodies and the specific material properties of chainmail. In short, these shimmering objects have the power to represent the shimmering nature of trans bodies. These ideas are also deepened by the photographic practice itself. Here, Heath's depictions of trans people are not static, tangible, or definable because they are *of* trans people, and other trans people can see themselves *reflected* in these representations. Many of the photographs of the collections are taken with multiple exposures, leading to overlapping layers where flesh and metal fuse with one another, and the glare of the armor is exaggerated through an overexposing of the images (Figure 5.6). For those whose

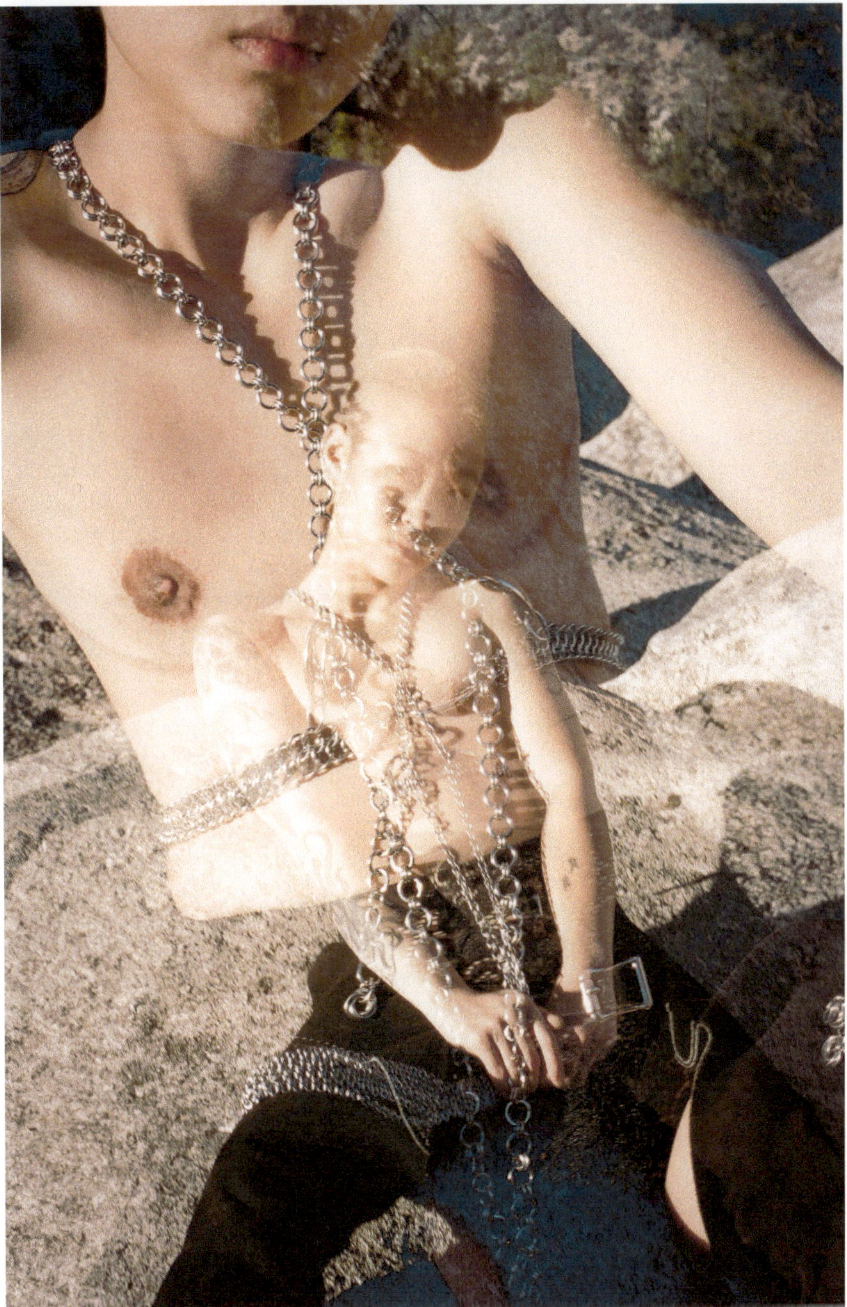

**Figure 5.6** Affect Metals, Equus Harness, 14 and 16 gauge stainless steel, stainless steel snaffle bit, dimensions variable (custom made to measure). Courtesy of Abe Heath.

bodies are continuously marginalized, vilified, and attacked, adornment and accessorizing may seem like a frivolous concern or a trivial location from which to imagine resistance to systems of oppression. Yet, rather than dwelling upon the negativity of queer and trans life, as is so easily done in today's political climate, the objects made by Affect Metals give agency to the wearer, encouraging them to move through life *shimmering*.

## Conclusion

This chapter has aimed to highlight multiple forms of queer adornment in relation to metalworking practices, from the jewelry of Hansel Tai to the queer armor of Affect Metals. It has shown the importance of craft in forms of fetish and the erotic, but fundamentally also one of self-expression and social signification. Both practitioners prioritize pleasure and foreground joy, conviviality, and belonging in their designs. The sexual politics and role of the fetish in Tai's work is undoubtedly more conceptual or at least material-driven, a process of fetishizing the material itself. Conversely, Heath's designs for Affect Metals provide a more sustained engagement with fetish, as many of the objects are designed for use within queer sexual cultures. Yet, both their practices demonstrate how the weight, texture, and feel of metal can provide specific sensory experiences and affects that contribute to the fetishistic nature of the object itself. They encourage their wearers and users to embrace play, joy, and pleasure, articulating that these, too, can be important sites of collective liberation.

# Chapter 6

## GLASS

## Handle with Care: Fragility and Viral Containment

### *Introduction*

"We had nothing, and now we have something."[1]

These were the words that Tim Tate, an American glass sculptor, said to me when I first spoke to him in 2022 about a rise in the use of terms such as "queer glass." It was a timely reminder that this book is, in part, about building an archive—a way to begin assembling the richness of queer craft as a field of research and practice. Over the past few years, I have had the pleasure of speaking with Tate regularly and have been working on curating a travelling exhibition of his work, "Imagining Utopia."[2] When I asked Tate about what queer glass meant to him, he replied: "queer glass is not just works made from glass by queer people, but rather works that are made from glass by queer people with queer *intent* and queer *content*."[3] He also echoed an excitement about situating his practice within this framework because "it demands that both parts of your identity and personhood – queer person and glass maker – be acknowledged and valued as equally important. It's this refusal to stay invisible," he said.[4] The recent proliferation of the term "queer glass," he noted, has allowed him to retrospectively examine this connection. Tate also pointed out that while "queer glass" is often presented as a new conceptual or scholarly field, its use within communities of practice is far from new. However, these communities have remained largely invisible until recently.

In contrast to invisibility which is "to be unseen, out of sight, and unknown," transparency signifies "the condition of being able to be seen through," offering "openness, visibility, or accessibility."[5] For queer individuals often forced into self-concealment for survival, the material and metaphorical qualities of glass hold resonance. Glass offers both physical clarity and a medium for personal expression. For queer glass practitioners, transparency can represent a movement beyond secrecy toward openness and authenticity, transforming the queer experience from invisibility to visibility—a chance to make the unseen, seen. Challenging the historical invisibility of queer artistic practices in glass and rendering them transparent—open, visible, and accessible—formed the central tenet of *Transparency: An LGBTQ+ Glass Art Exhibition*. Held at the National Liberty

Museum in Philadelphia during Pride Month 2017, this exhibition marked the first time a museum dedicated an entire show to queer glass, featuring over twenty LGBTQ+ practitioners, including Tate.[6] The exhibition marked the beginning of a wider appreciation of contemporary queer glass across a range of forms, including decorative glassware, glass sculptures, stained glass, mirror works, and mixed media approaches that incorporated found objects and digital technologies. It specifically focused on what has become known as "studio glass," signaling objects made as one-offs or in small quantities with conceptual purpose, as opposed to more industrial forms of glassmaking.[7]

The multiplicity and endless potentiality of glass make this field so truly exciting, with the resulting works being just as multifaceted and diverse as the community from which they emerge. In its molten state, glass is fluid and mutable, capable of being shaped, cast, blown, or molded into a dynamic range of forms. Glass can be transparent, colored, or opaque. It can be reflective, refractive, or both. It is mostly considered a delicate material, but it can also be made to be durable, often used to reflect both the fragility and resilience of the human body. This versatility allows queer practitioners to create a wide range of affects and expressions in their work, often playing on these very dualities. Many trans, non-binary, and gender nonconforming glass artists also find queerness within the making process itself. They articulate how working with glass in its molten, mutable state allows them to explore the fluidity of gender. For example, Grace Whiteside (b.1995, USA), who was a contestant on the hit Netflix reality TV show and glass competition *Blown Away* (2019–), showcases the "nonbinary properties of glass" and its "capacity to represent the gender spectrum" by embracing amorphous forms.[8]

Despite a vibrant and active field of practice, the field of queer glass as a subject of scholarly study is practically nonexistent. As American glass practitioner and curator Kim Harty observes in the *Transparency* exhibition catalog, "[q]ueer people have played important roles in the glass community since its inception, yet sexual orientation, gender expression, and non-normative identities are rarely, if ever, addressed in critical writing, reviews, bios, or exhibition themes."[9] This comes with devastating consequences. It is not just about the exclusion of those living and making but also the exclusion of queer practitioners in the past or those who have since passed away. How do we build an archive of queer craft when these practices and histories are not respected or preserved? The title of this chapter, "handle with care," is drawn from an instruction we often give for the handling of fragile goods, nominally those made from glass. Here, the phrase is used with a dual referent, signaling the material qualities of glass, but also a provocation and a warning—the need to handle these creative practices with care, respect, and due attention.

While this book focuses on living, actively working practitioners, it concludes with a reflection on the practice of British South Asian artist Hamad Butt, who died of AIDS-related illness in 1994 at the age of thirty-two. When I started writing this chapter, Butt's work was known to those working on contemporary British art and art history. Still, it had gone largely unpublished and unknown to the public, primarily because his works remained in storage. Initially kept in boxes under his bed, his surviving works, letters, and ephemera were later preserved in an attic by his brother, Jamal Butt.[10] He initially approached the Tate with the offer to donate his brother's work to the permanent collection, but the gallery was hesitant to accept the gift and refused the offer, most likely because of the fragile and toxic nature of the work, which made them quite complex and expensive to conserve and store. Though, institutional homophobia at the time may also have played a role in this decision. It was not until a letter co-signed by Butt's tutors and an international network of scholars, curators, writers, and artists, that Tate finally acquired and archived his work in 2015. Finally, as I write this chapter in 2023, Butt's work *Transmission* (1990) is on temporary display in the main galleries of Tate Britain after its first rehang in a decade. A traveling exhibition of his surviving works is also being organized for display at the Whitechapel Gallery and the Irish Museum of Modern Art (IMMA).[11] This marks a timely opportunity to shed further light on his practice, reminding us of the work still yet to be done to recognize the widespread contributions of queer-identifying practitioners across multiple spheres of making, and the care we need to take to ensure their legacy lives on and inspires future generations. The notion of care is also a thematic concern of both Tate and Butt's practice, relating to how they utilize blown glass to explore ideas of containment, contamination, and challenging societal stigmas around HIV/AIDS, particularly in late 1980s America and early 1990s Britain, respectively.

## *Tim Tate (b.1960, USA)*

Based in Washington, D.C., Tim Tate co-founded the Washington Glass School in 2001. Through his artistic practice and his work as an educator at the school, Tate remains dedicated to community engagement and widening access to the field. His journey with glass began after his HIV-positive diagnosis in 1989, when doctors gave him only a year to live. Realizing he might never otherwise have the chance, Tate decided to pursue a childhood dream, inspired by a visit to the Corning Museum of Glass at age nine, and enrolled at North Carolina's Penland School of Craft in 1990. He recalls that this period instilled a sense of urgency in his work, as he began to consider the legacy he would leave behind.

A leading figure in the field of queer glass, Tim Tate has spent over four decades using a wide range of glass techniques to explore his identity and advocate for LGBTQ+ rights. However, as he shared in our conversations, his work wasn't always met with the same acceptance it enjoys today. Following his diagnosis, Tate experienced discrimination from gallerists and curators, and faced vilification from the public and media. "One gallery that I showed my work in said that I could make glass with a gay narrative, but they would not exhibit those works in the gallery. They said they had no audience or clients for it, but of course, that was not true," he recalled.[12] He also began to seek out other LGBTQ+ practitioners working with glass, hoping to seek solace and develop a community, but found that "glass communities were, and sometimes still are, very heteronormative," often providing barriers to access.[13] The first and only fellow gay man working in glass that Tate knew at Penland died of suicide just a few days after they first met. Further, he began to witness many of his friends and colleagues dying from AIDS-related illnesses. Tate lost fourteen close friends during the early years of the AIDS epidemic in the United States, nine of those in just one year. This sense of loss is reflected in his work *9 Months, 9 Souls* (c.1992), one of Tate's earliest glass pieces.[14] This blown glass bowl, its blue surface crackled from layered powdered glass on molten clear glass, appears fractured and broken. Nine white, angel-like figures, each marked with a red positive symbol created using copper stencils and colored glass, adorn the bowl. The piece served as a tribute to his friends and marked the beginning of Tate's lifelong commitment to honoring those affected by HIV/AIDS through his art, using his craft to promote a more just and equitable society.

Tate was a director of the Triangle Artists Group (TAG) in Washington D.C., a collective formed in the mid-1990s for LGBTQ+ creatives primarily from the Washington and Baltimore area, including artists, craftspeople, designers, writers, poets, and many others. At its height, Tate recalls that over two hundred members curated exhibitions and showed together. Where galleries, museums, and collectors would not support queer work, TAG decided it would make spaces of their own. Many members of TAG were also active members of AIDS Coalition to Unleash Power (ACT UP), an international organization founded in the United States in 1987 which encouraged forms of radical and direct action to end AIDS. As a result, Tate describes TAG as a group where "politics and creative expression" coincided.[15] Tate was chairman of the "Art Against AIDS" event in Washington, D.C., and was also an active member of ACT UP, attending numerous protests and rallies in both Washington and New York.[16] Tate's work *Untouchable* (1997) reflects on an ACT UP rally that he attended with other TAG members. It is made from blown and cast glass elements (Figure 6.1). Created from blown and cast glass, the piece contains a pair of discarded yellow marigold gloves that Tate retrieved from the pavement after the rally. After seeing the bright yellow gloves contrasting against the dull gray pavement, Tate said he immediately knew he wanted to seek a way of preserving these seemingly mundane objects as a relic of that moment in time and how queer bodies were being treated.

For some readers, it may seem unusual that a pair of yellow marigold gloves, commonly used for washing up or domestic chores, would be present at a political rally. However, during this period, anti-LGBTQ+ activists and police officers often wore gloves, ostensibly to "protect" themselves from a misguided fear of "contamination" from touching LGBTQ+ and HIV-positive individuals.[17] This fear and anxiety surrounding AIDS, particularly within the heterosexual public in the United States, is explored by Leo Bersani in *Is the Rectum a Grave?* (2009). Bersani argues that public concern at the time centered not on examining, treating, and curing those dying from the disease, but rather on ensuring homosexual *containment* and heterosexual salvation.[18] This sentiment was reflected in several national polls at the time, where members of the US public even suggested that those

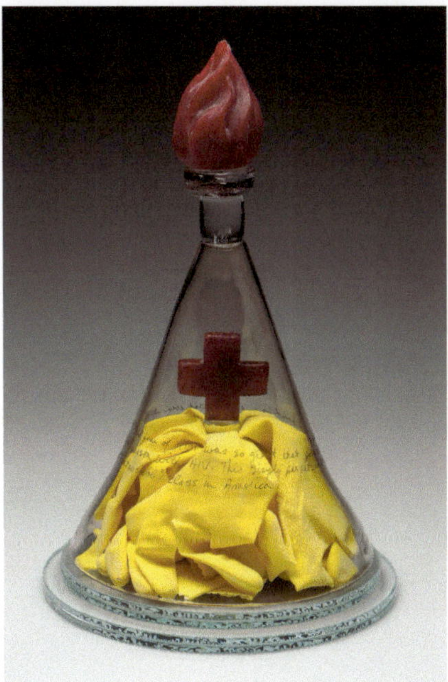

**Figure 6.1** Tim Tate, *Untouchable,* 1997. Blown glass, cast glass, found objects, and etched text, 18 × 10 × 10 inches. Courtesy of Tim Tate.

living with AIDS should be quarantined out of fear that LGBTQ+ would "infect" the majoritarian (cisgender and heterosexual) population.[19] President Ronald Reagan, who had been in office since 1981, did not even publicly mention HIV/AIDS until his second term, in April 1987.[20] This lack of public awareness contributed to widespread misunderstanding of HIV/AIDS transmission. Many believed it was airborne and could be transmitted through touch, particularly via glass objects and surfaces. In 1987, the California Medical Association, in collaboration with public health officials and community groups, launched the "Fight Fear with the Facts" campaign, a media-intensive program aimed at educating the public—not just high-risk groups—about HIV/AIDS. The campaign's objectives included presenting factual information, reducing fear, dispelling misconceptions, and directing audiences to further resources. Several posters featured the image of a glass accompanied with the headline "[s]ome people think you can catch AIDS from a glass," with the rebuttal—"[y]ou can't" (Figure 6.2).[21]

*Untouchable* reflects upon this discourse and takes the form of a container, specifically a reliquary. A reliquary is a traditional container used for preserving relics, such as the purported physical remains of saints, such as bone fragments and locks of hair, which are especially common in Christian, Buddhist, and other religious worship.[22] Reliquaries have existed since ancient times, including boxes, figureheads, altarpieces, caskets, lidded vessels, and even jewel-encrusted limb-

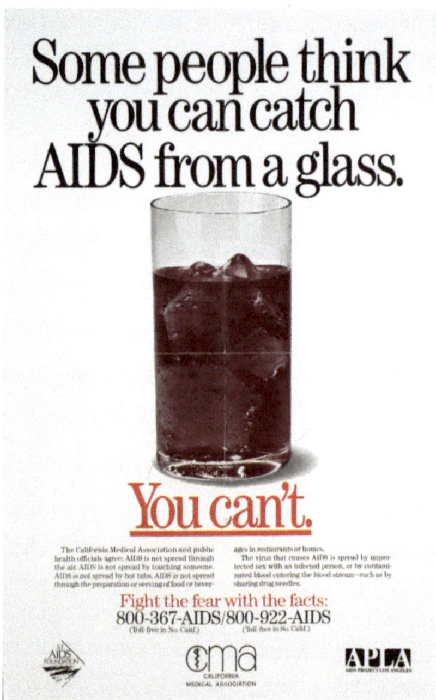


**Figure 6.2** California Medical Association and San Francisco AIDS Foundation, "Some people think you can catch AIDS from a glass: you can't," 1987, photomechanical print, 44 × 28 cm. Courtesy of San Francisco AIDS Foundation.

shaped objects. Often adorned with gilt metalwork and jewels, they typically featured a small glass window, allowing the relic to be visible and venerated as "evidence" of sacred bodies and lives. The properties of glass also aided in the relic's preservation, protecting it from damage and the elements. Later, entirely glass reliquary vessels became prevalent in much of Europe between the late sixteenth and early nineteenth centuries, particularly in Murano, Italy, a renowned hub for glassmaking.[23] Instead of body parts, Tate's reliquaries contain seemingly mundane objects from contemporary culture, offering new perspectives on ritual, remembrance, and sacredness. "My interests lie in finding the relics of the future while honoring the past," he observes.[24] In *Untouchable*, the marigold gloves are preserved as a worthy relic, a vital reminder for future generations of the hardships faced by HIV-positive and LGBTQ+ individuals, and a symbol of resistance against injustice. In many ways, these relics still comment on whose bodies are deemed sacred in society, with a simultaneous sense of intimacy and distance. Some of Tate's reliquaries also incorporate digital technologies, acknowledging that contemporary relics are often audiovisual rather than object-based. *The Moment* (2003), for example, is a small glass container housing a camera, screen, and speakers. As a viewer approaches, the camera captures their image, which is displayed on the screen. A motion sensor then triggers an audio clip: "I'm sorry.

The tests came back. You are HIV positive"—the same words spoken to Tate in 1989. Other works overtly play with invisibility/transparency by using sandblasted glass to create a frosted effect so that the actual relic is barely visible, encouraging viewers to peer and scrutinize it. Tate said that these works reflected how he found his entire identity was obscured when he would tell people he was HIV-positive and that everyone would only view him through the lens of his positive diagnosis.

Tate's glass reliquaries, as exemplified by *Untouchable*, also explore the interplay between container and contained. Instead of the traditional cylindrical dome or cloche shape often used for reliquaries, Tate's container is conical, subtly referencing the reappropriation of the triangular symbol (from which TAG also drew inspiration).[25] Inside, etched onto the glass surface and filled with black filament, is a short text, inscribed in Tate's handwriting using a rotary tool with a fine bit. The text describes how Tate and other HIV-positive individuals were treated as "untouchable class in America." A red cross, made from colored cast glass, is affixed to the dome's surface. While some might interpret this as a religious cross, a symbol of healing, salvation, or Christ's crucifixion, Tate intends it as a positive symbol, reflecting his positive diagnosis. The cast glass handle of the container takes the form of a burning red flame, referencing the sacred heat which a recurring motif in Tate's work, including a series of blown glass hearts dedicated to influential LGBTQ+ Americans who have died of HIV/AIDS. The sacred heart, a well-known Catholic devotion, represents Jesus's heart as a symbol of God's love and compassion, traditionally depicted as a flaming heart radiating divine light and surmounted by a cross. It is often shown as wounded or bleeding, reflective of Christ's sacrifice, sometimes with an arrow pierced through the heart or encircled with a crown of thorns. For Tate, the sacred heart here is less a symbol of religious sanctity and more a symbol of healing, reflecting his approach to craft as a form of "healing through making."[26]

Throughout the late 1990s and early 2000s, Tate made many versions of these containers, sometimes referring to them as "cell encasements" because containing or encasing something in glass became a way of processing his diagnosis. He explains, "They are an imaging exercise to help me materialize ways of containing the virus in my body."[27] Works such as *Imagine Caution* (2004) also encase found objects; in this case, several yellow billiard balls are used (Figure 6.3). In an eight-ball pool, the yellow ball is the first to be pocketed and bears a vertical line indicating a number one. With a marker pen, Tate drew a horizontal line over the number one to form a positive symbol. The spheres encased within the glass vessel symbolize the multiplication of positive cells within the body. This work seems to embody these ideas of containment most literally, for if the container were to be lifted from its glass stand, the balls or "cells" would spill out, likely smashing the glass base and causing destruction. The eight-ball specifically reoccurs throughout Tate's work and symbolizes how he felt chance had a crucial role in his HIV diagnosis. Another cell encasement, *Two Paths Taken* (2004), features a black eight-ball on a glass plinth encased by a double glass dome etched with text. The inner dome's text describes how Tate's life changed after his positive diagnosis, while the outer dome's text imagines what his life might have been like had the

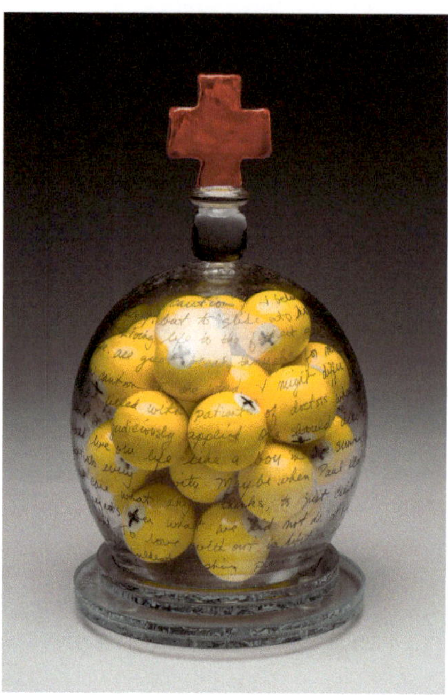

**Figure 6.3** Tim Tate, *Imagine Caution*, 2004. Blown glass, found objects, and etched text, 18 × 10 × 10 inches. Courtesy of Tim Tate.

diagnosis been negative. Tate explained that the work illustrates how "no one path was better than the other, both lives have their pros and cons . . . what I lost in one narrative I gained even more back in the second."[28] Tate says: "It was as if my life was a two-sided quilt. On one side lie sadness, animosity, hatred, lack of morality, and death. A bleak, grey, sad quilt. On the other, there was an explosion of color and joy. Only I could decide which side of the quilt I would display . . . ultimately, it was both sides."[29] The black eight-ball specifically references a Magic 8 Ball, a fortune-telling toy resembling a billiard eight-ball, reflecting how Tate felt his life was subject to fate. The black billiard ball also alludes to "blackballing," a traditional voting method using black and white balls, particularly in gentleman's clubs and Masonic lodges. A white ball would record a vote of support for a candidate, and a black ball would record an adverse vote. The result of a black ball would likely mean the member's expulsion and so the phrase is sometimes used to describe a process of excluding someone from society more broadly.[30] In this context, the work seems to contemplate how society might exclude Tate and other HIV-positive individuals, regardless of their diagnosis, simply based on their sexuality, identity, and existence, which is perceived as a threat to the status quo.

My initial encounter with Tate's work was while researching the intersections of queer craft, activism, and public memorialization. This led me to discover *The New Orleans AIDS Monument* (Figure 6.4), a project that Tate considers one

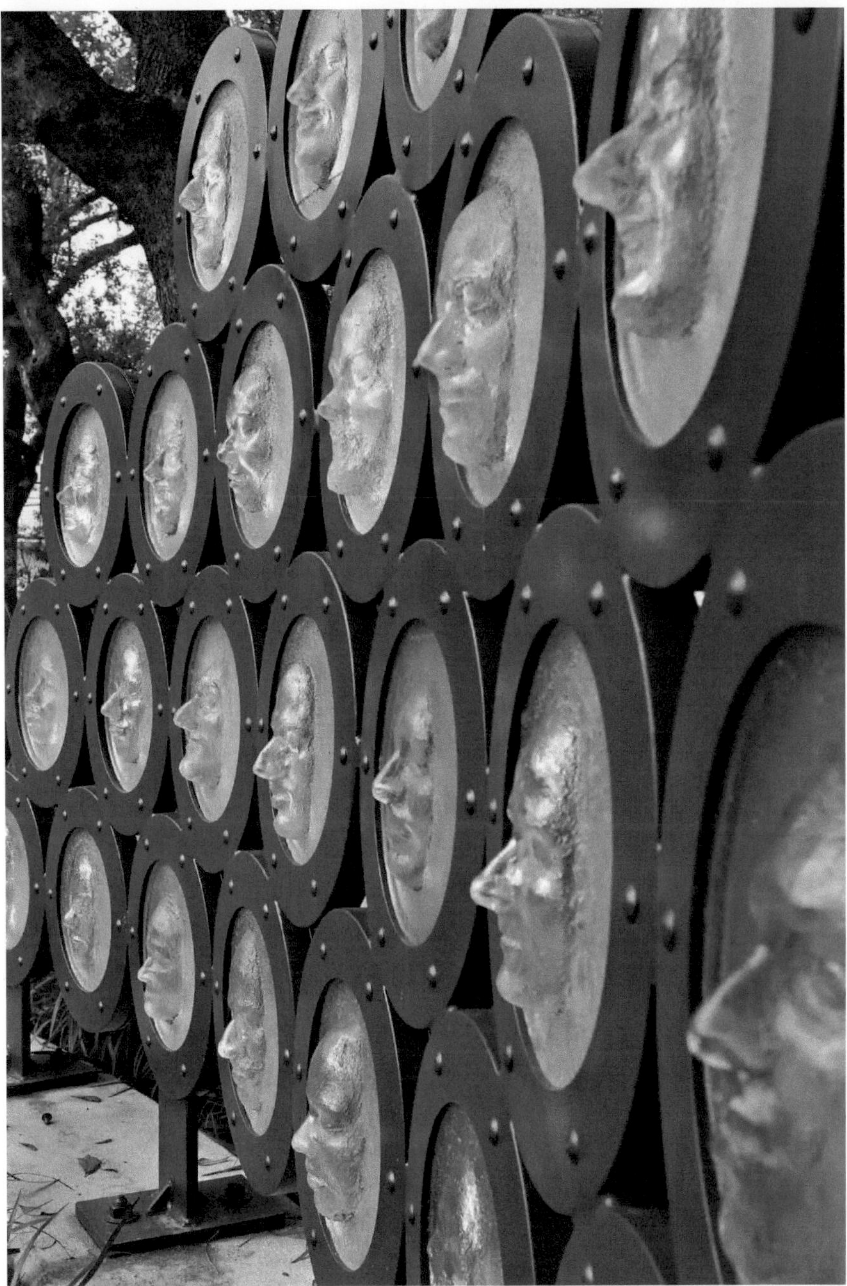

**Figure 6.4** Tim Tate, *The Guardian Wall (New Orleans AIDS Monument)*, 2008. Cast glass with steel frame, 8 ft × 35 ft.

of his "proudest achievements."[31] This public, outdoor sculpture of tempered glass was installed in November 2008 in Washington Square Park, Faubourg Marigny, New Orleans. Tate designed the monument in 1996 following a public competition to establish a public monument commemorating lives lost to HIV/AIDS. Tate revealed that there was urgency to establish the monument and as a result, no formal plans, schema, or archival materials exist. The design was simply drawn on a cocktail napkin while discussing the plans with those who had initiated the commission.[32] After the design was accepted, he worked closely with a friend and long-standing collaborator, Mitchell Gaudet, to help cast and build the monumental piece. The process took around eight years, largely due to the need for the organizing committee to secure funding after the commission was approved. Although Tate and others refer to it as the "AIDS Monument" its official title is *The Guardian Wall*. The 8-foot by 35-foot monument makes up a literal wall within the park, but rather than bricks and mortar, the work is made entirely from cast glass circles encased in concentric metal frames. Each of the thirty-four glass circles depicts a face and its "guardians." These were made by making molds from the faces of local HIV-positive people and their friends, family, and loved ones, then casting these in glass. Tate's selection of subjects—diverse in race, gender, sexuality, age, and background—underscores the message that "HIV/AIDS does not discriminate, potentially impacting a range of people's lives, both queer and non-queer."[33]

The cast glass faces, translucent and three-dimensional, peer outward from their circular frames, or "portals." This circular framing invites an intimate viewing experience, as if peering into another, endlessly repeating reality. The repetition of imagery and the sheer number of faces evoke the ongoing impact of HIV/AIDS, suggesting timelines stretching infinitely into the past and future—themes that recur in Tate's "endless mirror" works.[34] These "guardians" appear serene, their eyes closed, faces shimmering in the sunlight. Some even offer gentle smiles to passersby. Tate's original design featured a more staggered, randomized arrangement of the circles and included words such as "lover," "brother," "sister," "friend," and "teacher" stamped into the glass. These elements were ultimately omitted from the final version. However, the paving stones below are engraved with additional names and memorials. Nearby benches provide space for visitors to sit and contemplate the faces before them, with additional memorial plaques. The monument has become a focal point for queer activism in New Orleans, serving as a gathering place for vigils and protests advocating for LGBTQ+ rights. This has been particularly true in recent years, amid the Covid-19 pandemic, which disproportionately affected those with HIV/AIDS due to compromised immune systems, and the rise in violence against the queer community, including mass shootings at queer spaces across the United States, such as the Pulse nightclub in 2016 and Club Q in 2022.

While the field of queer glass has now gained significant traction, including many young practitioners who push the boundaries of the field in new and innovative ways, many of these practitioners are indebted to trailblazers like Tate. It is urgent to honor their practices and preserve their oral histories so that they can continue to inspire future generations to come. This is especially the case for other queer practitioners who have passed away and whose work largely lingers in archives. This is especially the case with Hamad Butt, whose work touches on themes similar to Tate's, especially relating to anxieties of contamination and using glass as a visualization of containing the virus.

## *Hamad Butt (b.1962, Pakistan, d.1994, UK)*

Born in Lahore, Pakistan, Hamad Butt moved to London with his family in 1964. Initially encouraged to pursue a career in biochemistry, he later followed his passion for creativity, graduating with a Fine Art degree from Goldsmiths, University of London, in 1990. Despite a tragically short, four-year career, Butt's practice is considered fundamental to contemporary British art. While often categorized as an "installation artist," Butt vehemently "disliked the term" and did not identify with the increasingly commercialized art world of the period, according to his friend and collaborator Stephen Foster, former Director of the John Hansard Gallery.[35] While most of Butt's work was undoubtedly designed to be shown within an installation setting, the surviving body of his work is made almost entirely of glass. Surprisingly, this central material focus has been largely overlooked by critics. This neglect contrasts sharply with the abundance of surviving designs, diagrams, drawings, diary entries, letters, and writings that demonstrate Butt's deep engagement with the materiality and affective potential of glass, particularly its associations with fragility and its capacity to contain toxic substances. He was deeply invested in understanding industrial and scientific glassmaking processes, conducting extensive experiments over an eighteen-month period in collaboration with glassblowers, technicians, and scientists—so much so that Foster joked with Butt that he only used his studio for reading.[36] Therefore, it seems fitting to posthumously situate some of Butt's works within the context of queer glass. This analysis will focus on three glass works from his *Familiars* (1992) series—*Substance Sublimation Unit*, *Hypostasis*, and *Cradle*—all blown in collaboration with chemistry research technicians and created during a period when Butt's health began to decline due to AIDS-related complications.

Butt's first major project, *Transmission* (1990), offers valuable insight into his conceptual development, which culminated in the *Familiars* series. While *Transmission* has been exhibited in various forms, it originated as part of his final-year exhibition. In this initial iteration, the work comprised a glass vitrine containing maggots and sugar-coated paper inscribed with nine of Butt's reflections on the human condition. The larvae would then transform into flies, consuming the paper, laying eggs, and ultimately dying, thus representing the cycle of life. The statements read:

*We have the 'Black light' that is Ultra-Violet.*
*A penetrative radiation that damages human sight.*
*A seductive invisibility that fascinates flies.*

*We have the eruption of the Triffid that obscures sex with death*
*A stigmata of an era with the fear of invasions*
*A mark of contagion that isolates others, defies intimacy*

*We have the blindness of fear and the books of fear.*
*We have the dangers of blind faith (prayer) and the*
*transmissions of faithlessness (distraction)*
*We have the apprehensions that regard these words*
*before strategic withdrawal.*[37]

*Transmission* drew significant inspiration from John Wyndham's post-apocalyptic science fiction novel, *The Day of the Triffids* (1951). In Wyndham's narrative, a meteor shower (initially believed to be a celestial event), blinds most of humanity, concealing the true threat—an invasion of carnivorous plants called Triffids, which proceed to dominate the planet, spreading disease and attacking people with retractable, venomous stingers. Butt etched illustrations of Triffids from the novel's original publication onto the surface of nine glass "books" that emitted ultraviolet light. Like the blaze of blinding green light that marks the arrival of the Triffids, the ultraviolet light given off by the tubing connected to the glass books would potentially harm viewers' retinas if viewed unprotected for too long. Butt described the glass books as a "kind of play with the whole notion of blind faith in written things from other places."[38] While the form of the glass books might evoke sacred texts, complete with spiritual and prayerful connotations (leading some critics to interpret it as a reconciliation with the Muslim faith), Butt clarified that the work primarily explored "disease transmission through the use of flies. In fact, the book when opened looks like a large moth or fly."[39]

Butt's work was replete with queer codes and references to the transmission of disease, and specifically the transmission of HIV, themes which are underscored by the very title of the work. Butt explained that he was interested in exploring that which "obscures sex with death," a concept that is reflected in the work's accompanying statements—including themes of "damages," "invasions," "contagion," "fear," "dangers," and "death" on the one hand, and "penetrative," "seductive," "sex," "intimacy," on the other. This duality mirrors the sexually transmitted nature of HIV, which, at the time, was widely perceived as a death sentence. The more ambiguous term "eruption" further complicates this duality, suggesting a range of meanings from explosion and outbreak (destruction) to emissions and ejaculatory discharge (pleasure). For Butt, this obscuring of sex and death is embodied most clearly by the figure of the Triffid. He even began to draw parallels between the "transparent, sharp, *penetrative*" nature of the glass— its sharp corners and potential to *prick* the skin—and the "penetrative" nature of the Triffid's who, in the original Penguin illustrations, the film posters, and the TV program, had long phallic tendrils which were "not anything as distant as the castrated male genitalia," Butt recalled.[40]

His invocation of the Triffid invasion can also be understood in the context of his diasporic queer identity. His use of the plural "invasions" is telling—it not only refers to the physical "invasion" of HIV into the bloodstream, but also to the "invasion" of communities migrating to the United Kingdom "from other places," as his statements suggest. This discourse reflects the intensely homophobic, racist, and inflammatory rhetoric directed at queer people of color during the late 1980s and early 1990s in the United Kingdom.[41] Butt extensively considered the queer and racialized discourses surrounding HIV/AIDS, particularly the "othering" of diseased bodies throughout history. In his writings, he cites the work of queer and gender studies scholar Martha Gever, who drew parallels between the nineteenth-century pathologizing of homosexuality by medical professionals and the racialized and sexualized constructions of the "exotic" by seventeenth- and eighteenth-century colonists.[42] These homophobic and racist tropes served interrelated ideological functions, with Gever noting that "the term 'exotic', sometimes used to describe a virus that appears to have originated 'elsewhere' . . . is an important theme that runs through AIDS literature," and by extension other cultural representations.[43] In essence, discourses surrounding HIV/AIDS became surrounding HIV/AIDS became "slotted into an existing colonial narrative of the mysterious, unknowable and, above all, different," with the framing of African and so-called "other" cultures as "dark" and "sick" with the potential to "invade" and "infect."[44] Butt specifically discussed these interrelated tropes when conceptualizing the stigmatization of HIV/AIDS as a "mark of contagion that isolates others" which refers to both a symbolic marker or "difference" and also a physical one, specifically referencing Kaposi's sarcoma—a cancer often associated with AIDS that manifests as visible skin lesions.[45] Much like the flora and fauna that colonists sought to categorize and collect, the Triffids become something mysterious and unidentifiable, emerging from an "elsewhere" and bringing new fears of sickness and societal collapse. Butt's invocation of the Triffid and narratives of alien invasion offer a powerful allegory for queer sexuality and HIV transmission, while also subverting colonizing, imperial tropes of racial superiority and anxieties about the "other."

Butt's ability to articulate such complex histories and cultural references earned him top marks at Goldsmiths. After graduation, *Transmission* was reconfigured and shown at London's Milch Gallery, which had previously been the site of the National Hospital for Nervous Diseases. At Milch, the pronouncements on sex and death weren't confined to the glass "books"; they were emblazoned across the glass windows in bold sandblasted lettering, visible to all who passed by, even those who dared not enter.[46] The original vitrine of flies was replaced, and the glowing glass "books" were arranged in a circle, bathing the gallery in ultraviolet light. The lighting made the gallery space look more like an underground club or illicit rave, a feeling only intensified by Milch's gritty architecture—consisting of raw brick, steel, and wood—as well as signs pasted at the entrance, reading "Dangerous!" and "Persons viewing this exhibition do so at their own risk." Milch occupied a unique position at the intersection of London's underground queer scene and emerging young artists, many of whom would become central figures in the Young British Artists (YBAs) movement.[47] Ros Carter, a curator at the John Hansard Gallery who later assisted with the installation of *Familiars*, drew direct parallels between the presentation of Butt's work at Milch and the surrounding cultural milieu, arguing that the themes of sex, death, fragility, and risk were only amplified. Carter particularly recalled the "extremity of the gay scene" in the local area at the time, describing its "overt and aggressive" vibe tied to the S&M subculture where risk was normalized as a part of lived and bodily practice. Carter describes the 1990s club scene as being "flooded by drugs," and recalls a "general culture of risk taking and doing things to your body" that extended beyond sexuality and risks of HIV transmission, including "a lot of chemicals going around" and a "general air of toxicity."[48] After running for only five months, the Milch Gallery closed on November 24, 1990, but the thriving culture surrounding it would live on.

For his first and only commissioned solo exhibition at the John Hansard Gallery in Southampton, Butt created *Familiars*.[49] Butt was invited to exhibit by Foster after he saw *Transmission at Milch*, and he wanted the display of *Familiars* to coincide with the British Association for the Advancement of Science's visit to the University of Southampton in 1992. *Familiars* expanded upon the themes of *Transmission*—contamination and containment, religion and science, life and death—but with a distinctly more dangerous edge, employing blown glass vessels designed to contain potentially toxic chemicals (Figure 6.5). *Familiars* marks a point where Butt's biochemical knowledge intersected with his creative practice, catalyzed by a profound understanding of the body's fragility—largely informed

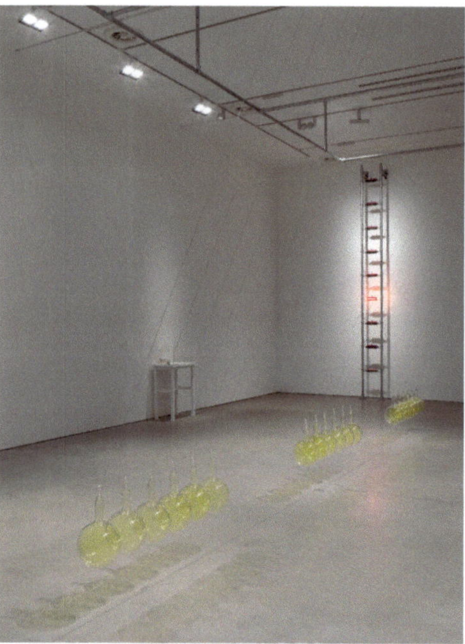

**Figure 6.5** Installation of *Familiars*, 1992. Vacuum-sealed glass, crystal iodine, liquid bromine, chlorine gas, water and steel, overall display dimensions variable. Courtesy of Tate. Copyright of Jamal Butt.

by his own declining health and the loss of his long-term partner, Nick Hodge, to AIDS-related cancer in 1993. Each of the three works in the series incorporates glass and a different halogen gas: iodine, bromine, and chlorine. While these elements occur naturally, exposure to certain quantities can be toxic or even lethal. Butt deliberately emphasizes their inherent instability, housing them within glass and activating them in ways that render them visible and tangible. Butt employs these chemicals as a device to convey the discourse about risk and the atmosphere of fear of so-called "polluting" and "contaminating" bodies during the early days of the AIDS epidemic in the United Kingdom. In his statement for the *Familiars* exhibition, Butt described his use of halogen gases: "[s]ubstances to ward of anxiety, fears, physical malfunctions and mental dysphoria. We are revisiting the alchemical ages with the notion of the body under siege and requiring fortification via familiars."[50] The series title, *Familiars*, carries multiple meanings. It not only denotes the elements' shared group within the periodic table (their "family") but also suggests "close association" or even "sexual intimacy." It could also refer to a witch's familiar, a supernatural spirit or animal believed in Western demonology to aid witches in divination and provide companionship. Additionally, it highlights the three closely related, or "familiar," works that comprise the series, each exploring the same concept in different forms.

*Substance Sublimation Unit* comprises six vacuum-sealed glass capsules containing iodine, arranged vertically like rungs on a ladder. Iodine, a dense, dark metallic crystal in its solid state, bypasses the liquid phase and transforms into a deep violet gas when heated to 113 degrees Celsius. In *Substance Sublimation Unit*, infrared lamps connected to an electrical source gradually raise the temperature within each capsule, vaporizing the iodine and causing each "rung" to glow red in ascending order. Given Butt's interest in the intersection of science and spirituality, this progression can be interpreted as a reflection on transubstantiation, the Catholic doctrine by which bread and wine in the Eucharist become the body and blood of Christ. More explicitly, the ascending light suggesting a spiritual ascent, evoking Jacob's Ladder, the staircase leading to heaven. However, Butt's glass "ladder" denies ascension, potentially burning and cutting the feet of any who try to climb it. While direct contact with iodine in its pure form can cause irritation, it is also a vital component of human medicine (most commonly as povidone-iodine), serving as a powerful antiseptic for skin disinfection. Like the other substances he uses, it technically cures by killing—a duality that was likely not lost on him.

*Hypostasis* comprises three long, curved steel tubes, each tipped with a blown glass vial containing six cubic inches of liquid bromine. Arranged equidistantly in a near-circle and held tentatively in place with supporting cables, the tubes bend inward, the chemically infused glass vials poised in tense proximity. The arrangement creates a cage-like structure, further hinting at ideas of containment. At room temperature, bromine appears as a dark, blood-red liquid that evaporates into a gas of the same hue. Its delayed reaction upon contact with skin makes it particularly dangerous; painful blisters and ulcers erupt only later. The work's title, *Hypostasis*, is rich with meaning. "Hypostasis" is a philosophical term that refers to the underlying makeup of reality, a scientific term describing the coexistence of liquid and solid states, a medical term denoting fluid accumulation in the lower body, and a religious term referring to each person of the Holy Trinity. The Trinity is referenced repeatedly throughout *Familiars*, including using the three chemical triads, exhibited in three different states (solid, liquid, gas), across three individual works that comprise the whole. Given these references, the bromine here could represent blood—that which makes up our bodies, that which coagulates after we die, and the metaphysical blood of Christ Beyond its Christian associations, the work's form also evokes Islamic arches and mosque architecture, designs Butt explored in preliminary sketches. Beyond references to the nexus between science and religion, Butt described *Hypostasis* as "a dark reservoir evoking and being... sexually conflating a penetrating appendage and an entrance, the arch unfolds the possibility of contamination between orality and anality," linking it to the themes of penetration and disease transmission previously explored in *Transmission*.[51] At the John Hansard Gallery, the work's association with a "penetrating appendage" was rendered more pronounced by its placement beneath a skylight. The glass tubes appeared to extend beyond the ceiling, penetrating the very fabric of the building and reaching towards the heavens. A large white triangle painted on the floor around *Hypostasis* during its Southampton exhibition was deemed significant enough to be listed as a material component in the exhibition catalog, suggesting a deliberate creative choice.[52] The triangle may have been another response to the gallery's angular architecture or a subtle way to manage viewer proximity to the work, it also potentially alludes to both the pink triangle in queer visual culture, as well as the Holy Trinity which is often represented by an equilateral triangle.

*Cradle* draws inspiration from Newton's cradle, the momentum-driven device designed by seventeenth-century French physicist Edme Mariotte and later named after English polymath, Sir Isaac Newton. It demonstrates the transfer of energy through a series of swinging spheres and miniaturized versions are widely marketed as a popular "desk toy." These smaller versions, typically consisting of five metal spheres, produce a therapeutic clacking sound with each collision, purportedly aiding concentration. Butt's reimagining of the cradle, however, is dramatically different. *Cradle consists* of eighteen individual glass spheres, each containing 4,825 cubic inches of chlorine gas and water. These are suspended from the ceiling by steel cables, creating a giant, potentially deadly version of Newton's cradle. The vacuum-sealed glass spheres are designed to maintain the toxic chemical at room temperature, where chlorine appears as an extremely reactive pale yellow-green gas. The glass spheres appear like beautiful, dimly glowing magical orbs, albeit potentially deadly. If inhaled, chlorine combines with the natural water in our bodies to produce hydrochloric acid and releases nitric oxides. In short, the combination of acid and oxides first causes chemical irritation, especially in the airways, and in extreme cases, would gradually dissolve the lungs and internal organs from within. As with the other elements of *Familiars*, a palpable tension exists between the various points of reference for the work. The title, while clearly referencing Newton's cradle, also evokes the more common image of a baby's cradle. Such cradles are often designed to swing, inducing peaceful sleep—much like the swinging pendulums of Newton's device, which also create a meditative sound. "Cradling" more broadly implies carefully holding something, providing rest, comfort, and protection which is in stark contrast to the lack of care shown towards people with HIV/AIDS at the time.

These three glass works create a compelling tension between invitation and threat, drawing the viewer in while simultaneously creating a sense of apprehension. The fragility of the blown glass underscores the potential danger, suggesting that even a minor incident could expose visitors to the hazardous contents—burning, cutting, asphyxiating, or blinding them. *Cradle* especially exemplifies this tension. At the John Hansard Gallery, Butt suspended nine of the chlorine-filled spheres from the ceiling's center in three groups of three, rather than a linear sequence, creating an illusion of potential motion. Foster recounted Butt's amusement at the gallery's provision of gas masks and asbestos suits for its installation. The work's stasis only amplifies the viewer's unease, the fear that a single broken sphere could initiate a chain reaction, releasing toxic gas and causing catastrophic asphyxiation. As British artist and writer Clement Page suggests in one of the only articles on Butt's work, dating from 1995, "Butt wanted his sculptures to induce a series of physiological states in his viewers, offering a defense against fear or fear inducing states of ecstasy and love."[53] The work hinges on a sense of stasis—not only the physical stasis between the spheres' stillness and anticipated movement, but also the metaphorical stasis between life and potential death, healing and killing. The anticipation of movement emphasizes our own vulnerability to contamination, fear, and the natural instability of the chemical world of which our bodies are a part. These works expose the precarious and threatened nature of the body's boundaries, its ultimate porosity and penetrability, drawing a parallel between the fear of leakage from the glass vessels and the anxiety of bodily "exposure"—a concept mirrored in Tate's cell encasements.

The glass vessels in *Familiars* reveal the meticulous process Butt employed to contain these chemicals. Each vessel features a small, pointed spout—the remnant of a sealed ampule. This extruded portion of the glass, where air was removed and chemical samples added, was sealed by heating and twisting the narrow neck under a flame. While these spouts were a practical necessity, their phallic appearance, protruding from the curved glass forms, further reinforces Butt's conceptual references to anality and penetration, as well as the intersection of science and religion. While some journalists have drawn parallels to myths of containing spirits in bottles, Butt's extensive knowledge of scientific equipment and chemistry suggests a more direct reference to the history of ampules.[54] Though now commonly used for single-dose medicines, ampules historically contained small samples of blood taken after death, often entombed with the body in Christian catacombs as tangible relics of the person. Given Butt's declining health, it is plausible that he viewed this practice as a potential record of his own existence, much like Tate's reflections on his HIV diagnosis.

Creating the technically complex glass works in *Familiars* was a collaborative endeavor. Butt worked closely with scientists, technicians, and glassblowers from Imperial College of Science, Technology and Medicine (University of London), including key collaborators Stephen Ramsay and Garry Rumbles. Laboratory-grade glassware and specialized scientific processes were crucial for ensuring the glass's resistance to thermal shock and maintaining chemical inertness. Ramsay's expertise in scientific glassblowing was essential in creating vessels robust enough for safe public display and for housing chemicals in a deliberately unstable state, a far cry from the controlled environment of a laboratory. Rumbles contributed his expertise in chemistry, studying the chemicals and their interaction with the glass, particularly the entropy of iodine during sublimation and recrystallization. The project's complexity was evident; in a letter to Butt dated May 5, 1992, Rumbles admitted, "The task was, I assure you, greater than I had anticipated."[55]

Viewing Butt's work through the lens of queer glass challenges conventional interpretations of contemporary glassmaking, particularly the notion of craft as a purely individual pursuit (as also discussed in Chapter 5 regarding metal and Tai's use of industrial processes). While some might argue that Butt's reliance on collaborators complicates his relationship to craft— often associated with a politicized resistance to industrial production through its ties to the personal, handmade, embodied, small-scale, and affective—this perspective is less relevant to glassmaking, a field historically embracing design and industrial processes. Even highly skilled glass practitioners rely on the support of technicians or assistants, to move glass objects. The inherent use of tools in shaping molten glass further complicates the traditional definition of "handmade" given that the hand is incredibly far removed from the material itself—glassmaking is more accurately experienced through the body, or rather, *bodies*. While caution regarding the appropriation of craft materials by contemporary fine artists remains valid, in "the current post-medium, post-studio environment," there is an increasing tendency across the field to "eschew making physical objects" or outsource fabrication. Regardless, Butt's exceptional knowledge of glassmaking is undeniable. His work demonstrates a profound understanding of the material, where the material itself becomes meaning. Trained in fine art yet utilizing meticulously designed industrial-grade techniques and traditional glassblowing crafts, Butt's work defies easy categorization. This very resistance to categorization forms part of its power and strength. Butt's art reveals the impermanence of such classifications, which prove as volatile as the chemicals he employs and as susceptible to fracture as the glass vessels themselves.

Butt's extensive writing on his work, some posthumously published at his request in the 1996 artist book *Familiars*, reveals a growing sense of vulnerability and anxiety. He describes "a penetrating fear triggered by something from outside, an unforeseen, dangerous event" and sought to explore "apprehensions"—the "seizure and arresting of perceptions" of fear which can lead us "to the point of understanding."[56] His collection of writings titled "Apprehensions" is structured into various headings, including "Apprehensions," "Stress," "Regard," "Scream," "Familiar," "Subjection," "Triffid," "Fluid," and "Strategic Withdrawal." Butt's decision to call these apprehensions was likely not a neutral or coincidental one. Apprehension denotes a feeling of anxiety or fear about the future, a feeling amplified through Butt's work and the ever-present possibility of exposure.

Even without the explicit mention of "Triffid," these descriptors could easily be mistaken for chapter titles in Wyndham's novel, suggesting the successive stages of an "alien" invasion of the body. "Apprehensions" also reveals Butt's extensive consideration of other real and imagined plagues throughout history, and a consideration of his own mortality. He cites various reference points, including the nursery rhyme "Ring a Ring o' Roses" (believed to originate from the Black Death), Daniel Defoe's *A Journal of the Plague Year* (1722), and Albert Camus's reflections on illness in *The Plague* (1947), among others. Ideas of fragility and the leaky body reoccur throughout Butt's writings as well as his work, including a reference to "fragile anus" syndrome and an acknowledgment that "the agenda of fear and the distraction of fear through its representations, evokes the most intimate sense of the self's fragility."[57] As viewers, we also become acutely aware of our materiality through the sense of stasis invoked in the work's display. We recognize what is most *familiar* to us—the vulnerable and penetrative nature of our flesh. In some instances, particularly with *Cradle,* where the spheres are larger, round, and polished, we even see ourselves *reflected* in the glass. The glass becomes a substitute for the body—both fragile and material, both with the potential to leak.

Butt adds "one of the risks in representing AIDS is the identification that the others of the social order, the others that the presumed healthy whole community can continue to 'scapegoat', scape . . . escape . . . (cappa) cloak . . . caput mortuum . . . the worthless residue after the alchemical distillation or sublimation."[58] Like the moral panic and hysteria that was fostered in the United States during the height of the AIDS epidemic, which Tate responded to through his work, there was a similar culture in the United Kingdom, which Butt also responded to through his. An ideology around the "impurity" or "contamination" of queer bodies as "worthless residue" or "disposable constituencies"—as Butt puts it—was firmly established during the late 1980s and early 1990s.[59] This was especially fueled by the Conservative governments under Margaret Thatcher (1979–1990) and John Major (1990–1997). Representations of AIDS became "derived from the image of mental and physical isolation of contamination," and a visual iconography relating to these ideas of needing to contain the virus began to emerge, creating waves of paranoia and sensationalized media reports.[60] Beyond homophobic policies like Section 28, which barred local authorities from "promoting" homosexuality in schools or publishing related material, this era was marked by a broader culture of exclusion. Anti-immigration rhetoric, including the Nationality Bill designed to restrict the entry of Black and Brown people, contributed significantly to this atmosphere. Scaremongering the public based on lack of medical evidence and research, the government believed that millions of "innocents" could be infected by AIDS and they distributed leaflets to every household and launched a widespread advertising and public health campaign called "AIDS: Don't Die of Ignorance."[61] Initiated by the government in 1986, the now infamous television advert featured melodramatic scenes of widespread destruction—a violently erupting volcano, huge tumbling boulders, an iceberg, and a gigantic monolith-cum-tombstone that topples over. The original version even opened with a civil defense siren, but

Thatcher, reportedly finding it too dramatic, had it removed.[62] The agency behind the advert, TBWA, explained that HIV/AIDS was perceived "like an Alien plague" at the time, and the advertisement was intentionally designed to frighten the public with a "doom and gloom sci-fi aesthetic."[63]

Butt, who would have received a pamphlet at his London home (and who explicitly references it in his writings), was likely offering a critique of the government's post-apocalyptic imagery by drawing upon the post-apocalyptic science fiction of *The Day of the Triffids*.[64] His writings demonstrate a deeper engagement with the idea that *Familiars* served to convey the fear of AIDS and a subtle form of activism. In the final section of his writing, "Strategic Withdrawal," Butt suggests: "We cannot respond to this epidemic without fear and confusion, without aching to know why. This is a fear of the here and now and to legislate, to speak for the order of apprehending AIDS and the fear of AIDS, in the sense of phenomenological arresting, enjoins one to deal with the elements of fear to appropriate the seduction of the visual experience, but also to ironize the privileged role of the eye."[65] American art historian and AIDS activist Douglas Crimp persuasively argued that AIDS "exists only in and through" the practices that "conceptualize, represent it, and respond to it."[66] He argues that it is necessary to "contest" the "notion that there is an underlying reality of AIDS, upon which are constructed the representations, or the culture, or the politics of AIDS. If we can recognize that AIDS exists only in and through these constructions, then hopefully we can also recognize the imperative to know them, analyze them, and wrest control of them."[67] Butt was acutely aware of the challenges of representing AIDS while simultaneously attempting to seize control of the harmful, homophobic, and racist cultural and political narratives circulating at the time. He likely sought to reclaim these narratives, recognizing that their meanings are never fixed but rather produced within the realm of the semiotic and the discursive.

Importantly, while Butt "struggled to come to terms with his own mortality through these works," as Foster argues, he "did so without falling to a spiral of hopeless solipsism, [and] they give us great hope for the future."[68] Although the highly toxic chemicals exhibited in their unstable chemical state is serious matter, these works cease to be purely apocalyptic. At any rate, there are just as many references to toys, ladders, and hungry plants as there are to decay, death, and destruction. Butt's works playfully highlight the absurdity, even impossibility, of visualizing the virus itself, just as they contemplate containing it. They represent not only a subtle form of activism then, but perhaps a playful resistance. As he himself summarized, "[t]he trauma of the body to which fantasy inures us, is the opposition to collective nightmares that might inspire a sense of humour."[69] While significant progress and medical advances have been made since the early 1990s, much work remains to challenge the stigmas and taboos associated with HIV/ AIDS, even within LGBTQ+ communities where HIV-positive status is often met with discrimination. Butt's work retains its urgency and resonance in the 2020s, just as it did in the 1990s.

## Conclusion

Through an engagement with the glass works by Tate and Butt, this chapter has illustrated how queer, HIV-positive artists have utilized glass to amplify and perform its potential for containment, reflecting the discourse and stigma surrounding HIV/AIDS in the late 1980s and early 1990s in both the United States and the United Kingdom. Tate's extensive body of work demonstrates the importance of craft within queer activism and consciousness-raising, proving that the personal is indeed political. Despite Butt's fine art training, his deep engagement with the medium and its properties should not be underestimated in its contribution to queer glass. This chapter also became somewhat about an ethics of care, towards getting to know the work of these practitioners, fundamentally understanding their tools, materials, concepts, and approaches—whether through interviewing and working with Tate or sensitively following traces in Butt's surviving work, writings, and archival materials. While the works featured in this chapter were created much earlier than others featured in this book, they still serve as an important reminder that against a continued backdrop of violence and discrimination towards LGBTQ+ people, we can reflect on a recent past to find a way forward. This call to action evidences the need to continue shedding light on these practices, highlighting their intuitive understanding of materials, materiality, and meaning, especially their intersections with queerness and the very making of it.

# NOTES

## *Preface*


1   Oxford English Dictionary, "Bent," accessed November 22, 2023, https://www.oed.com/search/dictionary/?scope=Entries&q=bent.
2   Ibid.
3   Eve Kosofsky Sedgwick, *Tendencies* (London: Routledge, 1993), xii.
4   "Daniel Fountain," accessed November 23, 2023, http://www.danielfountain.com.
5   Elizabeth Freeman persuasively argues that queer theory has always been a theory of kinship. See: Elizabeth Freeman, *Queer Kinship: Race, Sex, Belonging, Form* (Durham, NC: Duke University Press, 2022).


## *Introduction*


1   LJ Roberts, "Put Your Thing Down, Flip It, and Reverse It: Reimaging Craft Identities Using Tactics of Queer Theory," in *Extra/Ordinary: Craft and Contemporary Art*, ed. Maria Elena Buszek (Durham, NC: Duke University Press, 2011), 243–59 (247).
2   Jeanne Vaccaro, "Feelings and Fractals: Wooly Ecologies of Transgender Matter," *GLQ: A Journal of Lesbian and Gay Studies*, Vol. 21, No. 2–3 (2015): 273–93 (280).
3   Nikki Sullivan, *A Critical Introduction to Queer Theory* (New York: New York University Press, 2003), v.
4   Sedgwick, *Tendencies,* 105–6. Sedgwick made collages, textile works and many artist books, but these are still largely unfamiliar to many people. For more on her work, see: Eve Kosofsky Sedgwick, "Work," accessed February 11, 2023, https://evekosofskysedgwick.net/art/artworks/; Jason Edwards, *Queer and Bookish: Eve Kosofsky Sedgwick as Book Artist* (Santa Barbara, CA: Punctum Books, 2022).
5   Ibid.
6   David Halperin, *Saint Foucault: Towards a Gay Hagiography* (Oxford: Oxford University Press, 1997), 62.
7   bell hooks, "Are You Still a Slave? Liberating the Black Female Body," *The New School*, May 7, 2014, accessed February 8, 2023, https://www.youtube.com/watch?v=rJk0hNROvzs&t=5226s.
8   José Esteban Muñoz, *Disidentifications: Queers of Color and the Performance of Politics* (Minneapolis, MN: University of Minnesota Press, 1999), 170. Emphasis mine.
9   David L. Eng, Judith Halberstam, and José Esteban Muñoz, "What's Queer About Queer Studies Now?," *Social Text*, Vol. 23, No. 3–4 (2005): 1–17 (1). The term intersectionality was formalized by Professor Kimberlé Crenshaw in her landmark 1989 study of Black women's employment in the United States, which found that Black women were more likely to be discriminated against under the United States

legal system because of their intersecting identities as both Black and female. Intersectionality is now a term frequently used beyond legal studies and encompasses the study of overlapping or intersecting social identities and related systems of oppression, domination, or discrimination. In short, it considers how social inequalities relating to race, class, ethnicity, age, ability, sexuality, nationality, and religion can "intersect." See: Kimberlé Crenshaw, "Demarginalizing the Intersection of Race and Sex: A Black Feminist Critique of Antidiscrimination Doctrine, Feminist Theory and Antiracist Politics," *University of Chicago Legal Forum*, Issue 1 (1989): 139–67.

10  David Pye, *The Nature and Art of Workmanship* (London: The Herbert Press, 1968 [1995]), 20.

11  Glenn Adamson, *Thinking Through Craft* (London: Bloomsbury, 2007), 1.

12  Ibid., 4.

13  The term "sloppy craft" is explored in Chapter 1.

14  Adamson, *Thinking Through Craft*, 4.

15  David J. Getsy, *Queer* (Cambridge, MA: MIT Press, 2016), 15.

16  Cáel M. Keegan, "Transgender Studies, or How to Do Things with Trans," in *The Cambridge Companion to Queer Studies*, ed. Siobhan B. Somerville (Cambridge: Cambridge University Press, 2020), 66–78 (69); Hilary Malatino, "Pedagogies of Becoming: Trans Inclusivity and the Crafting of Being," *TSQ: Transgender Studies Quarterly*, Vol. 2, No. 3 (2015): 395–410 (399).

17  S. Godfrey, "Creeping; Collaborating;; and Not Calling it Trans Craft," in *TISSUE PAPERS #01 MAKING*, ed. Donna Marcus Duke and Sam Moore (London: TISSUE, 2023), 77–83 (79).

18  Following Sara Ahmed and the inclusive citational practices of many other scholars, I place "gender critical" in quotation marks throughout, as an acknowledgment that "most of the most critical work on sex and gender within the academy is happening in the very spaces […] many "gender critical" feminists oppose." Sara Ahmed, "Gender Critical = Gender Conservative," *feministkilljoys*, October 31, 2021, accessed October 21, 2022, https://feministkilljoys.com/2021/10/31/gender-critical -gender-conservative/comment-page-1/. Also see: Fran Amery, "'Gender Critical' Feminism as a Biopolitical Project," *Sexualities*, May 28, 2024, https://doi.org/10.1177 /13634607241257397.

19  Rozsika Parker, *The Subversive Stitch: Embroidery and the Making of the Feminine* (London and New York: I.B. Tauris & Co Ltd, 1984), 5.

20  Ibid., 5; Marcia Tucker, *A Labor of Love* (New York: The New Museum of Contemporary Art, 1996), 52.

21  Tami Katz-Freiman, "'Craftsmen in the Factory of Images', *from* BoysCraft," in The *Craft Reader*, ed. Glenn Adamson (Oxford: Berg, 2010), 599–600.

22  Parker, *The Subversive Stitch*, xix.

23  Elissa Auther, *String, Felt, Thread: The Hierarchy of Art and Craft in American Art* (Minneapolis, MN: University of Minnesota Press, 2010), 7.

24  Ibid., 29.

25  Ibid., xxx.

26  Joseph McBrinn, "'Male Trouble': Sewing, Amateurism, and Gender," in *Sloppy Craft: Postdisciplinarity and the Crafts*, ed. Elaine C. Paterson and Susan Surette (London: Bloomsbury, 2015), 27–44 (34).

27  Ibid., 30.

28  Joseph McBrinn, *Queering The Subversive Stitch: Masculinity and The Culture of Needlework* (London: Bloomsbury, 2021), xvii.

29  See: Rozsika Parker and Griselda Pollock, *Old Mistresses: Women, Art and Ideology* (London: I.B.Tauris, 1981); Linda Nochlin, "Why Have There Been No Great Women Artists? (1971)," in *Women, Art and Power and Other Essays* (Boulder, CO: Westview Press, 1988), 145–78.

30  Audre Lorde, "Age, Race, Class and Sex: Women Redefining Difference," in *Your Silence Will Not Protect You*, ed. Audre Lorde (London: Silver Press, 2017), 94–106 (94).

31  John Paul Morabito, "Weaving Beyond the Binary," *TEXTILE: Cloth and Culture*, Vol. 20 (2022): 424–38; matt lambert, "Craft Beyond the Binary," *Studio: Craft and Design in Canada*, Fall/Winter 2022, accessed February 8, 2023, https://www.studiomagazine .ca/articles/2022/2/provocations-craft-beyond-the-binary.

32  Jules Gill-Peterson, *A Short History of Trans Misogyny* (London and New York: Verso Books, 2024), 1.

33  Ibid.

34  See: Adamson, *Thinking Through Craft*; Elaine C. Paterson and Susan Surette, *Sloppy Craft: Postdisciplinarity and the Crafts* (London: Bloomsbury, 2015); Alex Coles and Catharine Rossi, *Post-Craft: EP Vol. 3* (London: Sternberg Press, 2022).

35  Kaneko Kenji, *Gendai Tōgei no Zōkei Shikō [Concepts of Creating Form in Contemporary Ceramics]* (Tokyo: Abe Shuppan 2001), 30–44, quoted in Yuko Kikuchi, "The Craft Debate at the Crossroads of Global Visual Culture: Re-centring Craft in Postmodern and Postcolonial Histories," *World Art*, Vol. 5, No. 1 (2015): 87–115 (96–7).

36  Julia Bryan-Wilson, *Fray: Art and Textile Politics* (Chicago, IL: The University of Chicago Press, 2017).

37  The Critical Craft Forum, co-founded by Namita Gupta Wiggers and Elisabeth Agro, has played a central role in facilitating many of these conversations. Critical Craft Forum, "About," accessed January 3, 2023, https://www.criticalcraftforum.com/ about. Also see: Clare M. Wilkinson-Weber and Alicia Ory DeNicola, *Critical Craft: Technology, Globalization, and Capitalism* (London: Routledge, 2016).

38  Glenn Adamson, "When Craft Gets Sloppy," *Crafts*, Vol. 211 (March/April 2008): 36–41 (36).

39  Matt Smith, "Making Things Perfectly Queer," in *Crafted with Pride: Queer Craft and Activism in Contemporary Britain*, ed. Daniel Fountain (Bristol and Chicago, IL: Intellect Books and The University of Chicago Press, 2023), 123–6 (125).

40  lambert, "Craft Beyond the Binary."

41  Daniel Fountain, "Survival of the Knittest: Craft and Queer-Feminist Worldmaking," *MAI: Feminism and Visual Culture*, Issue 8 (December 13, 2021), accessed January 24, 2023, https://maifeminism.com/survival-of-the-knittest-craft-and-queer-feminist -worldmaking/.

42  Bryan-Wilson, *Fray*, 60.

43  Vaccaro, "Feelings and Fractals," 274. Also see: Jeanne Vaccaro, "Handmade," *Transgender Studies Quarterly*, Vol. 1, No. 1–2 (2014): 96–7; Jeanne Vaccaro, "Out of Distracted Vision: Psychedelic Sexology and the Handmade Aesthetics of Transgender," *Art & Education*, April 2020, accessed July 14, 2021, https://www .artandeducation.net/classroom/video/328445/jeanne-vaccaro-out-of-distracted -vision-psychedelic-sexology-and-the-handmade-aesthetics-of-transgender.

44  Ibid., 274–5.

45  Ibid., 276.

46  Ibid., 275–6.

47  Ibid.

48  Getsy, *Queer*, 15.

49  Jenni Sorkin, "Hybrid Vessels: Nicki Green's Transmutations," *Cfile.Capscule*, February 6, 2021, accessed July 15, 2021. https://cfileonline.org/feature-hybrid-vessels -nicki-greens-transmutations/.

50  Nifemi Ogunro, "About," accessed June 26, 2024, https://nifemiogunro.com/About.

51  Sara Ahmed, *What's The Use?: On The Uses of Use* (Durham, NC and London: Duke University Press, 2019), 208.

## *Chapter 1: Textile*

1  See: Lesley Millar and Alice Kettle, *The Erotic Cloth: Seduction and Fetishism in Textiles* (London: Bloomsbury, 2018).

2  Parker, *The Subversive Stitch*. Although a fundamental text for the study of textiles, others have noted limitations of Parker's text, particularly that it largely focuses on White, upper-class, and Western European perspectives.

3  Parker, *The Subversive Stitch*, xii.

4  Amy E. Elkins, *Crafting Feminism from Literary Modernism to the Multimedia Present* (Oxford: Oxford University Press, 2022), 2. Emphasis mine.

5  McBrinn, *Queering the Subversive Stitch*.

6  See: Betsy Greer, *Craftivism: The Art of Craft and Activism* (Vancouver: Arsenal Pulp Press, 2014).

7  See: Daniel Fountain, *Crafted with Pride: Queer Craft and Activism in Contemporary Britain* (Bristol and Chicago, IL: Intellect Books and The University of Chicago Press, 2023); Andy Campbell, *Queer X Design: 50 Years of Signs, Symbols, Banners, Logos and Graphic art of LGBTQ* (New York: Black Dog & Leventhal Publishers, 2019).

8  Queer Threads ran from January 17 to March 16, 2014, at the Leslie-Lohman Museum in New York. It featured work by twenty-six artists and practitioners, including: Chris Bogia, Melanie Braverman, Jai Andrew Carrillo, Chiachio & Fiannone, Liz Collins, Ben Cuevas, Pierre Fouché, James Gobel, Jesse Harrod, Larry Krone, Rebecca Levi, Aubret Longley-Cook, Aaron McIntosh, Allyson Mitchell, John Thomas Paradiso, Sheila Pepe, Maria E. Piñeres, Allen Porter, LJ Roberts, Sonny Schneider, Buzz Slutzky, Nathan Vincent, and Jessica Whitbread. The exhibition then toured to the Maryland Institute College of Art in 2015 and the Boston Center for the Arts in 2016. There was then a second iteration of the show that launched at the San Jose Museum of Quilts & Textiles from May 10 to August 23, 2023, featuring works by thirty-seven artists and practitioners primarily from the West coast.

9  For more on fiber and the hierarchy of art and craft, specifically in American art, see: Auther, *String, Felt, Thread*.

10  John Chaich interview with Daniel Fountain, June 4, 2019.

11  John Chaich, *Queer Threads: Crafting Identity and Community*, accessed August 1, 2020, http://www.leslielohman.org/exhibitions/2013/queer-threads/QueerThreadsCat alogue_FINAL.pdf. Also see: John Chaich and Todd Oldham, *Queer Threads: Crafting Identity and Community* (Los Angeles, CA: AMMO Books, 2017).

12 John Chaich, "Queer Threads," *Queer Threads Catalog*, January 23, 2014, 3–4, accessed June 7, 2020, https://issuu.com/leslielohmanmuseum/docs/queerthreadscatalogue_final.

13 Lauren Berlant and Michael Warner, "Sex in Public," *Critical Inquiry*, Vol. 24, No. 2 (1998): 547–66 (548).

14 LJ Roberts interview with Daniel Fountain, February 2, 2020.

15 ACT UP was founded in 1987 by an American collective of artists and activists who utilized media, design, and advertising strategies to agitate for treatment, medication and draw attention to the widespread discrimination experienced by AIDS patients. Forms of creativity and craftivism were essential to many campaigns and a way to spread awareness, including zines, manifestos, banners, graphic design, badges, the creation of cardboard gravestones for a "die in," to name just several examples. See: ACT UP, *Actions*, accessed October 18, 2020, https://actupny.org/reports.1.html.; *Fight Back, Fight AIDS: 15 Years of ACT UP*, dir. by James Wentzy (Frameline, 2004); *How To Survive A Plague; United in Anger*, dir. by David France (Public Square Films, 2012).

16 The downward-pointing pink triangle (die Rosa-Winkel) was primarily used in the Second World War to distinguish those who had been identified by authorities as homosexual men but sometimes also any individuals whose sexuality and gender identity was deemed "deviant" by these forces, such as bisexuals and transgender men. An inverted version of the pink triangle has now become ubiquitous with the activism of groups such as ACT UP, as well as in the visual culture of the late 1980s and early 1990s more broadly, where it became a symbol of solidarity, strength, and collectivity.

17 Also see: Daniel Fountain and LJ Roberts, "LJ Roberts' Queer Epics," *Decorating Dissidence*, April 3, 2020, accessed June 3, 2020, https://decoratingdissidence.com/2020/04/03/lj-roberts-queer-craft-epics/; Fountain, "Survival of the Knittest."

18 Smithsonian American Art Museum, *40 Under 40: L.J.Roberts*, June 8, 2012, accessed June 4, 2020, https://www.youtube.com/watch?v=YxnyPQ7YATg&feature=emb_title. Also see: QuORUM, "Home," accessed December 5, 2023, https://quorumforum2011.wordpress.com.

19 Julia Bryan-Wilson makes a similar claim in relation to Harmony Hammond's 1973 series, *Floorpieces*. Exhibited on the floor, visitors need to bend over if they wish to see details of Hammond's "rag rugs." Bryan-Wilson suggests this invokes a form of queer and lesbian intimacy, interpreting this as a pun on "going down" (a term used to describe oral sex between women), and of being "on the rag" (a euphemism for menstruation). Julia Bryan-Wilson, "Queerly Made: Harmony Hammond's *Floorpieces*," *The Journal of Modern Craft*, Vol. 2, No. 1 (2009): 59–80.

20 LJ Roberts interview with Daniel Fountain, February 2, 2020; Buzz Slutzky, "Buttons for LJ Roberts," accessed June 1, 2024, http://www.buzzslutzky.com/drawing#/new-page-4/. Félix González-Torres' *Untitled* (Portrait of Ross in L.A.) from 1991 is one of series of participatory installation works that the artist created in honor of his partner, Ross Laycock, who died of AIDS-related illness that same year. The work consists of a pile of candy which weighs the same as Laycock did (175 pounds). Viewers are invited to take candies from the pile and the gradual diminishing of the weight of the pile is symbolic of the diminishing of Laycock's own body as his health deteriorated.

21 Katie Goldstein, "Queer Homes in a Non-Queer World," in *Mapping Queer Space(s) of Praxis and Pedagogy*, ed. Elizabeth McNeil, James E. Wermers, and Joshua O. Lunn (Cham: Palgrave Macmillan, 2018), 269–78 (269).

22 Ibid.

23 Ibid.

24 Fountain and Roberts, "LJ Roberts' Queer Epics."

25 These are documented in an illustrated book by Roberts, see: LJ Roberts, *Carry You With Me: Ten Years of Portraits* (Brooklyn, NY: Pioneer Works Press, 2021).

26 Ibid., 11.

27 Ibid.

28 Smithsonian American Art Museum, *40 Under 40*.

29 Although the idea of an AIDS Memorial Quilt originated in America and that other AIDS Quilts often take inspiration from Jones's concept, at the time of writing there are at least forty-two other AIDS Memorial Quilts worldwide which map a transnational response to HIV/AIDS.

30 Cleve Jones, *The Making of an Activist: Stitching a Revolution* (New York: Harper Collins, 2000), 105.

31 Ibid., 107.

32 In 2019, I conducted a range of archival research on the NAMES Project AIDS Memorial Quilt in New York. Collections I consulted included: the The Lesbian, Gay, Bisexual and Transgender Community Center Archive to view material relating to the New York Memorial Quilt (established in 1988) [Collection Number 2, b.1] and to document quilt blocks which were on temporary display at the Lincoln Center.

33 See: Nino Testa; "'If You Are Reading It, I am Dead': Activism, Local History, and the AIDS Quilt," *The Public Historian*, Vol. 44, No. 3 (2022): 24–57.

34 AIDS Quilt, "The AIDS Memorial Quilt," accessed June 25, 2020, https://www .aidsquilt.org/about/the-aids-memorial-quilt.

35 Peter S. Hawkins, "Naming Names: The Art of Memory and the NAMES Project AIDS Quilt," *Critical Inquiry*, Vol. 19, No. 4 (Summer 1993): 752–79 (757).

36 Bryan-Wilson, *Fray*, 190.

37 Hawkins, "Naming Names," 765.

38 Sarah Schulman, *The Gentrification of the Mind: Witness to a Lost Imagination* (Los Angeles, CA: University of California Press, 2012).

39 Ibid., 14.

40 Berlant and Warner, "Sex in Public," 558.

41 George Chauncey, "Privacy Could Only Be Had in Public: Gay Uses of the Streets," in *Stud: Architectures of Masculinity*, ed. Joel Sanders (New York: Princeton Architectural Press, 1996), 224–61; George Chauncey, *Gay New York: Gender, Urban Culture, and the Making of the Gay Male World, 1890–1940* (New York: Basic Books, 1994), 224. Also see: Adam Nathaniel Furnman and Joshua Mardell, eds., *Queer Spaces: An Atlas of LGBTQIA+ Places and Stories* (London: RIBA Publishing, 2022).

42 Fountain and Roberts, "LJ Roberts' Queer Epics"; Berlant and Warner, "Sex in Public," 561.

43 LJ Roberts, "Van Dykes," accessed October 26, 2023, https://www.ljroberts.net/ textiles/van-dykes.

45 Roberts, "Studio Views"; Ariel Levy, "Lesbian Nation," *The New Yorker*, February 23, 2009, accessed June 28, 2020, https://www.newyorker.com/magazine/2009/03/02/ lesbian-nation.

46 Ibid.

47  Ibid.

48  Ibid.

49  Ibid.

50  Sophie Saint Thomas, "Artists Sarah Zapata and LJ Roberts Use Textiles to Express Their Identities," *Allure*, September 13, 2017, accessed June 28, 2020, https://www.allure.com/story/queer-artists-exhibition-museum-of-arts-and-design.

51  Damien Luxe, *Vanifesto: A Mediation on Van Lust* (2011), 18, accessed June 26, 2020, http://www.damienluxe.com/wp-content/uploads/2014/05/VANIFESTO_final.pdf.

52  Damien Luxe, Heather María Ács, and Sabina Ibarrola, *Glitter & Grit: Queer Performance From the Heels on Wheels Femme Galaxy* (Portland, OR: Publication Studio, 2015), 19.

53  Roberts, *Carry You With Me*, 13.

54  Fountain and Roberts, "LJ Roberts' Queer Epics."

55  Berlant and Warner, "Sex in Public," 558. For more on queer kinship, see: Kath Weston, *Families We Choose: Lesbians, Gays, Kinship* (New York: Columbia University Press, 1997); Freeman, *Queer Kinship.*

56  Max Delany, "Paul Yore: WORD MADE FLESH," *Carriageworks*, accessed January 26, 2024, https://carriageworks.com.au/journal/paul-yore-word-made-flesh-interview/.

57  Nicola Heath, "Australian Artist Paul Yore Speaks About Censorship in Art, Queer Culture and Catholic Kitsch as ACCA Exhibition Surveys His Career," *ABC News*, November 5, 2022, accessed January 26, 2024, https://www.abc.net.au/news/2022-11-06/paul-yore-word-made-flesh-exhibition-acca-australian-artist/101610312. Also see Parker, *The Subversive Stitch*, for more on the gendering of textiles within education.

58  There is a much broader history of the use of textiles as a therapeutic and recuperative practice, especially during the First World War and the Second World War among recovering soldiers. For more, see: McBrinn, *Queering the Subversive Stitch.*

59  The exhibition ran from September 23 to November 20, 2022. The exhibition title is taken from the Gospel of John in the Bible and references Yore's religious upbringing. See: Daniel Fountain, "On the Queer Horizon: 'Welcome to Faggot Land'," in *Paul Yore: WORD MADE FLESH*, ed. Max Delany (Melbourne: Art Ink and Australian Centre for Contemporary Art, 2023), 264–315; Australian Centre for Contemporary Art, "Paul Yore: WORD MADE FLESH," accessed October 18, 2023, https://acca.melbourne/exhibition/paul-yore-word-made-flesh/.

60  Sarah Brown, "The Creative Process with Paul Yore and His Work 'The Rule of Lore'," March 1, 2022, accessed January 26, 2023, https://www.bendigoregion.com.au/bendigo-art-gallery/blogs/the-creative-process-with-paul-yore-and-his-work-the-rule-of-lore#:~:text=I%20build%20up%20structures%2C%20layers,parts%20of%20the%20creative%20process.

61  Ibid.

62  José Esteban Muñoz, *Cruising Utopia: The Then and There of Queer Futurity* (New York: New York University Press, 2009), 99.

63  Ibid., 1.

64  Ibid.

65  Ibid.

66  For example, American writer adrienne maree brown draws on Black feminist thought, queer theory, and science fiction to envision a future where pleasure is not a luxury but a necessity for social change. They use the term "pleasure activism" as

a framework for social justice that centers states of pleasure as a tool for healing and liberation. See: adrienne maree brown, *Pleasure Activism: The Politics of Feeling Good* (Chico, CA: AK Press, 2019).

67   Zygmunt Bauman has also explored similar concepts of social abjection. See: Zygmunt Bauman, *Wasted Lives: Modernity and its Outcasts* (Cambridge: Polity Press, 2004).

68   Max Delany, "Paul Yore: WORD MADE FLESH."

69   Alexia Petsinis, "Does My Ideology Look Big In This? Paul Yore on LET THEM EAT CAKE," July 12, 2021, accessed January 26, 2024, https://tobemagazine.com.au/does-my-ideology-look-big-in-this-paul-yore-on-let-them-eat-cake/.

70   Andrew Ross, *No Respect: Intellectuals and Popular Culture* (New York: Routledge, 1989), 121.

71   Susan Sontag, *Notes on Camp* (London: Penguin Random House, 2018), 8.

72   Ross, *No Respect*, 139–51.

73   Moe Meyer, *The Politics and Poetics of Camp* (London: Routledge, 2011), 7.

74   For more on camp and the abject, see: Ingrid Hotz-Davies, Georg Vogt, and Franziska Bergmann, *The Dark Side of Camp Aesthetics: Queer Economies of Dirt, Dust and Patina* (London: Routledge, 2018); Nicole Seymour, *Bad Environmentalism: Irony and Irreverence in the Ecological Age* (Minneapolis, MN and London: University of Minnesota Press, 2018).

75   Muñoz, *Disidentifications*.

76   Ibid., 31.

77   Heath, "Australian Artist Paul Yore Speaks about Censorship in Art, Queer Culture and Catholic Kitsch as ACCA Exhibition Surveys His Career."

78   Elaine Cheasley Paterson and Susan Surette, eds., *Sloppy Craft: Postdisciplinarity and the Crafts* (London: Bloomsbury, 2015).

79   Josh Faught, *Contact*, accessed October 26, 2023, https://www.joshfaught.com/contact.

80   Adamson, "When Craft Gets Sloppy," 36.

81   Joseph McBrinn, "'Male Trouble': Sewing, Amateurism, and Gender," in *Sloppy Craft: Postdisciplinarity and the Crafts*, ed. Elaine Cheasley Paterson and Susan Surette (London: Bloomsbury, 2015), 27–44; Elissa Auther and Elyse Speaks, "Sloppy Craft as Temporal Drag in the Work of Josh Faught," in *Sloppy Craft: Postdisciplinarity and the Crafts*, ed. Elaine Cheasley Paterson and Susan Surette (London: Bloomsbury, 2015), 45–59.

82   Adamson, *Thinking Through Craft*, 1.

83   For more on the intersections between textiles and colonialism more broadly, see Anna Arabindan-Kesson's essential book: Anna Arabindan-Kesson, *Black Bodies White Gold* (Durham, NC: Duke University Press, 2021).

84   Audre Lorde, *The Master's Tools Will Never Dismantle the Master's House* (London: Penguin Books, 2018); matt lambert, "Re-Tooling, Re-Using, Un-Mastering," *Decorating Dissidence*, July 11, 2022, accessed October 26, 2023, https://decoratingdissidence.com/2022/07/11/issue-fifteen-tools-use-mastery/.

85   LJ Roberts, "Bio," accessed July 2, 2020, https://www.ljroberts.net/about.

86   Also see: Julietta Singh, *Unthinking Mastery: Dehumanisim and Decolonial Entanglements* (Durham, NC: Duke University Press, 2017).

## *Chapter 2: Ceramic*

1   Bible Isa. 64.8; Quran Sad 38:71–2.

2   This appears in the Epic of Gilgamesh 1.2. Ninhursag (or Ninhursaga) is the most
    widely used name for the ancient Sumerian mother goddess today, but there are
    others in use. See: Don Nardo and Robert B. Kebric, *Ancient Mesopatomia* (New
    York: Greenhaven Press, 2007), 36.

3   Maya Barzilai, *Golem: Modern Wars and Their Monsters* (New York: NYU Press,
    2016), 3–6;

4   Andrew Livingstone and Kevin Petire, *The Ceramics* Reader (London: Bloomsbury,
    2017), 10.

5   Same-sex relations between men were commonplace in Ancient Greece and Rome.
    This is reflected in many ceramic objects, namely decorative cups and amphoras that
    depict anal sex and pederasty (sexual relationships between adult men and young
    boys). See: Holt Parker, "Vaseworld. Depiction and Description of Sex at Athens,"
    in *Ancient Sex: New Essays*, ed. Ruby Blondell and Kirk Ormand (Columbus, OH:
    The Ohio State University Press, 2015), 23–142; Richard B. Parkinson, *A Little Gay
    History: Desire and Diversity across the World* (London: British Museum Press, 2013),
    47.

6   The Moche lived on the North Coast of Peru c.150–900 CE and are now famed
    for their unique and playful approach to pottery, often encouraging forms of
    orality where pots become "activated" by blowing into them. In their extensive (re)
    examination of the Moche "sex pots," cultural anthropologist Mary Weismantel
    critiques the limitations of existing scholarship and argues that as transgender
    movements have recently gained traction across Peru, many of these pots have since
    been described by South American communities as intersex and transgender bodies
    (or *travesti*). See: Mary Weismantel, *Playing with Things: Engaging the Moche Sex Pots*
    (Austin, TX: University of Texas Press, 2021).

7   Lhamana are highly respected people who are biologically born male but who take
    on the social and ceremonial roles usually performed by women in traditional
    Zuni culture. Many Lhamana are considered to have spiritual responsibilities, often
    channeled through their crafts. For We'wah this most often included pottery, but
    also textile weaving and basketry. Many contemporary Lhamana now identify as part
    of the pan-Indian two-spirit (or 2S) community, and this term has sometimes been
    applied retrospectively. See: Bayu Kristanto, "Two-Spirits and The Decolonization of
    Gender," *Paradigma: Jurnal Kajian Budaya* 1, no. 2 (July 2011), 119–131.

8   The featured practitioners included Mark Burns, Dustin Yager, Ron Geibel, Jeremy
    Brooks, Kathy King, and Christina West. The exhibition ran from March 13 till April
    26, 2015.

9   Northern Clay Center, *Sexual Politics: Gender, Sexuality, and Queerness in
    Contemporary Ceramics* (Minneapolis, MN: Northern Clay Center, 2015), 6; Paul
    Mathieu, *Sex Pots: Eroticism in Ceramics* (New Brunswick, NJ: Rutgers University
    Press, 2003); Judith Schwartz, *Confrontational Ceramics* (London: A&C Black Visual
    Arts, 2008). For more on Foulem, Mathieu and Milette's work see Robin Metcalfe,
    *Camp Fires: The Queer Baroque of Léopold L. Foulem, Paul Mathieu and Richard
    Milette* (Toronto: Gardiner Museum, 2015).

10  The exhibition ran from May 6, 2023 to December 30, 2023. The exhibition was
    co-curated by Beth Ann Gerstein and Pam Aliaga. It included the work of Sascha

Brastoff, Howard Kottler, Mark Burns, Grayson Perry, Ramekon O'Arwisters, Larry Buller, Julia Kunin, Vick Quezada, Nicki Green, Alex Anderson, Karla Ekatherine Canseco, and Tamara Santibañez. The exhibition was part of a wider series called *Making in Between* which "brings together works by artists doing intersectional work and exploring common themes of identity, culture, and community." See: Beth Ann Gerstein, ed., *Making in Between: Queer Clay* (Pomona, CA: American Museum of Ceramic Art, 2023).

11 Matthew Limb, "An Archive in Clay: The Crafting of Queer Identities," in *Making in Between: Queer Clay*, ed. Beth Ann Gerstein (Pomona, CA: American Museum of Ceramic Art, 2023), 9–17 (11).

12 Maurice Merleau-Ponty, *Phenomenology of* Perception (London: Routledge, 2011), 151.

13 Gill-Peterson, *A Short History of Trans Misogyny*, ii–ix.

14 Vaccaro, *Handmade*, 97.

15 Ibid., 96.

16 For example, see Kenneth R. Beittel, "Clay as Elemental Wholeness," in *The Ceramics Reader*, ed. Andrew Livingstone and Kevin Petire (London: Bloomsbury, 2017), 14–17 (16).

17 Rose Schmits's interview with Daniel Fountain, November 15, 2022.

18 Jenni Sorkin, *Live Form: Women, Ceramics, and Community* (Chicago, IL: The University of Chicago Press, 2016).

19 Lois Stone, "Trans Craft and the Museum of Transology," in *Crafted with Pride: Queer Craft and Activism in Contemporary Britain*, ed. Daniel Fountain (Chicago, IL and Bristol: The University of Chicago Press and Intellect Books, 2023), 30–44.

20 Rose Schmits's interview with Daniel Fountain, November 15, 2022.

21 Vaccaro, "Handmade," 96.

22 Vaccaro, "Wooly Ecologies," 283.

23 Ibid., 275.

24 Vaccaro, "Handmade," 97.

25 Vaccaro, "Wooly Ecologies," 274.

26 Jay Prosser, *Second Skins: The Body Narratives of Transsexuality* (New York: Columbia University Press, 1998), 5.

27 Stone, "Trans Craft and the Museum of Transology," 31.

28 Rose Schmits's interview with Daniel Fountain, November 15, 2022.

29 Ibid.

30 Briony Hudson, ed., *English Delftware Drug Jars: The Collection of the Museum of the Royal Pharmaceutical Society of Great Britain* (London: Pharmaceutical Press, 2006). Hudson suggests that Delftware drug jars began to be produced in London around 1570 until about 1780 by which time tin-glazed earthenware began to be replaced by creamware, the forerunner of modern white earthenware or "whiteware" still used today.

31 This is especially the case in much of Europe and North America where the gendered associations with these colors was thought to have emerged in the mid-nineteenth century. Historically, it is suggested that this was the opposite, and that blue was traditionally associated with femininity and pink was associated with masculinity.

32 Emma Gray and Alanna Vagianos, "We Have A Navy Veteran To Thank For The Transgender Pride Flag," *Huffpost*, July 27, 2017, accessed October 24, 2022, https://www.huffingtonpost.co.uk/entry/we-have-a-navy-veteran-to-thank-for-the -transgender-pride-flag_n_5978c060e4b0e201d57a711f.

33  Michael Archer, *Delftware: The Tin-glazed Earthenware of the British Isles—A Catalogue of the Collection in the Victoria and Albert Museum* (London: Stationary Office Books, 1997), 4.

34  Rose Schmits, "About," accessed October 24, 2022, https://roseschmits.com/about.

35  Susan Stryker, Paisley Currah, and Lisa Jean Moore, "Introduction: Trans-, Trans, or Transgender?," *Women's Studies Quarterly,* Vol. 36, Nos. 3/4 (2008): 11–22 (13).

36  Reina Gossett, Eric Stanley, and Johanna Burton, *Trap Door: Trans Cultural Production and the Politics of Visibility* (Cambridge, MA: MIT Press, 2017).

37  Know Your Meme, "You Mess With Crabo, You Get a Stabbo," accessed October 25, 2022, https://knowyourmeme.com/memes/you-mess-with-crabo-you-get-a-stabo #fn1; Random Dude, "Gangster Crab With Knife," February 14, 2016, accessed October 25, 2022, https://www.youtube.com/watch?v=ebsvoRqPOMk&t=1s.

38  Ibid.

39  Avery Dame-Griff, *The Two Revolutions: A History of the Transgender Internet* (New York: New York University Press, 2023).

40  Rose Schmits's interview with Daniel Fountain, November 15, 2022.

41  Rose Schmits, "We Live in a Society," accessed October 24, 2022, https://roseschmits .com/we-live-in-a-society-collection.

42  Charlotte Jones and Jen Slater, "The Toilet Debate: Stalling Trans Possibilities and Defending 'Women's Protected Spaces'," *The Sociological Review*, Vol. 68, No. 4 (2020): 843–51 (835).

43  Given that this statistic is only reported crimes, and the Met Police have publicly acknowledged issues of institutionalized transphobia and homophobia, the actual figure is likely to be much higher. Home Office, *Hate Crime, England and Wales, 2022 to 2023* (second edition), GOV.UK., 2023 [online], accessed June 26, 2024, https:// www.gov.uk/government/statistics/hate-crime-england-and-wales-2022-to-2023/hate -crime-england-and-wales-2022-to-2023.

44  Christine Burns, *Trans Britain: Our Journey from The Shadows* (London: Unbound, 2018), 16.

45  Nicki Green, "About: Bio," accessed October 25, 2022, https://www.nickigreen.org.

46  Ibid.

47  Jori Finkel, "'Gender Alchemy' Is Transforming Art for the 21st Century," *The New York Times*, September 8, 2021, accessed October 24, 2022, https://www.nytimes.com /2021/09/08/arts/design/feminist-transgender-nonbinary-art.html.

48  Willemijn van Noord also points out that pseudo-Chinese ornamentation (especially invented script and symbols) were frequently used as if to legitimize these works as Chinese rather than Dutch imitations. See: Willemijn van Noord, "Between Script and Ornament: Delftware Decorated with Pseudo-Chinese Characters, 1680–1720," *Journal of Design History*, Vol. 31 (March 1, 2021): 1–20. For more on Delftware and colonialism, see: Susan Broomhall and Jacqueline Van Gent, *Dynastic Colonialism: Gender, Materiality and the Early Modern House of Orange-Nassau* (London and New York: Routledge, 2016); Dawn Odell, "Delftware and the Domestication of Chinese Porcelain," in *EurAsian Matters: China, Europe, and the Transcultural Object, 1600– 1800*, ed. Anna Grasskamp and Monica Juneja (New York: Springer, 2018), 175–202.

49  Sappho (c.630–c.570 BC) was a Greek poet from the island of Lesbos. Sappho's writing on the beauty of women led to both her name and nationality becoming intrinsically linked to women who love women, "sapphic" and "lesbian," respectively.

50  The term "Lavender Menace" originated as a derogatory term for the association of lesbianism with the feminist movement, but it was later reclaimed as a positive

term by lesbian feminists. The Lavender Menace was an informal group of lesbian radical feminists formed to protest the exclusion of lesbians and their issues from the feminist movement at the Second Congress to Unite Women in New York City on May 1, 1970. The "Lavender" aspect of the term stems back to the early twentieth century in which lavender shades became popular in women's fashion, and the color took on meaning as a slang term for gay men, with associations of effeminacy.

51  Eleanor Medhurst, "From Lavender to Violet: The Lesbian Obsession with Purple," *Dressing Dykes*, August 20, 2021, accessed October 2, 2022, https://dressingdykes.com /2021/08/20/from-lavender-to-violet/; Keava McMillan, "Violet Delights: A Queer History of Purple," *V&A Dundee*, accessed November 3, 2023, https://www.vam.ac.uk /dundee/articles/violet-delights-a-queer-history-of-purple.

52  Oscar Wilde popularised the trend of wearing a green carnation as a symbol of gay identity when he asked close friends to wear them on their lapels to his play *Lady Windermere's Fan* in 1892. Wearing a carnation on the left lapel then became a code among gay men. In the twentieth century, pansy was originally used as a derogatory term to refer to gay men, suggesting them to be non-masculine and delicate. See: Sarah Prager, "Four Flowering Plants That Have Been Decidedly Queered," *JSTOR Daily*, January 29, 2020, accessed November 3, 2023, https://daily.jstor.org/four -flowering-plants-decidedly-queered/. V&A Dundee, "The Language of Pride," accessed November 3, 2023, https://www.vam.ac.uk/dundee/articles/the-language -of-pride; Eddie Johnston, "Four Flowers That Have Become Queer Symbols," *Royal Botanic Gardens, Kew*, accessed November 3, 2023, https://www.kew.org/read-and -watch/plants-LGBTQ-symbols.

53  Even today, the Rijksmuseum online shop states: "This makes a great souvenir: it doesn't get more Dutch than this!". In addition to the fact that the designs and ornament were appropriated from Chinese ceramics, the tulip bulbs themselves were largely imported to Europe from Turkey and Central Asia. Rijksmuseum Shop, "Delftware," accessed November 7, 2023, https://www.rijksmuseumshop.nl/en/living /delftware; Frits Scholten and Michael Hoyle, ed., *Delft "Tulip Vases"* (Amsterdam: Rijksmuseum, 2013).

54  Louvre, "Les Trois Grâces," accessed October 20, 2023, https://collections.louvre.fr/en /ark:/53355/cl010091241.

55  The three graces have been the subject of numerous artists throughout history including Sandro Botticelli (c.1445–1510), Peter Paul Rubens (1557–1640), Raphael (1483–1520), and Antonio Canova (1757–1822), to name but a few. The appropriation of visual iconography of Greco-Roman culture is a recurring touchstone for many contemporary artists, such as the American genderqueer and intersex artist Del LaGrace Volcano (b.1957) who also drew inspiration from the three graces in the work *The Three Graces, Jasper, Suzie and Gill, London* (1992).

56  The term "trancestry" is particularly used among trans communities to describe the search for evidence that trans people existed historically—a process which can help to halt the continued erasure of trans history more broadly. The term also challenges the idea that ancestry is solely built on biological ties and acknowledges that people may feel a powerful connection to historical trans figures or material. MOT, based in the UK, and MOTHA, based in the United States, are examples of recent curatorial projects and collections that attempt to preserve trancestry. See: David Evans Frantz, Christina Linden, and Chris E. Vargas, *Trans Hirstory in 99 Objects,* (Pasadena,

CA and Munich: Museum of Trans Hirstory & Art and Hirmer Publishers, 2024); Museum of Transology, "About," accessed November 22, 2022, https://www .museumoftransology.com/about.

57    r/traaaaaaannnnnnnnnnns, "I Find This Image Super Empowering [NSFW][X-Post]," *Reddit*, accessed October 20, 2023, https://www.reddit.com/r/traaaaaaannnnnnnnnnns /comments/8ptatx/i_find_this_image_super_empowering_nsfwxpost_rgssp/.

58    MyMiniFactory, "The Three Graces, But They're Trans," accessed June 10, 2024, https://www.myminifactory.com/object/3d-print-the-three-graces-but-they-re-trans -151219.

59    KJ Rawson, "Archive," *Transgender Studies Quarterly*, Vol. 1, No. 1–2 (May 1, 2014): 24–6 (25).

60    Ibid.

61    Rose Schmits's interview with Daniel Fountain, November 15, 2022.

62    Mary Douglas, *Purity and Danger: An Analysis of the Concepts of Pollution and Taboo* (London and New York: Routledge, 1966), 36.

63    Eleanor Penny, "Filth: Trans Bathroom Panics May Be New, but Public Toilets Have Always Been a Political Battleground," *Novara Media*, April 8, 2020, accessed November 16, 2023, https://novaramedia.com/2020/04/08/filth-trans-bathroom -panics-may-be-new-but-public-toilets-have-always-been-a-political-battleground/.

64    Scholars such as Tara Atluri have drawn attention to the classed and racialised dimensions of the "hidden" labor that goes on within public toilets; often working-class, Black bodies, and migrant workers. Tara Atluri, "You Marxist, I Clean Toilet: Racism, Labor, and the Bathroom attendant," *Frame*, Vol. 1 (Spring 2011): 69–95.

65    The term "cottaging" has its roots in the ways self-contained lavatory blocks in Britain used to resemble small cottages in their appearance and this became used as a double entendre in Polari—the slang language used by gay men in Britain, predominantly in the mid-twentieth century. See: Alex Espinoza, *Cruising: An Intimate History of a Radical Pastime* (Los Angeles, CA: Unnamed Press, 2019).

66    These ideas have particularly been explored in the work of several queer contemporary artists, including Candice Lin's (b.1979) *A Hard White Body* (2017) and Prem Sahib's (b.1982) *Beneficiary* (2020), to name but a few examples.

67    James F. Deetz, "Material Culture and Worldview in Colonial Anglo-America," in *The Recovery of Meaning: Historical Archaeology in the Eastern United States*, ed. Mark P. Leone and Parker B. Potter Jr (Washington, DC and London: Smithsonian Institution Press, 1988), 219–34.

68    Sorkin, "Hybrid Vessels."

69    San Francisco NMWA, "Meet Nicki Green, NMWA 2024 Women to Watch Artist," June 2, 2023, accessed November 17, 2023, https://www.youtube.com/watch?v =IC4jYVJGq5s.

70    See: Myra J. Hird, "Naturally Queer," *Feminist Theory*, Vol. 5, No. 1 (2004): 85–9 (86); Myra J. Hird, *Sex, Gender and Science* (New York: Palgrave Macmillan, 2004); Patricia Kaishian and Hasmik Djoulakian, "The Science Underground: Mycology as a Queer Discipline," *Catalyst: Feminism, Theory, Technoscience*, Vol. 6, No. 2 (2020), 1–27.

71    Isabella Segalovich, "Queering the Jewish Mikvah," *Hyperallergic*, April 4, 2023, accessed October 23, 2023, https://hyperallergic.com/812775/queering-the-jewish -mikvah/.

## *Chapter 3: Wood*

1   Graham Gremore, "30 Extremely Accurate Tweets About Gay People Being Unable to Sit Properly," *Queerty*, September 8, 2019, accessed November 1, 2022, https://www.queerty.com/30-extremely-accurate-tweets-gay-people-unable-sit-properly-20190908. In 2024, another example went viral via Reddit of a modular piece of furniture with the caption "New bisexual chair just dropped," encouraging further conversation on the "nonconformist" nature of queer and "bi-sitting": r00giebeara, "Been Racking My Brain over This One for about a Week....," *Reddit*, December 28, 2023. accessed May 2, 2024, https://www.reddit.com/r/ExplainTheJoke/comments/18t84ou/been_racking_my_brain_over_this_one_for_about_a/.

2   Má Matiazi (@mamatiazi), "Have You Heard About Bi-sitting?," *Instagram*, July 26, 2019, accessed November 1, 2022, https://www.instagram.com/p/B0YfCHAAHIe/?utm_source=ig_embed&ig_rid=c8c3b839-b364-4e21-a49f-81922743b759.

3   Ibid.

4   Australian critic Ivana Brehas produced a short but informative popular article on queer sitting in film and television, citing examples of rebellious queers who refused to sit "straight," such as Katharine Hepburn. See: Ivana Brehas, "The Queer Art of Sitting," *Kill Your Darlings*, November 2, 2020, accessed November 1, 2022, https://www.killyourdarlings.com.au/article/the-queer-art-of-sitting/.

5   Ibid.

6   Sara Ahmed, *Queer Phenomenology: Orientations, Objects, Others* (Durham, NC: Duke University Press, 2006), 161.

7   Deirdre Visser, *Joinery, Joists and Gender: A History of Woodworking for the 21st Century* (New York: Routledge, 2022), 3. With fellow woodworker Laura Mays, Visser was also co-curator of *Making a Seat at the Table*, a significant exhibition that ran in October 2019 at the Center for Art in Wood in Philadelphia (now the Museum for Art in Wood) which was the largest exhibition of contemporary women and gender non-conforming makers in woodworking featuring forty-three practitioners from across North America. These included: Jennifer Anderson, Teresa Audet, Connie Chisholm, Vivian Chiu, Emma Chorostecki, Alex Clarke, Kate Davidson, Leigh Dotey, Heidi Earnshaw, Ashley Eriksmoen, Bec Evans, Annie Evelyn, Mollie Ferguson and Heather Trosdahl, Gail Fredell, Melanie Hamilton, BA Harrington, Katie Hudnall, Erin Irber, Laura Kishimoto, Yuri Kobayashi, Chris Lee, RH Lee and Would Works, Bowen Liu, Kristina Madsen, Sarah Marriage and A Workshop of Our Own, Heide Martin, Sarah Martin, Wendy Maruyama, Yvonne Mouser, Christy Oates, Jodie Prud'homme, SIOSI, Rosanne Somerson, Michaela Crie Stone, Tiny WPA, Katrina Tompkins, Briana Trujillo, Hannah Vaughan, Sarah Watlington, Leslie Webb, Folayemi Wilson, Kimberly Winkle, and Kat Wong.

8   Ibid.

9   Visser, *Joinery, Joists and Gender*, 2. Although Visser's book many focuses on women woodworkers, she does profile the work of KG MacKinnon (Limen Studio) who identifies as queer and trans, and Sean Desiree who identifies as non-binary.

10  Museum for Art in Wood, "Queering Wood Craft: An LGBTQIA+ Woodworkers Roundtable Part 6," accessed October 4, 2023, https://museumforartinwood.org/event/queering-wood-craft-an-lgbtqia-woodworkers-roundtable-part-6/.

11  Other panel chairs have included writer John Duane Kingsley, designer and builder Katherine Lam, "polydisciplinary practitioner" matt lambert, and furniture maker and fabricator Haniel Wides.

12  Here, I particularly invoke the work of Jack Halberstam who championed "low theory" as an alternative approach to thinking and writing, citing unconventional sources, perspectives and drawing on popular culture to defy expectations of academic knowledge, reflect the messiness of the queer experience, and to find new, perhaps unexpected, ways of understanding the world. See: Jack Halberstam, *The Queer Art of Failure* (Durham, NC and London: Duke University Press, 2011).

13  Eve Kosofsky Sedgwick, *Epistemology of the Closet* (Berkeley, CA: University of California Press, 1990), 65.

14  Kate Millett, *Sexual Politics* (New York: Columbia University Press, 2016).

15  Kate Millett, "From the Basement to the Madhouse," in *Kate Millett, Sculptor: The First 38 Years*, ed. Kathy O'Dell (College Park, MD: Fine Arts Gallery University of Maryland, 1997), 41–50 (41).

16  For recent press on Kate Millett's furniture, see: New-York Historical Society, "Kate Millett's Fantasy Furniture: Our Q&A with William J. Simmons," accessed October 5, 2023, https://salon94.com/exhibitions/fantasy-furniture-1967; Salon 94 S94D, "Kate Millett Fantast Furniture, 1967," accessed October 5, 2023, https://salon94 .com/exhibitions/fantasy-furniture-1967; Diana Budds, "The 'Fantasy Furniture' of a Feminist Icon," *Curbed,* January 20, 2022, accessed August 2, 2022, https://www .curbed.com/2022/01/kate-millett-fantasy-furniture-sculpture-salon-94-design.html.

17  Ahmed, *Queer Phenomenology,* 168.

18  The word furnish is said to be cognate with the Old High German *frumjan*, and the Old English *fremian*, both meaning "to perform."

19  Ibid.

20  Ahmed, *Queer Phenomenology,* 167.

21  In fact, several practitioners have been directly inspired by Ahmed's theorization. For example, "The Table" (2019) by a UK based duo known as Sophie + Kerri (Sophie Chapman and Kerri Jefferis), was developed in collaboration with carpenter Haroon Ishaq and architect Jon Orlek, and they cite Ahmed's *Queer Phenomenology* as a primary reference point. It is a modular table designed so that it can be reassembled and rearranged by those who use it, prompting participation and a host of orientations, inspired by histories of activism and groups sharing knowledge via the kitchen table. Sophie and Kerri, "The Table," accessed October 13, 2023, https:// sophiechapman.com/the-table.

22  Ahmed, *Queer Phenomenology,* 6.

23  Ibid., 1.

24  Raul De Lara interview with Daniel Fountain, June 11, 2024.

25  Ibid.

26  Ibid.

27  Ibid.

28  Ibid.

29  Raul De Lara (@rauldelaraa), "Soft Chair (M1) – 2023," *Instagram*, March 18, 2023, https://www.instagram.com/rauldelaraa/p/Cp7iCMoLGLV/.

30  Raul De Lara interview with Daniel Fountain, June 11, 2024.

31  Ibid.

32  Images of these works can be seen via De Lara's website: Raul De Lara, "Thinking Chair," accessed June 26, 2024, https://www.rauldelara.com/new-page-69; Raul De

Lara, "A Korean Affair," accessed June 26, 2024, https://www.rauldelara.com/new -page-5.

33 Raul De Lara interview with Daniel Fountain, June 11, 2024.

34 David Getsy, *Queer Behavior: Scott Burton and Performance Art* (Chicago, IL: The University of Chicago Press, 2022). For more on Getsy's work on Scott Burton, also see: David Getsy, *Scott Burton: Collected Writings on Art and Performance, 1965–1975* (Chicago, IL: Soberscove Press, 2012).

35 Raul De Lara interview with Daniel Fountain, June 11, 2024.

36 Ibid.

37 Ibid.

38 Ibid.

39 Ibid.

40 Ibid.

41 Sara Ahmed, *The Cultural Politics of Emotion* (Edinburgh: Edinburgh University Press, 2004), 155.

42 Ibid.,147.

43 Images can be seen via De Lara's website: Raul De Lara, "The Wait (Again)," accessed June 26, 2024, https://www.rauldelara.com/#/the-wait-again/.

44 Raul De Lara interview with Daniel Fountain, June 11, 2024.

45 Ibid.

46 Ibid.

47 The Hopper Prize, "Raul De Lara," accessed June 26, 2024, https://hopperprize.org/ raul-de-lara-interview/.

48 Ahmed, *Queer Phenomenology*, 167.

49 Yénika Castillo Muñoz, "Staying Diasporic: Centering Migrant and Diasporic Ways of Being in Design" (Paper Presented at Pivot 2021, Online, July 2021), 341–8 (341), https://dl.designresearchsociety.org/cgi/viewcontent.cgi?article=1071&context =pluriversaldesign.

50 Özlem Savaş, "Taste Diaspora: The Aesthetic and Material Practice of Belonging," *Journal of Material Culture*, Vol. 19, No. 2 (2014): 185–208 (185). Also see: Anne-Marie Fortier, "'Coming Home': Queer Migrations and Multiple Evocations of Home," *European Journal of Cultural Studies*, Vol. 4, No. 4 (2001): 405–24; B Camminga and John Marnell, eds., *Queer and Trans African Mobilities: Migration, Asylum and Diaspora* (London: Bloomsbury, 2022). Eithne Luibhéid and Karma R. Chávez, eds., *Queer and Trans Migrations: Dynamics of Illegalization, Detention, and Deportation* (Urbana, IL: University of Illinois Press, 2020).

51 Debika Ray, "Making Yourself At Home," *Financial Times*, July 29, 2023, 6.

52 Raul De Lara's interview with Daniel Fountain, June 11, 2024.

53 Maxwell Hanrahan Foundation, "2024 Awards in Craft: Raul De Lara," accessed June 26, 2024, https://www.maxwell-hanrahan.org/blog/2024-awards-in-craft-raul-de-lara.

54 Reynolds Gallery, "Raul de Lara," accessed October 5, 2023, https://www .reynoldsgallery.com/news/in-the-studio/raul-de-lara-2/#:~:text=Wood%20is %20generally%20my%20first,are%20smuggled%20into%20the%20country.

55 Ibid.

56 Raul De Lara's interview with Daniel Fountain, June 11, 2024.

57 For more on this, see: Jodi Frawley and Iain McCalman, eds., *Rethinking Invasion Ecologies from the Environmental Humanities* (London and New York: Routledge, 2014); Richard Grove, *Green Imperialism: Colonial Expansion, Tropical Island Edens and the Origins of Environmentalism, 1600–1860* (Cambridge: Cambridge University

Press, 1995); Reuben P. Keller, Marc W. Cadotte, and Glenn Sandiford, eds., *Invasive Species in a Globalised World: Ecological, Global, and Legal Perspectives on Policy* (Chicago, IL and London: The University of Chicago Press, 2014).

58 Visser, *Joinery, Joists and Gender*, 4.

59 Reynolds Gallery, "Raul de Lara."

60 Raul De Lara's interview with Daniel Fountain, June 11, 2024.

61 Images of these works can be seen via De Lara's website: Raul De Lara, "Live Laugh Love," accessed June 26, 2024, https://www.rauldelara.com/#/live-love-laugh/.

62 Raul De Lara's interview with Daniel Fountain, June 11, 2024.

63 Ogunro, "About"; Keren Dillard, "The Dwell 24: Nifemi Ogunro," accessed June 26, 2024, https://www.dwell.com/article/the-dwell-24-nifemi-ogunro-b9d958a5.

64 Nifemi Ogunro (@blonder.than.necessary), "A Lil Preview of Topé," *Instagram*, May 9, 2020, https://www.instagram.com/p/B_-HOUcFEeI/?igsh=d210NzN6dGN6MGdw.

65 Sight Unseen, "Nifemi Ogunro," accessed June 26, 2024, https://www.sightunseen .com/designers/nifemi-ogunro/

66 Sara Ahmed, "Queer Use," *Feministkilljoys*, November 8, 2018, https://feministkilljoys .com/2018/11/08/queer-use/

67 Sara Ahmed, *What's The Use?: On The Uses of Use* (Durham, NC: Duke University Press, 2019), 199.

68 Nifemi Ogunro's interview with Daniel Fountain June 27, 2024.

69 Ibid.

70 Marina Felix, "This Brooklyn Artist Wants to Change the Way You See Furniture," *Business of Home*, accessed October 5, 2023, https://businessofhome.com/articles/this -brooklyn-artist-wants-to-change-the-way-you-see-furniture#:~:text="I%20was%2 0able%20to%20not,long%20as%20it%20still1%20worked. Emphasis my own.

71 Nifemi Ogunro interview with Daniel Fountain June 27, 2024.

72 Felix, "This Brooklyn Artist Wants to Change the Way You See Furniture."

73 Nifemi Ogunro interview with Daniel Fountain June 27, 2024.

74 Camille Okhio, "Nifemi Ogunro Talks Design and Family," *Wallpaper*, August 1, 2022, accessed June 26, 2024, https://www.wallpaper.com/design/nifemi-ogunro -designer-profile.

75 Ibid.

76 Ibid.

77 Nifemi Ogunro's interview with Daniel Fountain June 27, 2024.

78 Annie Block, "Nifemi Ogunro Debuts Sculptural Wood Furnishings," *Interior Design*, June 1, 2021, https://interiordesign.net/products/nifemi-ogunro-debuts-sculptural -wood-furnishings/#:~:text="Textures%20are%20an%20interesting%20way,with %20herself%20as%20the%20model.

79 Shelter in Place Artist Residency, "BE U 2020," *YouTube*, accessed October 12, 2023, https://www.youtube.com/watch?v=xghneNqt9bM&t=1s; Shelter in Place Artist Residency, "Untitled, 2020," *YouTube*, accessed October 12, 2023, https://www .youtube.com/watch?v=sAXJtfi82fg.

80 Block, "Nifemi Ogunro Debuts Sculptural Wood Furnishings."

81 Ibid.

82 Michele Gorman, Yvette Chaparro, and Preeti Gopinath, eds., *The Decolonized Decarbonized Dinner Party* (New York: Parsons The New School, 2022), https://issuu .com/newschool/docs/d_d_workingdoc.

83 Nifemi Ogunro's interview with Daniel Fountain April 18, 2024.

84 Ibid.

85   The exhibition ran from the May 11 to July 14, 2023 and was curated by Luis Sendino
     at the gallery space in Barcelona. Side Gallery, "Nifemi Ogunro," accessed June
     26, 2024, https://side-gallery.com/nifemi_ogunro_aside_2023/#:~:text=Ogunro
     %20comments%20on%20her%20collaboration,soft%20enough%20to%20be
     %20inviting.
86   Ibid.
87   Nifemi Ogunro's interview with Daniel Fountain June 27, 2024.
88   Side Gallery, "Nifemi Ogunro."
89   Nifemi Ogunro's interview with Daniel Fountain April 18, 2024.
90   Ibid.
91   Ibid.
92   Culture Push, "Fall 2023 Black Utopian Fellow," accessed June 26, 2024, https://www
     .culturepush.org/nifemi-ogunro.
93   Ibid.


## *Chapter 4: Paper*


1    Historical sources largely credit the invention of paper and the papermaking process
     to a Chinese dignitary named Cai (Ts'ai) Lun (c.5062 – 121 CE), who, in 105 CE,
     began producing sheets of paper using mulberry and other bast fibres along with
     scraps of old rags, tree bark, hemp waste, and fishing nets. For more on papermaking
     history, see: Dard Hunter, *Papermaking: The History and Technique of an Ancient
     Craft* (New York: Dover Publications, Inc., 1978); Lisa Gitelman, *Paper Knowledge:
     Toward a Media History of Documents* (Durham, NC: Duke University Press, 2014);
     Neil Holt, Nicola von Velsen and Stephanie Jacobs, *Paper: Material, Medium and
     Magic* (London: Prestel, 2018); Mark Kurlansky, *Paper: Paging Through History* (New
     York: W.W.Norton & Company Ltd, 2016).
2    Adamson, *Thinking Through Craft*, 1.
3    The exhibition ran from October 7, 2009 to April 4, 2010. Museum of Arts and
     Design, "Slash: Paper Under the Knife," accessed July 23, 2022, https://madmuseum
     .org/exhibition/slash.
4    David Revere McFadden, *Slash: Paper Under the Knife* (New York: Museum of Arts
     and Design, 2009), 11.
5    Oliver Herring also knitted with other mundane materials such as tape, mylar, and
     plastic bags. For more on Herring's series *A Flower for Ethyl Eichelberger* (1991–
     2001), and his more recent life-size paper sculptures, see: Ian Berry, *Oliver Herring:
     Me Us Them* (Saratoga Springs, NY: The Frances Young Tang Teaching Museum
     and Art Gallery, 2010); Daniel Fountain, "All That Glitters Is Gold: Queering Waste
     Through Campy Craft" (PhD Thesis, Loughborough University, 2021), 165–75.
6    *Cock, Paper, Scissors* was on display from April 2 to July 10, 2016. See: David Evans
     Frantz, Lucas Hilderbrand, and Kayleigh Perkov, ed., *Cock, Paper, Scissors*, exh. cat.
     (Los Angeles, CA: One Archives, 2016).
7    Ibid., 7.
8    Ahmed, *What's The Use?*, 44.
9    Getsy, *Queer*, 15.
10   Ahmed, *What's The Use?*, 208. Emphasis in original.

11  Ibid., 198–208; Judith Butler, *Bodies That Matter: On the Discursive Limits of "Sex"* (London: Routledge, 1993), 228.

12  Ka-Ming Wu, *Reinventing Chinese Tradition: The Cultural Politics of Late Socialism* (Urbana, IL: University of Illinois Press, 2015), 35; Daoyi Zhang, *Zhongguo Minjian Jianzhi [Chinese Folk Paper-Cuts]* (Jiansu: Jinlin Shuhua Chubanshe, 1980), 7.

13  Ibid., 34.

14  Ibid.; Natalie Avella, "Introduction," in *Paper Cutting: Contemporary Artists, Timeless Craft*, ed. Laura Heyenga (San Francisco, CA: Chronicle Books LLC, 2011), 9–17 (9). For more on the traditions of paper cutting in China and East Asia more broadly see: Roderick Cave, *Chinese Paper Offerings* (Oxford: Oxford University Press, 1998); Hang Jian and Guo Qiuhui, *Chinese Arts and Crafts: History, Techniques and Legends* (Cambridge: Cambridge University Press, 2012).

15  Adamson, *Thinking Through Craft*, 5.

16  Yuko Kikuchi, "The Craft Debate at the Crossroads of Global Visual Culture: Re-centring Craft in Postmodern and Postcolonial Histories," *World Art*, Vol. 5, No. 1 (April 2015): 87–115 (90).

17  Wu, *Reinventing Chinese Tradition*, 31–63.

18  Ibid., 35.

19  Antonius-Tín Bui, "About," accessed August 1, 2022, http://www.antoniusbui.com/about.

20  Ibid.

21  moniquemeloche, "Antonius Bui: The Detour is To Be Where We Are," accessed August 1, 2022, https://www.moniquemeloche.com/exhibitions/187-antonius-bui-the-detour-is-to-be-where/press_release_text/.

22  Antonius-Tín Bui, "Not Sorry for the Trouble," accessed August 1, 2022, http://www.antoniusbui.com/2019-1#/not-sorry-for-the-trouble/.

23  See: Christopher T. Conner, "The Gay Gayze: Expressions of Inequality on Grindr," *The Sociological Quarterly*, Vol. 60, No. 3 (2019): 397–419 (409); Xiaofei Liu, "No Fats, Femmes, or Asian," *Moral Philosophy and Politics*, Vol. 2, No. 2 (2015): 255–76.

24  Muñoz, *Disidentifications*, 170. Emphasis mine.

25  moniquemeloche, "Antonius Bui: The Detour is To Be Where We Are."

26  Francesca Gavin, "The Personal is Political: A Conversation with Antonius-Tin Bui," *Independent*, April 2023, accessed June 23, 2024, https://www.independenthq.com/features/the-personal-is-political-a-conversation-with-antonius-tin-bui.

27  Ibid.

28  Amanda Quinn Olivar, "Antonius-Tin Bui," *Curator*, accessed August 1, 2021, http://curator.site/interviews/2019/4/1/antonius-bui.

29  For more on the importance of zines and queer print in queer culture, see: Allan Madden, "(Re)Collecting Queer Craft: Ownership, Identity and Remembrance in Queer Zine Collecting," in *Crafted with Pride: Queer Craft and Activism in Contemporary Britain*, ed. Daniel Fountain (Bristol and Chicago, IL: Intellect and The University of Chicago Press, 2023), 77–92; A. A. Bronson and Philip Aarons, "AA Bronson interviews Philip Aarons," in *Queer Zines*, ed. A. A. Bronson and P. Aarons (New York and Rotterdam: Printed Matter Inc. and Witte de With Center for Contemporary Art 2008), 10–13; Glyn Davis and Laura Guy, ed., *Queer Print in Europe* (London: Bloomsbury, 2022).

30  moniquemeloche, "Antonius Bui: The Detour is To Be Where We Are."

31  Staci Boris, *Antonius Bui: The Detour is To Be Where We Are* (Chicago, IL: Monique Meloche Gallery, 2021), 65.

32  Muñoz, *Cruising Utopia*, 11.

33  Laura Kina and Jan Christian Bernabe, *Queering Asian American Art* (Washington, DC: University of Washington Press, 2017), 8.

34  Grace Kyungwon Hong and Roderick A. Ferguson, *Strange Affinities: The Gender and Sexual Politics of Comparative Racialization* (Durham, NC: Duke University Press, 2011), 2. Emphasis mine.

35  Peggy McIntosh, "White Privilege: Unpacking the Invisible Knapsack," *Peace and Freedom*, July/August 1989 (1989): 10–12 (10).

36  Quinn Olivar, "Antonius-Tin Bui."

37  Staci Boris, *Antonius Bui: The Detour is To Be Where We Are*, 65.

38  Popular collage books such as *The Age of Collage* (2013) state that "Collage first emerged as an art form in Cubism" with the likes of Braque and Picasso." See: Silke Krohn, Dennis H. Busch, Henni Hellige, and Robert Klanten, eds., *The Age of Collage: Contemporary Collage in Modern Art* (Berlin: Die Gestalten Verlag, 2013), 4–5.

39  See: Elkins, *Crafting Feminism from Literary Modernism to the Multimedia Present*, 169–200.

40  I first wrote about queer collage in relation to the work of Hannah Höch, my own creative practice, and the writings of Jack Halberstam for the *Collage Research Network*: Daniel Fountain, "The Art of Hannah Höch: Queering Collage Via Jack Halberstam," *Collage Research Network*, June 13, 2019, accessed August 1, 2022, https://collageresearchnetwork.wordpress.com/2019/06/13/the-art-of-hannah-hoch -queering-collage-via-jack-halberstam/.

41  Jack Halberstam, *The Queer Art of Failure* (Durham, NC and London: Duke University Press, 2011), 136.

42  Ibid.

43  Ibid.; Fountain, "The Art of Hannah Höch: Queering Collage Via Jack Halberstam."

44  Company Gallery, "Troy Montes-Michie," accessed May 30, 2024, https:// companygallery.us/artists/troy-montes-michie.

45  Brent Hayes Edwards and Troy Montes-Michie, "The Alchemy of the Border," in *Troy Montes-Michie: Rock of Eye*, ed. Andrea Andersson and Lisa Pearson (New York: Siglio, 2021), 36–43 (39).

46  The exhibition ran from September 27, 2017 to January 21, 2018. New Museum, "Trigger: Gender as a Tool and a Weapon," acessed August 5, 2022, https://www .newmuseum.org/exhibitions/view/trigger-gender-as-a-tool-and-as-a-weapon.

47  Other featured practitioners in the exhibition who explore queer collage in their practice include Paul Mpagi Sepuya (b.1982, USA), Tschabalala Self (b.1990, USA), Candice Lin (b.1979, USA), Mickalene Thomas (b.1971, USA), and Chris E Vargas (b.1978, USA).

48  Rasheeda Saka, "The Beholder," *Alta*, December 20, 2021, accessed August 4, 2022, https://www.altaonline.com/books/photography/a38507995/troy-montes-michie -rock-of-eye-book-review/.

49  Edwards and Montes-Michie, "The Alchemy of the Border," 39.

50  Russel Tovey and Robert Diament, "Troy Michie (QuarARTine Special Episode)," *Talk Art* (podcast), Season 6, Episode 1, April 10, 2020, accessed 1 November, 2022, https://podcasts.apple.com/gb/podcast/troy-michie-quarartine-special-episode/ id1439567112?i=1000477238479.

51  André-Naquian Wheeler, "Troy Michie is Making Collage Art a Little More Queer," *i-D*, March 30, 2018, accessed August 4, 2022, https://i-d.vice.com/en_uk/article /9kg3yp/troy-michie-is-making-collage-art-a-little-more-queer.

52   Halberstam, *The Queer Art of Failure*, 140.
53   Edwards and Montes-Michie, "The Alchemy of the Border."
54   Kathy Peiss, *Zoot Suit: The Enigmatic Career of an Extreme Style* (Philadelphia, PA: University of Pennsylvania Press, 2011).
55   Although the zoot suit was much more popular among men, it was sometimes a style worn by both men and women. In Montes-Michie's 2022 solo exhibition at Company Gallery in New York titled *Dishwater Holds No Images*, he drew attention to the relationships between the zoot suit and gender, specifically through several collages referencing female zoot suiters, including in *Versatility* (2022) and *Romona* (2022). For more on gender and the zoot suit, see: Catherine S. Ramírez, *The Woman in the Zoot Suit: Gender, Nationalism, and the Cultural Politics of Memory* (Durham, NC: Duke University Press, 2009).
56   *Rock of Eye* ran from February 16 to September 4, 2022.
57   Sharon Mizota, "Fugitive Practice: Troy Montes-Michie's *Rock of Eye*," *BOMB*, March 16, 2022, accessed August 5, 2022, https://bombmagazine.org/articles/fugitive -practice-troy-montes-michies-rock-of-eye-reviewed/.
58   Penrose later taught at a range of other institutions too, such as the Eastern Command Camouflage School in Norwich, and at the Camouflage Development and Training Centre at Farnham Castle, Surrey.
59   Wheeler, "Troy Michie is Making Collage Art a Little More Queer."
60   See: David J. Getsy and Jennifer Doyle, "Queer Formalisms: David J. Getsy and Jennifer Doyle in Conversation," *Art Journal*, Vol. 72, No. 4 (2013): 58–71; David J. Getsy, *Abstract Bodies: Sixties Sculpture in the Expanded Field of Gender* (New Haven, CT: Yale University Press, 2015); David J. Getsy, "Ten Queer Theses on Abstraction," in *Queer Abstraction*, exh. cat., ed. Jared Ledesma (Des Moines: Des Moines Art Center, 2019), 65–75; Lex Morgan Lancaster, *Dragging Away: Queer Abstraction in Contemporary Art* (Durham, NC: Duke University Press, 2022).

## Chapter 5: Metal

1   This acronym stands for Two-Spirit, Lesbian, Gay, Bisexual, Transgender, Queer and/ or Questioning, Intersex, and Asexual. The plus symbol indicates the range of other ways a person may self-identify. Although I use LGBTQ+ throughout the book, Queer Metalsmiths use this specific acronym in their "about us" statement and so it is replicated here.
2   Queer Metalsmiths, "About," accessed February 8, 2023, https://www .queermetalsmiths.com; Society of Inclusive Blacksmiths, accessed February 8, 2023, https://www.inclusiveblacksmiths.com. Both these organizations were founded in the United States, but they have had international reach and in recent years have connected with wider communities through digital platforms and opportunities.
3   Craftspace, "Queer + Metals," accessed February 28, 2023, https://craftspace.co.uk/ queer-metals/.
4   This was co-curated by Craftspace Director Deirdre Figueiredo in collaboration with Rebekah Frank and Dauvit Alexander. Exhibitors included in the Queer + Metals exhibition were Annie Higgins, Fei Hei, Dauvit Alexander, Gilbert Hadden, John Moore, Theo Somerville-Scott, Mark Newman, and Roxanne Simone.

5   Roxanne Simone, "Bio," accessed November 23, 2023, https://www.roxannesimone
    .com/bio. Hydroforming involves using highly pressurized liquid (usually water)
    to adapt the shape and form of metal. In Simone's work, it gives the impression of
    "inflating" two sheets of welded metal. Simone likes to push the metal beyond its
    limits, embracing the concept of "imperfect" objects and they revealed that they see
    this process as a way of conceptually "exploding" boundaries within contemporary
    craft.

6   For more on queer jewelry adjacent practices, see Rebekah Frank's three-part article
    series for *Art Jewelry Forum* which covers the adorned boxing gloves of Demetri
    Broxton, the synthetic and human hair works by Angela Hennessy, and the Native
    beadwork of Hollis Chitto. Rebekah Frank, "Jewelry||Adjacent: Demetri Broxton's
    Beaded Boxing Gloves, Investigating Race, Masculinity, and Sport in the United
    States," *Art Jewelry Forum*, March 8, 2021, accessed February 2, 2023, https://
    artjewelryforum.org/articles/demetri-broxtonaes-beaded-boxing-gloves/; Rebekah
    Frank, "Jewlery||Adjacent: Angela Hennessy, The Presence of Absence," *Art Jewelry
    Forum*, May 17, 2021, accessed February 2, 2023, https://artjewelryforum.org/articles
    /angela-hennessy/; Rebekah Frank, "Jewlery||Adjacent: Hollis Chitto, Blurring
    Traditions in Native Beadwork," November 15, 2021, accessed February 2, 2023,
    https://artjewelryforum.org/articles/hollis-chitto/.

7   Hansel Tai interview with Daniel Fountain, January 30, 2023.

8   Ibid.

9   Ibid.

10  The earliest recorded use of the term "faggot" I found in print dates from 1914 in
    Louis E. Jackson and C. R. Hellyer, *A Vocabulary of Criminal Slang, With Some
    Examples of Common Usages* (Portland, OR: Modern Printing Co., 1914), 80. The
    term has been widely used by many gay writers, artists and activists, most notably in
    Larry Mitchell's infamous novel *The Faggots and Their Friends Between Revolutions*
    which draws on his experience of queer communal living in the 1970s, and his
    solidarity with feminist activists: Larry Mitchell, *The Faggots and Their Friends
    Between Revolutions* (New York: Calamus Books, 1977).

11  NRTN, "Major General II Brooch," accessed October 25, 2023, https://nrtnlab.com/
    product/major-general-ii-brooch/.

12  BDSM is a variety of often erotic practices or roleplaying involving bondage,
    discipline, dominance and submission, sadomasochism, and other related
    interpersonal dynamics and subcultures. The acronym 'BDSM' is often used and
    interpreted as a combination of the abbreviations B/D (Bondage and Discipline), D/s
    (Dominance and submission), and S/M (Sadism and Masochism). See: Adam Geczy
    and Vicki Karaminas, "Kiss of the Whip: Bondage, Discipline and Sadomasochism,
    or BDSM Style," in *Queer Style*, ed. Adam Geczy and Vicki Karaminas (London:
    Bloomsbury, 2013), 99–110. "Military Realness" has also been one of the main
    categories in American ballroom and drag. See: Martha Gever, Pratibha Parmar, and
    John Greyson, eds., *Queer Looks: Perspectives on Lesbian and Gay Film and Video*
    (New York: Routledge, 1993), 109.

13  See: Paul Baker, *Polari: The Lost Language of Gay Men* (London: Routledge, 2002),
    123; J. Raúl Cornier, "Hanky Panky: An Abridged History of the Hanky Code," *The
    History Project*, April 23, 2019, accessed November 14, 2020, https://historyproject
    .org/news/2019-04/hanky-panky-abridged-history-hanky-code-0.

14  For more, see: Eleanor Medhurst, "Lez Accessorise: Carabiners and Rings as
    Lesbian Signals," *DressingDykes*, May 14, 2021, accessed February 26, 2024, https://

dressingdykes.com/2021/05/14/lez-accessorise/; Christina Cauterucci, "Lesbians and Key Rings: A Cultural Love Story," *Slate*, December 21, 2016, accessed April 19, 2024, https://slate.com/human-interest/2016/12/the-lesbian-love-of-key-rings-and-carabiners-explained.html; Eleanor Medhurst, *Unsuitable: A History of Lesbian Fashion* (London: C. Hurst & Co Publishers Ltd, 2024).

15  Hansel Tai's interview with Daniel Fountain, January 30, 2023.

16  Ibid.

17  For more on queer identity and body modifications, see: Victoria Pitts, *In the Flesh: The Cultural Politics of Body Modification* (New York: Palgrave Macmillan, 2003); Mike Featherstone, *Body Modification* (London: SAGE Publications, 2000); Lisiunia A. Romanienko, *Body Piercing and Identity Construction: A Comparative Perspective—New York, New Orleans, Wroclaw* (New York: Palgrave Macmillan, 2011).

18  Victoria Pitts, "Visibly Queer: Body Technologies and Sexual Politics," *The Sociological Quarterly*, Vol. 41, No. 3 (2000): 443–63 (446).

19  Although rarely discussed in the field of craft studies, this conversation has, of course, played out in the field of fashion theory for decades. See: Frenchy Lunning, *Fetish Style* (New York: Bloomsbury, 2013); Valerie Steele, *Fetish: Fashion, sex, and power* (New York: Oxford University Press, 1996).

20  Tom Cubbin, "Crafting Fetish Across Materials and Sexual Styles: An Interview with Skeeter of Mr. S Leather," *The Journal of Modern Craft*, Vol. 13, No. 2 (2020): 179–87 (180).

21  Hansel Tai's interview with Daniel Fountain, January 30, 2023.

22  See: Richard Sennett, *The Craftsman* (London: Penguin Books, 2008), 149; Raymond Tallis, *The Hand: A Philosophical Inquiry in Human Being* (Edinburgh: Edinburgh University Press, 2003).

23  David Pye, *The Nature and Art of Workmanship* (London: The Herbert Press, 1968 [1995]), 26.

24  Ibid., 25.

25  Hansel Tai's interview with Daniel Fountain, January 30, 2023.

26  Ibid.

27  Ibid.

28  Malcolm McCullough, *Abstracting Craft: The Practiced Digital Hand* (Cambridge, MA: MIT Press, 1998), 35–6.

29  For examples of these works, see: Hansel Tai, "Dirt Container / ON," accessed February 26, 2024. https://hanseltai.com/Dirt-Container-ON.

30  Hansel Tai's interview with Daniel Fountain, January 30, 2023.

31  Ibid.

32  Abe Heath's interview with Daniel Fountain, June 6, 2024.

33  Ibid.

34  Ibid.

35  Affect Metals, "Metal Flogger," accessed October 19, 2023, https://www.affectmetals.com/product-page/metal-flogger.

36  Abe Heath's interview with Daniel Fountain, June 6, 2024.

37  Ibid.

38  Ibid.

39  Tattoodo, "Queer Armor: Collector and Creator Abe Heath of Affect Metals," February 4, 2020, accessed October 19, 2023, https://www.tattoodo.com/articles/queer-armor-collector-and-creator-abe-of-affect-metals-150032.

40   Transgender activist and writer Leslie Feinberg especially popularized the notion
     of Joan of Arc as being an important trans historical figure in the book *Transgender
     Warriors*. See: Leslie Feinberg, *Transgender Warriors: Making History From Joan of
     Arc to Dennis Rodman* (Boston, MA: Beacon Press, 1996).
41   Abe Heath's interview with Daniel Fountain, June 6, 2024.
42   Affect Metals (@affect.metals), "One of My Favorite and Most Enduring Creations is
     the Strap on Harness . . .," *Instagram*, February 25, 2022, accessed February 7, 2024,
     https://www.instagram.com/affect.metals/p/Caa1x1zP5GM/.
43   Berlant and Warner, "Sex in Public," 558.
44   Ibid., 562.
45   Ibid.
46   Ibid., 563.
47   Bryan-Wilson, *Fray*, 40.
48   Ibid.; Dorothy Allison, *Skin: Talking about Sex, Class, and Literature* (Ithaca, NY:
     Firebrand Books, 1994), 130–1.
49   Affect Metals, "Strap on Harness," accessed October 19, 2023, https://www
     .affectmetals.com/product-page/strap-on-harness.
50   Ibid.
51   Voyage LA, "Meet Abe Heath of Affect Metals in Northeast LA (Glassell Park),"
     September 16, 2019, accessed February 7, 2024, https://voyagela.com/interview/meet
     -abe-heath-affect-metals-northeast-la/.
52   Audre Lorde, *Uses of the Erotic: The Erotic as Power* (Trumansburg, NY: Out and Out
     Books, 1978), 1–10.
53   Abe Heath's interview with Daniel Fountain, 6 June, 2024.
54   Ibid.
55   Ibid.
56   Ibid.
57   Erin J. Rand, "'Soft Armour' for Ugly Bodies," in *The Routledge Handbook of Queer
     Rhetoric*, ed. Jacqueline Rhodes and Jonathan Alexander (London and New York:
     Routledge, 2022), 365–74 (365).
58   Ibid., Emphasis mine.
59   Abe Heath's interview with Daniel Fountain, June 6, 2024.
60   Leonard Diepeveen and Timothy van Laar, *Shiny Things: Reflective Surfaces and Their
     Mixed Meanings* (Bristol: Intellect Books, 2021), 22.
61   Ibid.
62   Ibid., 40.
63   Abe Heath's interview with Daniel Fountain, June 6, 2024.
64   See: Roland Barthes, *The Neutral*, trans. Rosalind E. Krauss and Denis Hollier (New
     York: Columbia University Press, [2002] 2005); Michel Foucault, *The History of
     Sexuality*, Vol. 1: *An Introduction [Will to Knowledge]* [1976], trans. Robert Hurley
     (New York: Vintage Books, 1978), 59 ; Susan Stryker, "Christine in the Cutting Room:
     Cinema, Surgery and Celebrity in the Career of Christine Jorgensen" (Paper Presented
     at the Department of Media, Music, Communication and Cultural Studies Public
     Lecture Series, Macquarie University, Sydney, Australia, May 1, 2013), August 16, 2013,
     accessed March 19, 2023, https://www.youtube.com/watch?v=XlqJ8B9dKCs.
65   Eliza Steinbock, *Shimmering Images: Trans Cinema, Embodiment, and the Aesthetics of
     Change* (Durham, NC: Duke University Press, 2019), ix.
66   Ibid., 12.
67   Ibid., 9.

## *Chapter 6: Glass*

1   Tim Tate's interview with Daniel Fountain, December 5, 2022. For more information on Tate's work, see: Tim Tate, "About," accessed April 19, 2024, https://www.timtateglass.com/about.

2   At the time of writing, we are working together on a traveling exhibition titled "Imagining Utopia." The exhibition marks an exciting new direction for Tate's practice and explores themes of queer worldmaking, imagining what a queer, inclusive and socially just future would look like.

3   Tim Tate's interview with Daniel Fountain, December 5, 2022.

4   Ibid.

5   Kim Harty, "Foreword: Consequences of Transparency," in *Transparency*, ed. National Liberty Museum (Philadelphia, PA: National Liberty Museum, 2017), 5–7 (5).

6   The exhibition then traveled to the Museum of Glass in Tacoma, Washington, in 2019. In addition to Tim Tate, the exhibition also included works by Tamás Ábel, Nancy Callan, Joseph Cavalieri, Pearl Dick, Sarah Gilbert, Kim Harty, Joshua Hershman, Eric Hess, Niki Hildebrand, Carmichael Jones, Sabrina Knowles/Jenny Pohlman, Drew Mattei, Natalie Hope McDonald, Amanda Nardone, Ronnie Phillips, Brandon Robinson (Glass Munky), Joseph Sircoulomb, Davis Thal, Wes Valdez, Jeff Zimmer, and Walter Zimmerman.

7   Many scholars situate the origins of "glass art" or "studio glass" in the mid twentieth century and claim that it particularly arose in post-war Europe, but it does have origins worldwide. Geoffrey Edwards, *Art of Glass: Glass in the Collection of the National Gallery of Victoria* (Melbourne: National Gallery of Victoria, 1998), 182.

8   In 2020, Whiteside also launched Sticky Glass, a design company that specializes in multi-functional, performative, and collaborative glasswork, entirely hand-blown by Whiteside and a team of LGBTQ+, POC, and female-identifying practitioners in Brooklyn, New York. See: Grace Whiteside, "Homosilica: Glass Is Gay," accessed May 1, 2024, https://gracewhiteside.com/section/509671-Homosilica-Glass-is-Gay.html; Sticky Glass, "About," accessed May 1, 2024, https://stickyglass.com.

9   Harty, "Foreword," 5.

10  The Tate Gallery Archive (Reference TGA 201,919,) hold the archive of Hamad Butt which dates from 1980–1994, comprising of preparatory and documentary material for *Transmission* (1990) and *Familiars* (1992), as well as other work. Also see: Tate Archive and Public Records Catalogue, "Butt, Hamad," accessed May 1, 2024, https://archive.tate.org.uk/Record.aspx?src=CalmView.Catalog&id=TGA+201,919&pos=1; Hamad Butt, "About," accessed May 1, 2024, https://hamadbutt.co.uk/about.

11  At the time of completing this book, Dominic Johnson is in the process of organizing a forthcoming travelling exhibition of Butt's work in collaboration with the IMMA and the Whitechapel Gallery. The display at IMMA will be Butt's first exhibition outside of the UK.

12  Tim Tate's interview with Daniel Fountain, December 5, 2022.

13  Ibid.

14  Ibid. Tate cannot remember the exact date of the work, but suggested it was made some time in the early 1990s, around 1992.

15  Ibid.

16  Art Against AIDS was a series of exhibitions and auctions that aimed to promote awareness of HIV/AIDS while also raising money for various charities and

organizations. Recipients of proceeds included the American Foundation for AIDS Research and Best Friends, Clinical Trials Expanded Access Project, DC Coalition of Black Gay Men and Women, Grandma's House, Us Helping Us, Inc., and the Whitman-Walker Clinic. See: Anne Livet, ed., *Art Against AIDS, Washington, D.C.: A Sale Exhibition of Contemporary Works of Art* (New York: American Foundation for AIDS Research, 1990).

17  Images featuring New York Police Department (NYPD) officers at the time often show black rubber or black leather gloves being worn, as opposed to yellow gloves. However, the yellow marigolds may have been used among civilians and anti-LGBTQ+ protestors. This also became a running joke among AIDS activists who highlighted the ridiculousness of this act. In 1987, British comedian Paul O'Grady was arrested in drag, as his stage persona Lily Savage, while performing at the Royal Vauxhall Tavern in London. When police raided the venue wearing rubber gloves, he said: "Well well, looks like we've got help with the washing up!", he recalled in an Instagram comment. Royal Vauxhall Tavern [@rvtofficial], "It's a New Week," *Instagram,* January 25, 2021, https://www.instagram.com/p/CKd2BSSlPrC/.

18  Leo Bersani, *Is The Rectum a Grave? And Other Essays* (Chicago, IL and London: The University of Chicago Press, 2009), 5. It is also important to note that notions of containment are not limited to heterosexual culture alone but are also present within the gay community today where there is still a stigma associated with HIV-positive men.

19  John Balzar, "The Times Poll: Touch New Government Action on AIDS Backed," *Los Angeles Times,* December 19, 1985, accessed November 16, 2020, https://www.latimes.com/archives/la-xpm-1985-12-19-mn-30337-story.html; Robert Steinbrook, "The Times Poll: 42% Would Limit Civil Rights in AIDS Battle," *Los Angeles Times*, July 31, 1987, accessed November 16, 2020, https://www.latimes.com/archives/la-xpm-1987-07-31-mn-217-story.html.

20  Reagan mentioned AIDS for the first time in public on September 17, 1985, but this was only in response to a reporter's question. The first major speech he gave which mentioned AIDS was not until April 2, 1987 when he addressed the College of Physicians in Philadelphia. See: James Gerstenzang and Marlene Cimons, "Reagan Asks Abstinence in Remarks About AIDS," *Los Angeles Times*, April 2, 1987, accessed October 14, 2020, https://www.latimes.com/archives/la-xpm-1987-04-02-mn-1950-story.html.

21  National Library of Medicine, "Some People Think You Can Catch AIDS from a Glass," accessed April 19, 2024, https://collections.nlm.nih.gov/catalog/nlm:nlmuid-101584655X73-img.

22  See: Joan Carroll Cruz, *Relics: What They Are and Why They Matter* (Charlotte, NC: TAN Books, 2015); Peter Brown, *The Cult of the Saints: Its Rise and Function in Latin Christianity* (Chicago, IL: The University of Chicago Press, 2014).

23  Ibid.

24  Tim Tate's interview with Daniel Fountain, December 5, 2022.

25  For further discussion of the pink triangle, see Chapter 1.

26  Tim Tate's interview with Daniel Fountain, 2022.

27  Ibid.

28  Ibid.

29  Ibid. Tate also references the AIDS Quilt, which greatly inspired him. When he visited the AIDS Quilt for the first time in his hometown of Washington, DC, there was a ceremony where people took turns reading all the names memorialized as

part of the quilt. He recalled an epiphany of hearing Keith Haring reading Robert Mapplethorpe's name, and it was then he realized he wanted to make a tangible legacy through making.

30  Oxford English Dictionary, "Blackball," accessed April 19, 2024, https://www.oed.com /dictionary/blackball_v?tab=meaning_and_use&tl=true#19,433,991.

31  Tim Tate interview with Daniel Fountain, 2022.

32  Ibid.

33  Ibid.

34  "Infinity" mirrors are made by a configuration of two or more parallel or angled mirrors, which are arranged in such a way that they create a sort of "tunnel" effect where reflections get smaller and smaller and appear to repeat endlessly. They were first by Tate as a way of imagining the countless lives lost to HIV/AIDS during the early years of the epidemic but also of remembering and commemorating them, such as in *We Rose Up* (2007).

35  Foster and Tawadros (eds.), *Familiars*, 10. For example, Kevil Brazil and Nathan Ladd, position him an installation artist contrary to Butt's own rejection of this label. Kevin Brazil, "The Uses of Queer Art," October 2018, accessed May 2, 2024, https:// www.thewhitereview.org/feature/uses-queer-art/.; Nathan Ladd, "Transmission," Tate, March 2019, accessed May 1, 2024, https://www.tate.org.uk/art/artworks/butt -transmission-t15512.

36  Foster and Tawadros (eds.), *Familiars*, 10.

37  Ladd, "Transmission."

38  Butt in Sophia Charalambous, "The British Artist Who Helped Pioneer the Use of Science in Art," July 9, 2019, accessed May 2, 2024, https://elephant.art/british-artist -helped-pioneer-use-science-art/.

39  Ibid.

40  Foster and Tawadros (eds.), *Familiars*, 50.

41  Ibid., 41; Martha Gever, "Pictures of Sickness: Stuart Marshall's Bright Eyes," in *AIDS Cultural Analysis/Cultural Activism*, ed. Douglas Crimp (Cambridge, MA: October Books, 1987), 109–26 (111).

42  Foster and Tawadros (eds.), *Familiars*, 41; Ibid.

43  Ibid.

44  Adrian Flint and Vernon Hewitt, "Colonial Tropes and HIV/AIDS in Africa: Sex, Disease and Race," *Commonwealth & Comparative Politics*, Vol. 53, No. 3 (2015): 294–314.

45  Kaposi's sarcoma or "KS" is a type of cancer that forms in the lining of blood and lymph vessels, forming lesions on the skin that are usually red or brown in color. It is often caused by immune suppression and as a result is relatively common among people living with HIV/AIDS. Foster and Tawadros (eds.), *Familiars*, 41.

46  Due to the limitations of image printing in academic publications, I have been unable to reproduce installation images of the exhibition here, but they are freely available to view online.

47  The YBAs are a loosely defined group of British visual artists who began to exhibit together in the late 1980s. They were largely recognized for their unconventional or "shock" tactics, referred to in some circles as the "hazardists." Many of them graduated from Goldsmiths (or had training at other London based institutions, such as the Royal College of Art), well known examples include the likes of Tracey Emin, Sarah Lucas, and Damien Hirst.

48  Carter in Brazil, "The Uses of Queer Art."

49 The exhibition ran from August 3, 1992 till September 11, 1992. After the exhibition, the John Hansard Gallery and Iniva published an artist's book of the same name which was released posthumously. See: Stephen Foster and Gilane Tawadros, eds., *Familiars: Hamad Butt* (London and Southampton: Institute of International Visual Arts and John Hansard Gallery, 1996).

50 Butt in Page, "Hamad Butt," 38.

51 Ibid., 41.

52 For the 1992 exhibition at the John Hansard Gallery, the catalogue lists the materials as bromine, glass, steel, steel wire, white paint. Foster and Tawadros (eds.), *Familiars*, 34.

53 Page, "Hamad Butt," 36.

54 Charalambous, "The British Artist Who Helped Pioneer the Use of Science in Art."

55 Foster and Tawadros (eds.), *Familiars*, 56.

56 Butt in Clement Page, "Hamad Butt: The art of metachemics," *Third Text*, Vol. 9, No. 32 (1995): 33–42 (35); Foster and Tawadros (eds.), *Familiars*, 36.

57 Foster and Tawadros (eds.), *Familiars*, 43–6.

58 Ibid., 53.

59 Ibid., 39.

60 Ibid., 41.

61 Scholars such as Simon Watney and Douglas Crimp have noted that one of the key reasons there was such a lack of AIDS awareness at the time was because the British government actively banned gay materials coming from the United States. See: Douglas Crimp. "How to Have Promiscuity in an Epidemic," *October*, Vol. 43 (1987): 237–71; Simon Watney, *Policing Desire: Pornography, AIDS, and the Media*, (Minneapolis, MN: University of Minnesota Press, 1987), 13.

62 The volcano appeared in the first iteration of the campaign, while the iceberg was featured in the second, referencing the "hidden" danger, like the submerged portion of an iceberg. Norman Fowler, then Secretary of State for Health and Social Services, felt that Thatcher "wasn't a natural supporter" of the campaign, believing that informing people about HIV and unprotected sex would encourage such practices. See: BFI, "AIDS: Monolith (1987)," *YouTube Video*, May 20, 2016, https://www .youtube.com/watch?v=iroty5zwOVw. Tim Jonze, "It Was a Life-and-Death Situation. Wards Were Full of Young Men Dying: How We Made the Don't Die of Ignorance Aids Campaign," *The Guardian*, September 4, 2017; Norman Fowler, *AIDS: Don't Die of Prejudice* (Hull: Biteback Publishing, 2014).

63 Jonze, "It was a life-and-death situation." Also see Gever's analysis of Stuart Marshall's videotape, *Bright Eyes*, which was produced for Channel Four and was first broadcast in December 1984 and portrayed AIDS as both highly infectious and a national emergency in true hyperbolic fashion, referencing "The Gay Plague," and "Gay Bug." Gever, "Pictures of Sickness: Stuart Marshall's Bright Eyes," 109–26.

64 Foster and Tawadros (eds.), *Familiars*, 43.

65 Ibid., 53.

66 Douglas Crimp, "AIDS: Cultural Analysis/Cultural Activism," *October*, Vol. 43 (Winter 1987): 3–16 (3).

67 Ibid.

68 Foster and Tawadros (eds.), *Familiars*, 11.

69 Ibid., 45.

BIBLIOGRAPHY

ACT UP. "Actions." Accessed October 18, 2020. https://actupny.org/reports.1.html.

Adamson, Glenn. *Thinking Through Craft*. London: Bloomsbury, 2007.

Adamson, Glenn. "When Craft Gets Sloppy." *Crafts*, Vol. 211 (March/April 2008): 36–41.

Affect Metals. "Metal Flogger." Accessed October 19, 2023. https://www.affectmetals.com/product-page/metal-flogger.

Affect Metals. "One of My Favorite and Most Enduring Creations is the Strap on Harness…" *Instagram*, February 25, 2022. Accessed February 7, 2024. https://www.instagram.com/affect.metals/p/Caa1x1zP5GM/.

Affect Metals. "Strap on Harness." Accessed October 19, 2023. https://www.affectmetals.com/product-page/strap-on-harness.

Ahmed, Sara. "Gender Critical = Gender Conservative." *Feministkilljoys*, October 31, 2021. Accessed October 21, 2022. https://feministkilljoys.com/2021/10/31/gender-critical-gender-conservative/comment-page-1/.

Ahmed, Sara. *Queer Phenomenology: Orientations, Objects, Others*. Durham, NC: Duke University Press, 2006.

Ahmed, Sara. "Queer Use." *Feministkilljoys*, November 8, 2018. Accessed October 21, 2022. https://feministkilljoys.com/2018/11/08/queer-use.

Ahmed, Sara. *The Cultural Politics of* Emotion. Edinburgh: Edinburgh University Press, 2004.

Ahmed, Sara. *What's The Use?: On The Uses of Use*. Durham, NC and London: Duke University Press, 2019.

AIDS Quilt. "The AIDS Memorial Quilt." Accessed June 25, 2020. https://www.aidsquilt.org/about/the-aids-memorial-quilt.

Allison, Dorothy. *Skin: Talking about Sex, Class, and Literature*. Ithaca, NY: Firebrand Books, 1994.

Amery, Fran. "'Gender Critical' Feminism as Biopolitical Project." *Sexualities*, May 28, 2024. https://doi.org/10.1177/13634607241257397.

Arabindan-Kesson, Anna. *Black Bodies White Gold*. Durham, NC: Duke University Press, 2021.

Archer, Michael. *Delftware: The Tin-glazed Earthenware of the British Isles – A Catalogue of the Collection in the Victoria and Albert Museum*. London: Stationary Office Books, 1997.

Atluri, Tara. "You Marxist, I Clean Toilet: Racism, Labor, and the Bathroom Attendant." *Frame*, Vol. 1 (Spring 2011): 69–95.

Australian Centre for Contemporary Art. "Paul Yore: WORD MADE FLESH." Accessed October 18, 2023. https://acca.melbourne/exhibition/paul-yore-word-made-flesh.

Auther, Elissa. *String, Felt, Thread: The Hierarchy of Art and Craft in American Art*. Minneapolis, MN: University of Minnesota Press, 2010.

Auther, Elissa, and Elyse Speaks. "Sloppy Craft as Temporal Drag in the Work of Josh Faught." In *Sloppy Craft: Postdisciplinarity and the Crafts*, edited by Elaine C. Paterson and Susan Surette, 45–59. London: Bloomsbury, 2015.

Avella, Natalie. "Introduction." In *Paper Cutting: Contemporary Artists, Timeless Craft*, edited by Laura Heyenga, 9–17. San Francisco, CA: Chronicle Books LLC, 2011.

Baker, Paul. *Polari: The Lost Language of Gay Men*. London: Routledge, 2002.

Balzar, John. "The Times Poll: Touch New Government Action on AIDS Backed." *Los Angeles Times*, December 19, 1985. Accessed November 16, 2020. https://www.latimes.com/archives/la-xpm-1985-12-19- mn-30337-story.html.

Barthes, Roland. *The Neutral*. Translated by Rosalind E. Krauss and Denis Hollier. New York: Columbia University Press, [2002] 2005.

Barzilai, Maya. *Golem: Modern Wars and Their Monsters*. New York: NYU Press, 2016.

Bauman, Zygmunt. *Wasted Lives: Modernity and its Outcasts*. Cambridge: Polity Press, 2004.

Beittel, Kenneth R. "Clay as Elemental Wholeness." In *The Ceramics Reader*, edited by Andrew Livingstone and Kevin Petire, 14–17. London: Bloomsbury, 2017.

Berlant, Lauren, and Michael Warner. "Sex in Public." *Critical Inquiry*, Vol. 24, No. 2 (1998): 547–66.

Berry, Ian. *Oliver Herring: Me Us Them*. Saratoga Springs, NY: The Frances Young Tang Teaching Museum and Art Gallery, 2010.

Bersani, Leo. *Is The Rectum a Grave? And Other Essays*. Chicago, IL: The University of Chicago Press, 2009.

BFI. "AIDS: Monolith (1987)." *YouTube Video*, May 20, 2016. Accessed May 2, 2024. https://www.youtube.com/watch?v=iroty5zwOVw.

Block, Annie. "Nifemi Ogunro Debuts Sculptural Wood Furnishings." *Interior Design*, June 1, 2021, https://interiordesign.net/products/nifemi-ogunro-debuts-sculptural-wood-furnishings/#:~:text="Textures%20are%20an%20interesting%20way,with%20herself%20as%20the%20model.

Boris, Staci. *Antonius Bui: The Detour is To Be Where We Are*. Chicago, IL: Monique Meloche Gallery, 2021.

Brazil, Kevin. "The Uses of Queer Art." October 2018. Accessed May 2, 2024. https://www.thewhitereview.org/feature/uses-queer-art/.

Brehas, Ivana. "The Queer Art of Sitting." *Kill Your Darlings*, November 2, 2020. Accessed November 1, 2022. https://www.killyourdarlings.com.au/article/the-queer-art-of-sitting/.

Bronson, A. A., and Philip Aarons. "AA Bronson interviews Philip Aarons." In *Queer Zines*, edited by A. A. Bronson and Philip Aarons, 10–13. New York and Rotterdam: Printed Matter Inc. and Witte de With Center for Contemporary Art, 2008.

Broomhall, Susan, and Jacqueline Van Gent. *Dynastic Colonialism: Gender, Materiality and the Early Modern House of Orange-Nassau*. London and New York: Routledge, 2016.

brown, adrienne maree. *Pleasure Activism: The Politics of Feeling Good*. Chico, CA: AK Press, 2019.

Brown, Peter. *The Cult of the Saints: Its Rise and Function in Latin Christianity*. Chicago, IL: The University of Chicago Press, 2014.

Brown, Sarah. "The Creative Process with Paul Yore and His Work; The Rule of Lore." *Bendigo Art Gallery*, March 1, 2022. Accessed January 26, 2023. https://www.bendigoregion.com.au/bendigo-art-gallery/blogs/the-creative-process-with-paul-yore-and-his-work-the-rule-of-lore#:~:text=I%20build%20up%20structures%2C%20layers,parts%20of%20the%20creative%20process.

Bryan-Wilson, Julia. *Fray: Art and Textile Politics*. Chicago, IL: The University of Chicago Press, 2017.

Bryan-Wilson, Julia. "Queerly Made: Harmony Hammond's *Floorpieces*." *The Journal of Modern Craft*, Vol. 2, Issue 1 (2009): 59–80.

Budds, Diana. "The 'Fantasy Furniture' of a Feminist Icon." *Curbed*, January 20, 2022. Accessed August 2, 2022. https://www.curbed.com/2022/01/kate-millett-fantasy -furniture-sculpture-salon-94-design.html.

Bui, Antonius-Tín. "About." Accessed August 1, 2022. http://www.antoniusbui.com/about.

Bui, Antonius-Tín. "Not Sorry for the Trouble." Accessed August 1, 2022. http://www .antoniusbui.com/2019-1#/not-sorry-for-the-trouble/.

Burns, Christine. *Trans Britain: Our Journey from The Shadows*. London: Unbound, 2018.

Butler, Judith. *Bodies That Matter: On The Discursive Limits of "Sex."* London: Routledge, 1993.

Butt, Hamad. "About." Accessed April 19, 2024. https://hamadbutt.co.uk/about.

Camminga, B., and John Marnell, eds. *Queer and Trans African Mobilities: Migration, Asylum and Diaspora*. London: Bloomsbury, 2022.

Campbell, Andy. *Queer X Design: 50 Years of Signs, Symbols, Banners, Logos and Graphic art of LGBTQ*. New York: Black Dog & Leventhal Publishers, 2019.

Carroll Cruz, Joan. *Relics: What They Are and Why They Matter*. Charlotte, NC: TAN Books, 2015.

Castillo Muñoz, Yénika. "Staying Diasporic: Centering Migrant and Diasporic Ways of Being in Design." Paper Presented at Pivot 2021, Online, July 2021, 341–8 (341). https://dl.designresearchsociety.org/cgi/viewcontent.cgi?article=1071&context =pluriversaldesign.

Cauterucci, Christina. "Lesbians and Key Rings: A Cultural Love Story." *Slate*, December 21, 2016. Accessed April 19, 2024. https://slate.com/human-interest/2016/12/the -lesbian-love-of-key-rings-and-carabiners-explained.html.

Cave, Roderick. *Chinese Paper Offerings*. Oxford: Oxford University Press, 1998.

Chaich, John. "Queer Threads Catalogue." Accessed June 7, 2020. https://issuu.com/ leslielohmanmuseum/docs/queerthreadscatalogue_final.

Chaich, John. "Queer Threads: Crafting Identity and Community." Accessed August 1, 2020. http://www.leslielohman.org/exhibitions/2013/queer- threads/QueerThreadsCat alogue_FINAL.pdf.

Chaich, John, and Todd Oldham. *Queer Threads: Crafting Identity and Community*. Los Angeles, CA: AMMO Books, 2017.

Charalambous, Sophia. "The British Artist Who Helped Pioneer the Use of Science in Art." July 9, 2019. Accessed May 2, 2024. https://elephant.art/british-artist-helped -pioneer-use-science-art/.

Chauncey, George. *Gay New York: Gender, Urban Culture, and the Making of the Gay Male World, 1890-1940*. New York: Basic Books, 1994.

Chauncey, George. "Privacy Could Only Be Had in Public: Gay Uses of the Streets." In *Stud: Architectures of Masculinity*, edited by Joel Sanders, 224–61. New York: Princeton Architectural Press, 1996.

Coles, Alex, and Catharine Rossi. *Post-Craft: EP Vol. 3*. London: Sternberg Press, 2022.

Company Gallery. "Troy Montes-Michie." Accessed May 30, 2024. https://companygallery .us/artists/troy-montes-michie .

Conner, Christopher T. "The Gay Gayze: Expressions of Inequality on Grindr." *The Sociological Quarterly*, Vol. 60, No. 3 (2019): 397–419.

Cornier, J. Raúl. "Hanky Panky: An Abridged History of the Hanky Code." *The History Project*, April 23, 2019. Accessed 14 November, 2020. https://historyproject.org/news /2019-04/hanky-panky-abridged-history-hanky-code-0.

Craftspace. "Queer + Metals." Accessed February 28, 2023. https://craftspace.co.uk/queer
-metals/.

Crenshaw, Kimberlé. "Demarginalizing the Intersection of Race and Sex: A Black Feminist
Critique of Antidiscrimination Doctrine, Feminist Theory and Antiracist Politics."
*University of Chicago Legal Forum*, Vol. 1 (1989): 139–67.

Crimp, Douglas. "AIDS: Cultural Analysis/Cultural Activism." *October*, Vol. 43 (Winter
1987): 3–16.

Crimp, Douglas. "How to Have Promiscuity in an Epidemic." *October,* Vol. 43 (1987):
237–71. https://doi.org/10.2307/3397576.

Critical Craft Forum. "About." Accessed January 3, 2023. https://www.criticalcraftforum
.com/about.

Cubbin, Tom. "Crafting Fetish Across Materials and Sexual Styles: An Interview with
Skeeter of Mr. S Leather." *The Journal of Modern Craft*, Vol. 13, No. 2 (2020): 179–87.

Culture Push. "Fall 2023 Black Utopian Fellow." Accessed June 26, 2024. https://www
.culturepush.org/nifemi-ogunro.

Dame-Griff, Avery. *The Two Revolutions: A History of the Transgender Internet*. New York:
New York University Press, 2023.

Davis, Glyn, and Laura Guy. *Queer Print in Europe*. London: Bloomsbury, 2022.

De Lara, Raul. "A Korean Affair." Accessed June 26, 2024. https://www.rauldelara.com/new
-page-5.

De Lara, Raul. "Live Laugh Love." Accessed June 26, 2024. https://www.rauldelara.com/#/
live-love-laugh/.

De Lara, Raul. "Soft Chair (M1) – 2023." *Instagram*, March 18, 2023. https://www
.instagram.com/rauldelaraa/p/Cp7iCMoLGLV/.

De Lara, Raul. "The Wait (Again)." Accessed June 26, 2024. https://www.rauldelara.com/#
/the-wait-again/.

De Lara, Raul. "Thinking Chair." Accessed June 26, 2024. https://www.rauldelara.com/new
-page-69.

Deetz, James F. "Material Culture and Worldview in Colonial Anglo-America." In *The
Recovery of Meaning: Historical Archaeology in the Eastern United States*, edited
by Mark P. Leone and Parker B. Potter Jr, 219–34. Washington, DC and London:
Smithsonian Institution Press, 1988.

Delany, Max. "Paul Yore: WORD MADE FLESH." n.d. *Carriageworks*. Accessed January
26, 2024. https://carriageworks.com.au/journal/paul-yore-word-made-flesh-interview/.

Diepeveen, Leonard, and Timothy van Laar. *Shiny Things: Reflective Surfaces and Their
Mixed Meanings*. Bristol: Intellect Books, 2021.

Dillard, Keren. "The Dwell 24: Nifemi Ogunro." Accessed June 26, 2024. https://www
.dwell.com/article/the-dwell-24-nifemi-ogunro-b9d958a5.

Douglas, Mary. *Purity and Danger: An Analysis of the Concepts of Pollution and Taboo*.
London and New York: Routledge, 1966.

Edwards, Brent Hayes, and Troy Montes-Michie. "The Alchemy of the Border." In *Troy
Montes-Michie: Rock of Eye*, edited by Andrea Andersson and Lisa Pearson, 36–43.
New York: Siglio, 2021.

Edwards, Geoffrey. *Art of Glass: Glass in the Collection of the National Gallery of Victoria*.
Melbourne: National Gallery of Victoria, 1998.

Edwards, Jason. *Queer and Bookish: Eve Kosofsky Sedgwick as Book Artist*. Santa Barbara,
CA: Punctum Books, 2022.

Elkins, Amy E. *Crafting Feminism from Literary Modernism to the Multimedia Present*.
Oxford: Oxford University Press, 2022.

Eng, David L., Judith Halberstam, and José Esteban Muñoz, "What's Queer About Queer Studies Now?" *Social Text*, Vol. 23, No. 3–4 (2005): 1–17.

Espinoza, Alex. *Cruising: An Intimate History of a Radical Pastime.* Los Angeles, CA: Unnamed Press, 2019.

Faught, Josh. "Contact." Accessed October 26, 2023. https://www.joshfaught.com/contact.

Featherstone, Mike. *Body Modification.* London: SAGE Publications, 2000.

Feinberg, Leslie. *Transgender Warriors: Making History From Joan of Arc to Dennis Rodman.* Boston, MA: Beacon Press, 1996.

Felix, Marina. "This Brooklyn artist wants to change the way you see furniture." *Business of Home,* September 15, 2022. Accessed October 5, 2023. https://businessofhome .com/articles/this-brooklyn-artist-wants-to-change-the-way-you-see-furniture#:~ :text="I%20was%20able%20to%20not,long%20as%20it%20still%20worked.

*Fight Back, Fight AIDS: 15 Years of ACT UP.* Directed by James Wentzy. Frameline, 2004.

Finkel, Jori. "'Gender Alchemy' Is Transforming Art for the 21st Century." *The New York Times,* September 8, 2021. Accessed October 24, 2022. https://www.nytimes.com/2021 /09/08/arts/design/feminist-transgender-nonbinary-art.html.

Flint, Adrian, and Vernon Hewitt. "Colonial Tropes and HIV/AIDS in Africa: Sex, Disease and Race." *Commonwealth & Comparative Politics,* Vol. 53, No. 3 (2015): 294–314.

Fortier, Anne-Marie. "'Coming Home': Queer Migrations and Multiple Evocations of Home." *European Journal of Cultural Studies,* Vol. 4, No. 4 (2001): 405–24.

Foster, Stephen, and Gilane Tawadros. *Familiars: Hamad Butt.* London and Southampton: Institute of International Visual Arts and John Hansard Gallery, 1996.

Foucault, Michel. *The History of Sexuality, Vol. 1: An Introduction [Will to Knowledge].* Translated by Robert Hurley. New York: Vintage, [1976] 1978.

Fountain, Daniel. Accessed 23 November 2023. http://www.danielfountain.com.

Fountain, Daniel. "All That Glitters Is Gold: Queering Waste Through Campy Craft." PhD Thesis, Loughborough University, 2021.

Fountain, Daniel. *Crafted with Pride: Queer Craft and Activism in Contemporary Britain.* Chicago, IL and Bristol: The University of Chicago Press and Intellect Books, 2023.

Fountain, Daniel. "On the Queer Horizon: 'Welcome to Faggot Land." In *Paul Yore: WORD MADE FLESH,* edited by Max Delany, 264–315. Melbourne: Art Ink and Australian Centre for Contemporary Art.

Fountain, Daniel. "Survival of the Knittest: Craft and Queer-Feminist Worldmaking." *MAI: Feminism and Visual Culture* 8 (Autumn 2021). Accessed January 24, 2023. https://maifeminism.com/survival-of-the-knittest-craft-and-queer-feminist -worldmaking.

Fountain, Daniel. "The Art of Hannah Höch: Queering Collage Via Jack Halberstam." *Collage Research Network,* June 13, 2019. Accessed August 1, 2022. https://collagerese archnetwork.wordpress.com/2019/06/13/the-art-of-hannah-hoch-queering-collage-via -jack-halberstam.

Fountain, Daniel, and LJ Roberts. "LJ Roberts' Queer Epics." *Decorating Dissidence,* April 3, 2020. Accessed June 3, 2020. https://decoratingdissidence.com/2020/04/03/lj-roberts -queer-craft-epics/.

Fowler, Norman, *AIDS: Don't Die of Prejudice.* Hull: Biteback Publishing, 2014.

Frank, Rebekah. "Jewlery||Adjacent: Angela Hennessy, the Presence of Absence." *Art Jewelry Forum,* May 17, 2021. Accessed February 2, 2023. https://artjewelryforum.org/ articles/angela-hennessy/.

Frank, Rebekah. "Jewelry||Adjacent: Demetri Broxton's Beaded Boxing Gloves, Investigating Race, Masculinity, and Sport in the United States." *Art Jewelry Forum,*

March 8, 2021, Accessed February 2023. https://artjewelryforum.org/articles/demetri
-broxtonaes-beaded-boxing-gloves/.

Frank, Rebekah. "Jewlery||Adjacent: Hollis Chitto, Blurring Traditions in Native
Beadwork." November 15, 2021. Accessed February 2, 2023. https://artjewelryforum
.org/articles/hollis-chitto/.

Frantz, David Evans, Lucas Hilderbrand, and Kayleigh Perkov. *Cock, Paper, Scissors.* Los
Angeles, CA: ONE Archives, 2016.

Frantz, David Evans, Christina Linden, and Chris E. Vargas. *Trans Hirstory in 99 Objects.*
Pasadena, CA and Munich: Museum of Trans Hirstory & Art and Hirmer Publishers,
2024.

Frawley, Jodi, and Iain McCalman, eds. *Rethinking Invasion Ecologies from the
Environmental Humanities.* London and New York: Routledge, 2014.

Freeman, Elizabeth. *Queer Kinship: Race, Sex, Belonging, Form.* Durham, NC: Duke
University Press, 2022.

Furnman, Adam Nathaniel, and Joshua Mardell, eds. *Queer Spaces: An Atlas of LGBTQIA+
Places and Stories.* London: RIBA Publishing, 2022.

Gavin, Francesca. "The Personal is Political: A Conversation with Antonius-Tin Bui."
*Independent*, April 2023. Accessed June 23, 2024. https://www.independenthq.com/
features/the-personal-is-political-a-conversation-with-antonius-tin-bui.

Geczy, Adam, and Vicki Karaminas. "Kiss of the Whip: Bondage, Discipline and
Sadomasochism, or BDSM Style." In *Queer Style*, edited by Adam Geczy and Vicki
Karaminas, 99–110. London: Bloomsbury, 2013.

Gerstein, Beth Ann. *Making in Between: Queer Clay.* Pomona, CA: American Museum of
Ceramic Art, 2023.

Gerstenzang, James, and Marlene Cimons. "Reagan Asks Abstinence in Remarks About
AIDS." *Los Angeles Times*, April 2, 1987. Accessed October 14, 2020. https://www
.latimes.com/archives/la-xpm-1987-04-02-mn-1950-story.html.

Getsy, David J. *Abstract Bodies: Sixties Sculpture in the Expanded Field of Gender.* New
Haven, CT: Yale University Press, 2015.

Getsy, David J. *Queer.* Cambridge, MA: MIT Press, 2016.

Getsy, David J. *Queer Behavior: Scott Burton and Performance Art.* Chicago, IL: The
University of Chicago Press, 2022.

Getsy, David J. *Scott Burton: Collected Writings on Art and Performance, 1965-1975.*
Chicago, IL: Soberscove Press, 2012.

Getsy, David J. "Ten Queer Theses on Abstraction." In *Queer Abstraction*, edited by Jared
Ledesma, 65–75. Des Moines: Des Moines Art Center, 2019.

Getsy, David J., and Jennifer Doyle. "Queer Formalisms: David J. Getsy and Jennifer Doyle
in Conversation." *Art Journal*, Vol. 72, No. 4 (2013): 58–71.

Gever, Martha. "Pictures of Sickness: Stuart Marshall's Bright Eyes." In *AIDS Cultural
Analysis/Cultural Activism*, edited by Douglas Crimp, 109–26. Cambridge, MA:
October Books, 1987.

Gever, Martha, Pratibha Parmar, and John Greyson. *Queer Looks: Perspectives on Lesbian
and Gay Film and Video.* New York: Routledge, 1993.

Gill-Peterson, Jules. *A Short History of Trans Misogyny.* London and New York: Verso
Books, 2024.

Gitelman, Lisa. *Paper Knowledge: Toward a Media History of Documents.* Durham, NC:
Duke University Press, 2014.

Godfrey, S. "Creeping;; Collaborating;; and Not Calling It Trans Craft." In *TISSUE PAPERS #01 MAKING*, edited by Donna Marcus Duke and Sam Moore, 77–83. London: TISSUE, 2023.

Goldstein, Katie. "Queer Homes in a Non-Queer World." In *Mapping Queer Space(s) of Praxis and Pedagogy*, edited by Elizabeth McNeil, James E. Wermers, and Joshua O. Lunn, 269–78. Cham: Palgrave Macmillan, 2018.

Gorman, Michele, Yvette Chaparro, and Preeti Gopinath, eds. *The Decolonized Decarbonized Dinner Party*. New York: Parsons The New School, 2022. https://issuu .com/newschool/docs/d_d_workingdoc.

Gossett, Reina, Eric Stanley, and Johanna Burton. *Trap Door: Trans Cultural Production and the Politics of Visibility*. Cambridge, MA: MIT Press, 2017.

Gray, Emma, and Alanna Vagianos. "We Have a Navy Veteran to Thank for the Transgender Pride Flag." *Huffpost*, July 27, 2017. Accessed October 24, 2022. https://www.huffingtonpost.co.uk/entry/we-have-a-navy-veteran-to-thank-for-the -transgender-pride-flag_n_5978c060e4b0e201d57a711f.

Green, Nicki. "About: Bio." Accessed October 25, 2022. https://www.nickigreen.org.

Greer, Betsy. *Craftivism: The Art of Craft and Activism*. Vancouver: Arsenal Pulp Press, 2014.

Gremore, Graham. "30 Extremely Accurate Tweets about Gay People Being Unable to Sit Properly." *Queerty*, September 8, 2019. Accessed November 1, 2022. https://www .queerty.com/30-extremely-accurate-tweets-gay-people-unable-sit-properly-20190908.

Grove, Richard. *Green Imperialism: Colonial Expansion, Tropical Island Edens and the Origins of Environmentalism, 1600-1860*. Cambridge: Cambridge University Press, 1995.

Halberstam, Jack. *The Queer Art of Failure*. Durham, NC and London: Duke University Press, 2011.

Halperin, David. *Saint Foucault: Towards a Gay Hagiography*. Oxford: Oxford University Press, 1997.

Harty, Kim. "Foreword: Consequences of Transparency." In *Transparency*, edited by National Liberty Museum, 5–7. Philadelphia, PA: National Liberty Museum, 2017.

Hawkins, Peter S. "Naming Names: The Art of Memory and the NAMES Project AIDS Quilt." *Critical Inquiry*, Vol. 19, No. 4 (Summer, 1993): 752–79.

Heath, Nicola. "Australian Artist Paul Yore Speaks about Censorship in Art, Queer Culture and Catholic Kitsch as ACCA Exhibition Surveys His Career." *ABC News*, November 5, 2022. Accessed 26 January, 2024. https://www.abc.net.au/news/2022-11-06/paul-yore -word-made-flesh-exhibition-acca-australian-artist/101610312.

Hird, Myra J. "Naturally Queer." *Feminist Theory*, Vol. 5, No. 1 (2004): 85–9.

Hird, Myra J. *Sex, Gender and Science*. New York: Palgrave Macmillan, 2004.

Holt, Neil, Nicola von Velsen, and Stephanie Jacobs, *Paper: Material, Medium and Magic*. London: Prestel, 2018.

Home Office. Hate Crime, England and Wales, 2022 to 2023 (second edition). GOV.UK., 2023 [online]. Accessed June 26, 2024. https://www.gov.uk/government/statistics/ hate-crime-england-and-wales-2022-to-2023/hate-crime-england-and-wales-2022-to -2023.

Hong, Grace Kyungwon, and Roderick A. Ferguson. *Strange Affinities: The Gender and Sexual Politics of Comparative Racialization*. Durham, NC: Duke University Press, 2011.

hooks, bell. "Are You Still a Slave? Liberating the Black Female Body." *The New School,* May 7, 2014. Accessed February 8, 2023. https://www.youtube.com/watch?v=rJk0hNROvzs &t=5226s.

Hotz-Davies, Ingrid, Georg Vogt, and Franziska Bergmann. *The Dark Side of Camp Aesthetics: Queer Economies of Dirt, Dust and Patina.* London: Routledge, 2018.

*How To Survive A Plague; United in Anger.* Directed by David France. Public Square Films, 2012.

Hudson, Briony. *English Delftware Drug Jars: The Collection of the Museum of the Royal Pharmaceutical Society of Great Britain.* London: Pharmaceutical Press, 2006.

Hunter, Dard. *Papermaking: The History and Technique of an Ancient Craft.* New York: Dover Publications, Inc., 1978.

Jackson, Louis E., and C. R. Hellyer. *A Vocabulary of Criminal Slang, With Some Examples of Common Usages.* Portland, OR: Modern Printing Co., 1914.

Jian, Hang, and Guo Qiuhui. *Chinese Arts and Crafts: History, Techniques and Legends.* Cambridge: Cambridge University Press, 2012.

Johnston, Eddie. "Four Flowers That Have Become Queer Symbols." *Royal Botanic Gardens, Kew.* Accessed November 3, 2023. https://www.kew.org/read-and-watch/ plants-LGBTQ-symbols.

Jones, Charlotte, and Jen Slater. "The Toilet Debate: Stalling Trans Possibilities and Defending 'Women's Protected Spaces.'" *The Sociological Review,* Vol. 68, no. 4 (2020): 843–51.

Jones, Cleve. *The Making of an Activist: Stitching a Revolution.* New York: HarperCollins, 2000.

Jonze, Tim. "It Was a Life-and-Death Situation. Wards Were Full of Young Men Dying': How We Made the Don't Die of Ignorance Aids Campaign." *The Guardian,* September 4, 2017.

Kaishian, Patricia, and Hasmik Djoulakian. "The Science Underground: Mycology as a Queer Discipline." *Catalyst: Feminism, Theory, Technoscience,* Vol. 6, No. 2 (2020).

Katz-Freiman, Tami. "'Craftsmen in the Factory of Images', *from* BoysCraft." In The *Craft Reader,* edited by Glenn Adamson, 599–600. Oxford: Berg, 2010.

Keegan, Cáel M. "Transgender Studies, or How to Do Things with Trans." In *The Cambridge Companion to Queer Studies,* edited by Siobhan B. Somerville, 66–78. Cambridge: Cambridge University Press, 2020.

Keller, Reuben P., Marc W. Cadotte, and Glenn Sandiford, eds. *Invasive Species in a Globalised World: Ecological, Global, and Legal Perspectives on Policy.* Chicago, IL and London: The University of Chicago Press, 2014.

Kenji, Kaneko. *Gendai Tōgei no Zōkei Shikō [Concepts of Creating Form in Contemporary Ceramics].* Tokyo: Abe Shuppan, 2001. Quoted in Yuko Kikuchi, "The Craft Debate at the Crossroads of Global Visual Culture: Re-centring Craft in Postmodern and Postcolonial Histories." *World Art,* Vol. 5, No. 1 (2015): 87–115.

Kina, Laura, and Jan Christian Bernabe. *Queering Asian American Art.* Washington, DC: University of Washington Press, 2017.

Know Your Meme. "You Mess With Crabo, You Get a Stabbo." Accessed October 25, 2022. https://knowyourmeme.com/memes/you-mess-with-crabo-you-get-a-stabo#fn1.

Kristanto, Bayu. "Two-Spirits and The Decolonization Of Gender." *Paradigma: Jurnal Kajian Budaya,* Vol. 1, No. 2 (July 2011): 119–31.

Krohn, Silke, Dennis H. Busch, Henni Hellige, and Robert Klanten, *The Age of Collage: Contemporary Collage in Modern Art.* Berlin: Die Gestalten Verlag, 2013.

Kurlansky, Mark. *Paper: Paging Through History*. New York: W. W. Norton & Company, 2016.

Ladd, Nathan. "Transmission." *Tate*, March 2019. Accessed May 1, 2024. https://www.tate.org.uk/art/artworks/butt-transmission-t15512.

lambert, matt. "Craft Beyond the Binary." *Studio: Craft and Design in Canada*, Fall/Winter 2022. Accessed February 8, 2023. https://www.studiomagazine.ca/articles/2022/2/provocations-craft-beyond-the-binary.

lambert, matt. "Re-Tooling, Re-Using, Un-Mastering." *Decorating Dissidence*, July 11, 2022. Accessed October 26, 2023. https://decoratingdissidence.com/2022/07/11/issue-fifteen-tools-use-mastery/.

Lancaster, Lex Morgan. *Dragging Away: Queer Abstraction in Contemporary Art*. Durham, NC: Duke University Press, 2022.

Levy, Ariel. "Lesbian Nation." *The New Yorker*, February 23, 2009. Accessed June 28, 2020. https://www.newyorker.com/magazine/2009/03/02/lesbian-nation.

Limb, Matthew. "An Archive in Clay: The Crafting of Queer Identities." In *Making in Between: Queer Clay*, edited by Beth Ann Gerstein, 9–17. Pomona, CA: American Museum of Ceramic Art, 2023.

Liu, Xiaofei. "No Fats, Femmes, or Asians." *Moral Philosophy and Politics*, Vol. 2, No. 2 (2015): 255–76.

Livet, Anne. *Art Against AIDS, Washington, D.C.: A Sale Exhibition of Contemporary Works of Art*. New York: American Foundation for AIDS Research, 1990.

Livingstone, Andrew, and Kevin Petire. *The Ceramics* Reader. London: Bloomsbury, 2017.

Lorde, Audre. "Age, Race, Class and Sex: Women Redefining Difference." In *Your Silence Will Not Protect* You, edited by Audre Lorde, 94–106. London: Silver Press, 2017.

Lorde, Audre. *The Master's Tools Will Never Dismantle the Master's House*. London: Penguin Books, 2018.

Lorde, Audre. *Uses of the Erotic: The Erotic as Power*. Trumansburg, NY: Out and Out Books, 1978.

Louvre. "Les Trois Grâces." Accessed October 20, 2023. https://collections.louvre.fr/en/ark:/53355/cl010091241.

Luibhéid, Eithne, and Karma R. Chávez, eds. *Queer and Trans Migrations: Dynamics of Illegalization, Detention, and Deportation*. Urbana, IL: University of Illinois Press, 2020.

Lunning, Frenchy. *Fetish Style*. New York: Bloomsbury, 2013.

Luxe, Damien. "Vanifesto: A Mediation on Van Lust." 2011. Accessed June 26, 2020. http://www.damienluxe.com/wp-content/uploads/2014/05/VANIFESTO_final.pdf.

Luxe, Damien, Heather María Ács, and Sabina Ibarrola. *Glitter & Grit: Queer Performance From the Heels on Wheels Femme Galaxy*. Portland, OR: Publication Studio, 2015.

Madden, Allan. "(Re)Collecting Queer Craft: Ownership, Identity and Remembrance in Queer Zine Collecting." In *Crafted with Pride: Queer Craft and Activism in Contemporary Britain*, edited by Daniel Fountain, 77–92. Chicago, IL and Bristol: The University of Chicago Press and Intellect Books, 2023.

Malatino, Hilary. "Pedagogies of Becoming: Trans Inclusivity and the Crafting of Being." *TSQ: Transgender Studies Quarterly*, Vol. 2, No. 3 (2015): 395–410.

Mathieu, Paul. *Sex Pots: Eroticism in Ceramics*. New Brunswick, NJ: Rutgers University Press, 2003.

Matiazi, Má (@mamatiazi). "Have You Heard About Bi-sitting." *Instagram*, July 26, 2019. Accessed November 1, 2022. https://www.instagram.com/p/B0YfCHAAHIe/?utm_source=ig_embed&ig_rid=c8c3b839-b364-4e21-a49f-81922743b759.

Maxwell Hanrahan Foundation. "2024 Awards in Craft: Raul De Lara." Accessed June 26, 2024. https://www.maxwell-hanrahan.org/blog/2024-awards-in-craft-raul-de-lara.

McBrinn, Joseph. "'Male Trouble': Sewing, Amateurism, and Gender." In *Sloppy Craft: Postdisciplinarity and the Crafts*, edited by Elaine C. Paterson and Susan Surette, 27–44. London: Bloomsbury, 2015.

McBrinn, Joseph. *Queering The Subversive Stitch: Masculinity and The Culture of Needlework*. London: Bloomsbury, 2021.

McCullough, Malcolm. *Abstracting Craft: The Practiced Digital Hand*. Cambridge, MA: MIT Press, 1998.

McFadden, David Revere. *Slash: Paper Under The Knife*. New York: Museum of Arts and Design, 2009.

McIntosh, Peggy. "White Privilege: Unpacking the Invisible Knapsack." *Peace and Freedom*, Vol. 1989 (July/August 1989): 10–12.

McMillan, Keava. "Violet Delights: A Queer History of Purple." *V&A Dundee*. Accessed November 3, 2023. https://www.vam.ac.uk/dundee/articles/violet-delights-a-queer -history-of-purple.

Medhurst, Eleanor. "From Lavender to Violet: The Lesbian Obsession with Purple." *Dressing Dykes*, August 20, 2021. Accessed October 2, 2022. https://dressingdykes.com /2021/08/20/from-lavender-to-violet/.

Medhurst, Eleanor. "Lez Accessorise: Carabiners and Rings as Lesbian Signals." *DressingDykes*, May 14, 2021. Accessed April 19, 2024. https://dressingdykes.com/2021 /05/14/lez-accessorise/.

Medhurst, Eleanor. *Unsuitable: A History of Lesbian Fashion*. London: C. Hurst & Co Publishers, 2024.

Merleau-Ponty, Maurice. *Phenomenology of* Perception. London: Routledge, 2011.

Metcalfe, Robin. *Camp Fires: The Queer Baroque of Léopold L. Foulem, Paul Mathieu and Richard Milette*. Toronto: Gardiner Museum, 2015.

Meyer, Moe. *The Politics and Poetics of Camp*. London: Routledge, 2011.

Millar, Lesley, and Alice Kettle. *The Erotic Cloth: Seduction and Fetishism in Textiles*. London: Bloomsbury, 2018.

Millett, Kate. "From the Basement to the Madhouse." In *Kate Millett, Sculptor: The First 38 Years*, edited by Kathy O'Dell, 41–50. College Park, MD: Fine Arts Gallery University of Maryland, 1997.

Millett, Kate. *Sexual Politics*. New York: Columbia University Press, 2016.

Mitchell, Larry. *The Faggots and Their Friends Between Revolutions*. New York: Calamus Books, 1977.

Mizota, Sharon. "Fugitive Practice: Troy Montes-Michie's *Rock of Eye*." *Bomb*, March 16, 2022. Accessed 5 August, 2022. https://bombmagazine.org/articles/fugitive-practice -troy-montes-michies-rock-of-eye-reviewed/.

moniquemeloche. "Antonius Bui: The Detour is To Be Where We Are." Accessed August 1, 2022. https://www.moniquemeloche.com/exhibitions/187-antonius-bui-the-detour-is -to-be-where/press_release_text/.

Morabito, John Paul. "Weaving Beyond the Binary." *Textile: Cloth and Culture*, Vol. 20 (2022): 424–38.

Muñoz, José Esteban. *Cruising Utopia: The Then and There of Queer Futurity*. New York: NYU Press, 2009.

Muñoz, José Esteban. *Disidentifications*: New York: NYU Press, 1999.

Museum for Art in Wood. "Queering Wood Craft: An LGBTQIA+ Woodworkers Roundtable Part 6." Accessed October 4, 2023. https://museumforartinwood.org/event/queering-wood-craft-an-lgbtqia-woodworkers-roundtable-part-6.

Museum of Arts and Design. "Slash: Paper Under The Knife." Accessed July 23, 2022. https://madmuseum.org/exhibition/slash.

Museum of Transology. "About." Accessed November 22, 2022. https://www.museumoftransology.com/about.

MyMiniFactory. "The Three Graces, But They're Trans." Accessed June 10, 2024. https://www.myminifactory.com/object/3d-print-the-three-graces-but-they-re-trans-151219.

Nardo, Don, and Robert B. Kebric. *Ancient Mesopatomia*. New York: Greenhaven Press, 2007.

National Library of Medicine. "Some People Think You Can Catch AIDS from a Glass." Accessed April 19, 2024. https://collections.nlm.nih.gov/catalog/nlm:nlmuid-101584655X73-img.

New Museum. "Trigger: Gender as a Tool and a Weapon." Accessed August 5, 2022. https://www.newmuseum.org/exhibitions/view/trigger-gender-as-a-tool-and-as-a-weapon.

New-York Historical Society. "Kate Millett's Fantasy Furniture: Our Q&A with William J. Simmons." Accessed October 5, 2023. https://salon94.com/exhibitions/fantasy-furniture-1967.

Nochlin, Linda. "Why Have There Been No Great Women Artists? (1971)." In *Women, Art and Power and Other Essays*, 145–78. Boulder, CO: Westview, 1988.

Northern Clay Center. *SEXUAL POLITICS: Gender, Sexuality, and Queerness in Contemporary Ceramics*. Minneapolis, MN: Northern Clay Center, 2015.

NRTN. "Major General II Brooch." Accessed October 25, 2023. https://nrtnlab.com/product/major-general-ii-brooch/.

Odell, Dawn. "Delftware and the Domestication of Chinese Porcelain." In *EurAsian Matters: China, Europe, and the Transcultural Object, 1600-1800*, edited by Anna Grasskamp and Monica Juneja, 175–202. New York: Springer, 2018.

Ogunro, Nifemi (@blonder.than.necessary). "A Lil Preview of Topé." *Instagram*, May 9, 2020. https://www.instagram.com/p/B_-HOUcFEeI/?igsh=d210NzN6dGN6MGdw.

Ogunro, Nifemi. "About." Accessed June 26, 2024. https://nifemiogunro.com/About.

Okhio, Camille. "Nifemi Ogunro Talks Design and Family." *Wallpaper*, August 1, 2022. Accessed June 26, 2024. https://www.wallpaper.com/design/nifemi-ogunro-designer-profile.

Olivar, Amanda Quinn. "Antonius-Tin Bui." *Curator*. Accessed August 1, 2021. http://curator.site/interviews/2019/4/1/antonius-bui.

Oxford English Dictionary. "Bent." Accessed November 22, 2023. https://www.oed.com/search/dictionary/?scope=Entries&q=bent.

Oxford English Dictionary. "Blackball." Accessed April 19, 2024. https://www.oed.com/dictionary/blackball_v?tab=meaning_and_use&tl=true#19433991.

Page, Clement. "Hamad Butt: The Art of Metachemics." *Third Text*, Vol. 9, No. 32 (1995): 33–42.

Parker, Holt. "Vaseworld. Depiction and Description of Sex at Athens." In *Ancient Sex: New Essays*, edited by Ruby Blondell and Kirk Ormand, 23–142. Columbus, OH: The Ohio State University Press, 2015.

Parker, Rozsika. *The Subversive Stitch: Embroidery and the Making of the Feminine*. London and New York: I.B. Tauris & Co Ltd, 1984.

Parker, Rozsika, and Griselda Pollock. *Old Mistresses: Women, Art and Ideology.* London: I.B.Tauris, 1981.

Parkinson, Richard B. *A Little Gay History: Desire and Diversity across the World.* London: British Museum Press, 2013.

Paterson, Elaine C., and Susan Surette. *Sloppy Craft: Postdisciplinarity and the Crafts.* London: Bloomsbury, 2015.

Peiss, Kathy. *Zoot Suit: The Enigmatic Career of an Extreme Style.* Philadelphia, PA: University of Pennsylvania Press, 2011.

Penny, Eleanor. "Filth: Trans Bathroom Panics May Be New, but Public Toilets Have Always Been a Political Battleground." *Novara Media,* April 8, 2020. Accessed November 16, 2023. https://novaramedia.com/2020/04/08/filth-trans-bathroom-panics -may-be-new-but-public-toilets-have-always-been-a-political-battleground/.

Petsinis, Alexia. "Does My Ideology Look Big In This? Paul Yore on LET THEM EAT CAKE," July 12, 2021. Accessed January 26, 2024. https://tobemagazine.com.au/does -my-ideology-look-big-in-this-paul-yore-on-let-them-eat-cake/.

Pitts, Victoria. *In The Flesh: The Cultural Politics of Body Modification.* New York: Palgrave Macmillan, 2003.

Pitts, Victoria. "Visibly Queer: Body Technologies and Sexual Politics." *The Sociological Quarterly*, Vol. 41, No. 3 (2000): 443–63.

Prager, Sarah. "Four Flowering Plants That Have Been Decidedly Queered." *JSTOR Daily,* January 29, 2020. Accessed November 3, 2023. https://daily.jstor.org/four-flowering -plants-decidedly-queered/.

Prosser, Jay. *Second Skins: The Body Narratives of Transsexuality.* New York: Columbia University Press, 1998.

Pye, David. *The Nature and Art of Workmanship.* London: The Herbert Press, 1968 [1995].

Queer Metalsmiths. "About." Accessed February 8, 2023. https://www.queermetalsmiths .com.

QuORUM. "Home." Accessed December 5, 2023. https://quorumforum2011.wordpress .com.

r/traaaaaaannnnnnnnnns. "I Find This Image Super Empowering [NSFW][X-Post]." *Reddit.* Accessed October 20, 2023. https://www.reddit.com/r/traaaaaaannnnnnnnnns/ comments/8ptatx/i_find_this_image_super_empowering_nsfwxpost_rgssp/.

r00giebeara. "Been Racking My Brain over This One for about a Week..." *Reddit,* December 28, 2023. Accessed May 2, 2024. https://www.reddit.com/r/ExplainTheJoke/ comments/18t84ou/been_racking_my_brain_over_this_one_for_about_a/.

Ramírez, Catherine S. *The Woman in the Zoot Suit: Gender, Nationalism, and the Cultural Politics of Memory.* Durham, NC: Duke University Press, 2009.

Rand, Erin J. "'Soft Armour' for Ugly Bodies." In *The Routledge Handbook of Queer Rhetoric,* edited by Jacqueline Rhodes and Jonathan Alexander, 365–74. London and New York: Routledge, 2022.

Random Dude. "Gangster Crab With Knife," February 14, 2016. Accessed October 25, 2022. https://www.youtube.com/watch?v=ebsvoRqPOMk&t=1s.

Rawson, KJ. "Archive." *Transgender Studies Quarterly*, Vol. 1, No. 1–2 (May 1, 2014): 24–6.

Ray, Debika. "Making Yourself at Home." *Financial Times,* July 29, 2023, 6.

Reynolds Gallery. "Raul de Lara." Accessed October 5, 2023. https://www.reynoldsgallery .com/news/in-the-studio/raul-de-lara-2/#:~:text=Wood%20is%20generally%20my %20first,are%20smuggled%20into%20the%20country.

Rijksmuseum Shop. "Delftware." Accessed November 7, 2023. https://www .rijksmuseumshop.nl/en/living/delftware.

Roberts, LJ. "Bio." Accessed July 2, 2020. https://www.ljroberts.net/bio.

Roberts, LJ. *Carry You With Me: Ten Years of Portraits*. Brooklyn, NY: Pioneer Works Press, 2021.

Roberts, LJ. "Put Your Thing Down, Flip It, and Reverse It: Reimaging Craft Identities Using Tactics of Queer Theory." In *Extra/Ordinary: Craft and Contemporary Art*, edited by Maria Elena Buszek, 243–59. Durham, NC: Duke University Press, 2011.

Roberts, LJ. "Studio Views @ MAD." Accessed June 26, 2020. http://ljroberts.net/index .php?/work/studio-views-craft-and-the-expanded-field/.

Roberts, LJ. "Van Dykes." Accessed October 26, 2023. https://www.ljroberts.net/van-dykes.

Romanienko, Lisiunia A. *Body Piercing and Identity Construction: A Comparative Perspective–New York, New Orleans, Wroclaw*. New York: Palgrave Macmillan, 2011.

Ross, Andrew. *No Respect: Intellectuals and Popular Culture*. New York: Routledge, 1989.

Royal Vauxhall Tavern [@rvtofficial]. "It's a New Week." *Instagram*, January 25, 2021. Accessed April 19, 2024. https://www.instagram.com/p/CKd2BSSlPrC/.

Saint Thomas, Sophie. "Artists Sarah Zapata and LJ Roberts Use Textiles to Express Their Identities." *Allure*, September 13, 2017. Accessed June 28, 2020. https://www.allure.com /story/queer-artists-exhibition-museum-of-arts-and-design.

Saka, Rasheeda. "The Beholder." *Alta*. December 20, 2021. Accessed August 4, 2022. https://www.altaonline.com/books/photography/a38507995/troy-montes-michie-rock -of-eye-book-review/.

Salon 94 S94D. "Kate Millett Fantast Furniture, 1967." Accessed October 5, 2023. https:// salon94.com/exhibitions/fantasy-furniture-1967.

San Francisco NMWA. "Meet Nicki Green, NMWA 2024 Women to Watch Artist." June 2, 2023. Accessed November 17, 2023. https://www.youtube.com/watch?v=IC4jYVJGq5s.

Savaş, Özlem. "Taste Diaspora: The Aesthetic and Material Practice of Belonging." *Journal of Material Culture*, Vol. 19, No. 2 (2014): 185–208 (185).

Schmits, Rose. "About." Accessed October 24, 2022. https://roseschmits.com/about.

Schmits, Rose. "We Live in a Society." Accessed October 24, 2022. https://roseschmits.com /we-live-in-a-society-collection.

Scholten, Frits, and Michael Hoyle. *Delft "Tulip Vases."* Amsterdam: Rijksmuseum, 2013.

Schulman, Sarah. *The Gentrification of the Mind: Witness to a Lost Imagination*. Los Angeles, CA: University of California Press, 2012.

Schwartz, Judith. *Confrontational Ceramics*. London: A&C Black Visual Arts, 2008.

Sedgwick, Eve Kosofsky. *Epistemology of the Closet*. Berkeley, CA: University of California Press, 1990.

Sedgwick, Eve Kosofsky. *Tendencies*. London: Routledge, 1993.

Sedgwick, Eve Kosofsky. "Work." Accessed April 19, 2024. https://evekosofskysedgwick .net/art/artworks/.

Segalovich, Isabella. "Queering the Jewish Mikvah." *Hyperallergic*, April 4, 2023. Accessed 23 October, 2023. https://hyperallergic.com/812775/queering-the-jewish-mikvah/.

Sennett, Richard. *The Craftsman*. London: Penguin Books, 2008.

Seymour, Nicole. *Bad Environmentalism: Irony and Irreverence in the Ecological Age*. Minneapolis, MN and London: University of Minnesota Press, 2018.

Shelter in Place Artist Residency. "BE U 2020." YouTube. Accessed October 12, 2023. https://www.youtube.com/watch?v=xghneNqt9bM&t=1s.

Shelter in Place Artist Residency. "Untitled, 2020." YouTube. Accessed October 12, 2023. https://www.youtube.com/watch?v=sAXJtfi82fg.

Shiner, Larry. "'Blurred Boundaries?' Rethinking the Concept of Craft and its Relation to Art and Design." *Philosophy Compass*, Vol. 7 (2012): 230–44.

Side Gallery. "Nifemi Ogunro." Accessed June 26, 2024. https://side-gallery.com/nifemi _ogunro_aside_2023/#:~:text=Ogunro%20comments%20on%20her%20collaboration ,soft%20enough%20to%20be%20inviting.

Sight Unseen. "Nifemi Ogunro." Accessed June 26, 2024. https://www.sightunseen.com/ designers/nifemi-ogunro/.

Simone, Roxanne. "Bio." Accessed November 23, 2023. https://www.roxannesimone.com /bio.

Singh, Julietta. *Unthinking Mastery: Dehumanisim and Decolonial Entanglements*. Durham, NC: Duke University Press, 2017.

Slutzky, Buzz. "Buttons for LJ Roberts." Accessed June 1, 2024. http://www.buzzslutzky .com/drawing#/new-page-4/.

Smith, Matt. "Making Things Perfectly Queer." In *Crafted with Pride: Queer Craft and Activism in Contemporary Britain*, edited by Daniel Fountain, 123–26 (125). Bristol and Chicago, IL: Intellect Books and The University of Chicago Press, 2023.

Smith, Matt. "Making Things Perfectly Queer: Art's Use of Craft to Signify LGBT Identities." PhD Thesis, University of Brighton, 2015.

Smithsonian American Art Museum. "40 Under 40: L.J. Roberts." June 8, 2012. Accessed June 4, 2020. YouTube video. https://www.youtube.com/watch?v=YxnyPQ7YATg &feature=emb_title.

Society of Inclusive Blacksmiths. Accessed February 8, 2023. https://www.inclusivebl acksmiths.com.

Sontag, Susan. *Notes on Camp*. London: Penguin Random House, 2018.

Sophie and Kerri. "The Table." Accessed October 13, 2023. https://www.sophieandkerri .com/the-table.

Sorkin, Jenni. "Hybrid Vessels: Nicki Green's Transmutations." *Cfile*, February 6, 2021. Accessed July 15, 2021. https://cfileonline.org/feature-hybrid-vessels-nicki-greens -transmutations/.

Sorkin, Jenni. *Live Form: Women, Ceramics, and Community*. Chicago, IL: The University of Chicago Press, 2016.

Steele, Valerie. *Fetish: Fashion, Sex, and Power*. Oxford: Oxford University Press, 1996.

Steinbock, Eliza. *Shimmering Images: Trans Cinema, Embodiment, and the Aesthetics of Change*. Durham, NC: Duke University Press, 2019.

Steinbrook, Robert. "The Times Poll: 42% Would Limit Civil Rights in AIDS Battle." *Los Angeles Times*, July 31, 1987. Accessed November 16, 2020. https://www.latimes.com/ archives/la-xpm-1987-07-31-mn-217-story.html.

Sticky Glass. "About." Accessed May 1, 2024. https://stickyglass.com.

Stone, Lois. "Trans Craft and the Museum of Transology." In *Crafted with Pride: Queer Craft and Activism in Contemporary Britain*, edited by Daniel Fountain, 30–44. Chicago, IL and Bristol: The University of Chicago Press and Intellect Books, 2023.

Stryker, Susan. "Christine in the Cutting Room: Cinema, Surgery and Celebrity in the Career of Christine Jorgensen." YouTube, August 16, 2013. Accessed March 19, 2023. https://www.youtube.com/watch?v=XlqJ8B9dKCs.

Stryker, Susan, Paisley Currah, and Lisa Jean Moore. "Introduction: Trans-, Trans, or Transgender?" *Women's Studies Quarterly*, Vol. 36, Nos. 3/4 (2008): 11–22.

Sullivan, Nikki. *A Critical Introduction to Queer Theory*. New York: New York University Press, 2003.

Tai, Hansel. "Dirt Container / ON." Accessed April 19, 2024. https://hanseltai.com/Dirt-Container-ON.

Tallis, Raymond. *The Hand: A Philosophical Inquiry in Human Being*. Edinburgh: Edinburgh University Press, 2003.

Tate Archive and Public Records Catalogue. "Butt, Hamad." Accessed April 19, 2024. https://archive.tate.org.uk/Record.aspx?src=CalmView.Catalog&id=TGA+201919&pos=1.

Tate, Tim. "About." Accessed April 19, 2024. https://www.timtateglass.com/about.

Tate, Tim. "Queer Glass: A Personal History." June 3, 2019. Accessed April 19, 2024. http://washingtonglassschool.com/queer-glass-a-personal-history.

Tattoodo. "Queer Armor: Collector and Creator Abe Heath of Affect Metals." February 4, 2020. Accessed October 19, 2023. https://www.tattoodo.com/articles/queer-armor-collector-and-creator-abe-of-affect-metals-150032.

Testa, Nino. "'If You Are Reading It, I am Dead': Activism, Local History, and the AIDS Quilt." *The Public Historian*, Vol. 44, No. 3 (2022): 24–57.

The Hopper Prize. "Raul De Lara." Accessed June 26, 2024. https://hopperprize.org/raul-de-lara-interview/.

Tovey, Russell, and Robert Diament. "Troy Michie (QuarARTine Special Episode)." *Talk Art* (podcast), Season 6, Episode 1, April 10, 2020. Accessed November 1, 2022. https://podcasts.apple.com/gb/podcast/troy-michie-quarartine-special-episode/id1439567112?i=1000477238479.

Tucker, Marcia. *A Labor of Love*. New York: The New Museum of Contemporary Art, 1996.

V&A Dundee. "The Language of Pride." Accessed November 3, 2023. https://www.vam.ac.uk/dundee/articles/the-language-of-pride.

Vaccaro, Jeanne. "Feelings and Fractals: Wooly Ecologies of Transgender Matter." *GLQ: A Journal of Lesbian and Gay Studies*, Vol. 21, No. 2–3 (2015): 273–93.

Vaccaro, Jeanne. "Handmade." *Transgender Studies Quarterly*, Vol. 1, No. 1–2 (2014): 96–7.

Vaccaro, Jeanne. "Out of Distracted Vision: Psychedelic Sexology and the Handmade Aesthetics of Transgender." Art & Education, April 2020. Accessed July 14, 2021. https://www.artandeducation.net/classroom/video/328445/jeanne-vaccaro-out-of-distracted-vision-psychedelic-sexology-and-the-handmade-aesthetics-of-transgender.

van Noord, Willemijn. "Between Script and Ornament: Delftware Decorated with Pseudo-Chinese Characters, 1680–1720." *Journal of Design History*, Vol. 31, No. 1 (March 2021): 1–20.

Visser, Deirdre. *Joinery, Joists and Gender: A History of Woodworking for the 21st Century*. New York: Routledge, 2022.

VoyageLA. "Meet Abe Heath of Affect Metals in Northeast LA (Glassell Park)." September 16, 2019. Accessed February 7, 2024. https://voyagela.com/interview/meet-abe-heath-affect-metals-northeast-la/.

Watney, Simon. *Policing Desire: Pornography, AIDS, and the Media*. Minneapolis, MN: University of Minnesota Press, 1987.

Weismantel, Mary. *Playing with Things: Engaging the Moche Sex Pots*. Austin, TX: University of Texas Press, 2021.

Weston, Kath. *Families We Choose: Lesbians, Gays, Kinship*. New York: Columbia University Press, 1997.

Wheeler, André-Naquian. "Troy Michie is Making Collage Art a Little More Queer." *i-D*, March 30, 2018. Accessed August 4, 2022. https://i-d.vice.com/en_uk/article/9kg3yp/troy-michie-is-making-collage-art-a-little-more-queer.

Whiteside, Grace. "Homosilica: Glass is Gay." Accessed May 1, 2024. https://gracewhiteside.com/section/509671-Homosilica-Glass-is-Gay.html.

Wilkinson-Weber, Clare M., and Alicia Ory DeNicola. *Critical Craft: Technology, Globalization, and Capitalism*. London: Routledge, 2016.

Wu, Ka-Ming. *Reinventing Chinese Tradition: The Cultural Politics of Late Socialism*. Urbana, IL: University of Illinois Press, 2015.

Zhang, Daoyi. *Zhongguo Minjian Jianzhi [Chinese Folk Paper-Cuts]*. Jiansu: Jinlin Shuhua Chubanshe, 1980.

# GLOSSARY

As the Introduction outlines, these terms are subjective, vary across cultures, and are continuously contested, re-evaluated, and added to over time. They are not exhaustive, but they are intended to give readers a better idea of the terms used in this book and those used at the time of publication.

## I: Key LGBTQ+ Terms

**AAPI** an acronym that refers to Asian American Pacific Islanders. It is often used to include all people of Asian, Asian American, or Pacific Islander ancestry who trace their origins to the countries, states, jurisdictions, and/or diasporic communities of these geographic regions.

**Agender** a person who identifies as having no gender identity.

**Ally** someone who actively supports the movements and rights of a marginalized group of people (such as the LGBTQ+ community) but who does not identify as such.

**Aromantic (Aro)** a term for people who have non or varying degrees of romantic attraction to others. Someone who identifies as both Aromantic and Asexual, or along that spectrum, may use the term "AroAce."

**Asexual (Ace)** a term for people who have no or varying degrees of sexual attraction to others. Someone who identifies as both Aromantic and Asexual, or along that spectrum, may use the term "AroAce."

**Bigender** a person who identifies with two (or more) genders, often simultaneously.

**BIPOC** this acronym refers to Black, Indigenous, and other people of color.

**Bisexual (Bi)** a term for people who have romantic and/or sexual orientation toward more than one gender.

**Butch** a term used in queer culture to describe someone who often (but not always) expresses themselves in a typically "masculine" way.

**Chosen Family** a term used in queer culture to describe support systems constructed by choice and social ties rather than biological or legal ones.

**Cisgender (Cis)** a term used to describe someone whose gender identity matches the sex they were assigned at birth.

**Cisnormative** a concept that delegitimizes any gender that is not cisgender and assumes all people should have the same gender identity as the sex they were assigned at birth.

**Cruising** the act of searching for sex, often in public spaces such as parks, public bathrooms, and alleyways.

**Dyke** a historically derogatory term for lesbian and bisexual women, typically seen as "masculine." In some contexts, the term has been reclaimed as a positive identity when used in self-reference.

**Femme** a term used in queer culture to describe someone who often (but not always) expresses themselves in a typically "feminine" way.

**Gay** a term for a man who has a romantic and/or sexual orientation towards other men. Some lesbians, trans, and non-binary people may also identify as gay.

**Gender** gender can be considered gender identity (a person's definition of their gender) and gender expression (how they outwardly express their gender) Gender is culturally determined and is often assumed based on sex assigned at birth.

**Gender dysphoria** when a person experiences discomfort or distress because they feel a disconnect between their sex assigned at birth and their gender identity.

**Gender euphoria** when a person experiences comfort or joy because they feel a connection between their gender identity and gender expression, or when their perceived gender aligns with their sense of self.

**Gender non-conforming** a term for people who do not conform to the binary gender categories that cisnormative society prescribes (man and woman) through their gender identity/expression.

**Genderfluid** a person who sees their gender identity as fluid.

**Genderqueer** a broad term for genders that do not conform to a binary of male or female.

**Heteronormative** the concept that heterosexuality is the preferred form of sexual orientation. There is an assumption that heterosexuality is superior or the "normal." It also reinforces the gender binary by suggesting that sexual and/or marital relations are most fitting between those of the opposite sex (also see cisnormative).

**Heterosexual/straight** a term for a man who has a romantic and/or sexual orientation toward women, or, a woman who has a romantic and/or sexual orientation toward men.

**HIV/AIDS** HIV (Human Immunodeficiency Virus) is a virus that attacks the body's immune system. If HIV is not treated, it can lead to AIDS (Acquired Immunodeficiency Syndrome). A range of drugs now exist to prevent and treat HIV, leading many to live a healthy and long life with undetectable and untransmutable status (U=U).

**Homophobia** prejudice, discrimination, or antagonism against LGBTQ+ people.

**Homosexual** this might be considered a more medical term used to describe someone who has a romantic and/or sexual orientation towards someone of the same gender. The term "gay" is now more generally used.

**Intersectionality** intersectionality encompasses the study of overlapping or intersecting social identities and related systems of oppression, domination, or discrimination. In short, it considers how social inequalities relating to race, class, ethnicity, age, ability, sexuality, nationality, and religion can intertwine and shape one another. Professor Kimberlé Crenshaw formalized the term in a 1989 study of Black women's employment in the United States.

**Intersex** a term used to describe people who may have biological attributes that do not conform to societal assumptions of what constitutes "male" or "female." The term specifically relates to biological characteristics and is distinct from a person's sexual orientation or gender identity.

**Lesbian** a term for a woman who has a romantic and/or sexual orientation toward a woman. Some trans and non-binary people may also identify as lesbian.

**LGBTQ+** an acronym for Lesbian, Gay, Bisexual, Trans, and Queer and/or Questioning. This is not exhaustive; the plus symbol nods to the varying sexual orientations and gender identities worldwide. Other popular variations in use include LGBT (just Lesbian, Gay, Bisexual, and Trans) and LGBTQIA+ (which specifically recognizes Intersex and Asexual identities).

**Non-Binary** an umbrella term for people whose gender identity doesn't sit comfortably with "man" or "woman."

**Pansexual (Pan)** a term used to describe people whose romantic and/or sexual attraction towards others is not limited by sex or gender.

**Passing** if someone is regarded, based on appearance, to be cisgender and/or heterosexual.

**POC** an acronym for people of color, a term used to denote someone not considered white. The term is used to emphasize the common experiences of systematic racism among all people of color.

**QTIPOC** an acronym that stands for queer, transgender, and intersex people of color. The term is used to emphasize both the common experiences of systematic racism as well as homophobia and/or transphobia among LGBTQ+ people of color.

**Queer** historically, this was used as a derogatory term to mean "odd" or "strange"and usually targeted toward LGBTQ+ people, but it was reclaimed as a positive source of identity by activists in the 1980s. It is often used in self-reference by people who do not identify with the restrictive and binary terms that have traditionally described sexual orientation and/or gender identity. It is sometimes used as an umbrella term for LGBTQ+ people, as in the queer community.

**Questioning** the process of exploring one's sexual orientation and/or gender identity.

**Racism** prejudice, discrimination, or antagonism against someone based on their race or ethnicity.

**Sex** categories into which people are divided based on their reproductive functions, including male, female, or intersex.

**Transgender (Trans)** an umbrella term used to describe people whose gender is not the same or does not sit comfortably with the sex they were assigned at birth. Some trans people may identify as non-binary or gender nonconforming.

**Transition/Transitioning** the steps a trans person may take to live as the gender with which they identify. Each person's transition will involve different things. For some, this involves medical intervention, such as hormone replacement therapy (HRT) and gender-affirming surgeries, but not all trans people want or can have this. Transitioning also might include telling friends and family, dressing in new ways, or changing legal documents.

**Transphobia** a rejection of trans identity and a refusal to acknowledge that it could be real or valid.

**Two Spirit (2S)** a contemporary umbrella term used by some Indigenous people to describe gender, sexual, and spiritual identities that do not conform to the male/female binary. Traditionally, two-spirit people have held special and ceremonial roles in their communities. Two-spirit is an English language term, and it is important to recognize that the term itself is not universal  some Indigenous cultures have their own languages and terms to describe similar identities. In some contexts, two-spirit people may identify as part of the LGBTQIA+ community, often using the acronym LGBTQIA2S+.

## *II: Key Technical Terms*

### *Textile*

**Appliqué** a method that involves using individual pieces of fabric and adding them to another piece of fabric. It is primarily used in sewn projects to add dimension or to construct a composition.

**Batting** a layer between layers of fabric commonly used in quilting for insulation, also known as wadding.

**Beading** the process of attaching beads by stringing them onto a thread, a piece of string, or a thin wire, and often used in sewing projects.

**Binding** in sewing, this refers to finishing a seam or hem of a garment, usually by rolling or pressing, then stitching on an edging or trim. The term is also used as a broad category to signify a range of processes involving wrapping or "binding" material.

**Bobbin** a bobbin is a holder of thread. In weaving, it refers to a cylinder or cone holding thread, yarn, or other material held in the shuttle. In machine sewing, it refers to the holder that feeds the thread to the machine that appears on the underside of each stitch.

**Braiding** interlacing three or more strands of material (such as yarn or strips of fabric) at a diagonal angle so they cross over each other, forming a cord or narrow fabric known as a "braid" or a "plait."

**Cloth** a generic term to describe a piece of material made by the interweaving of fibers. Rather than fabric, cloth refers to fabric specifically used to make clothing.

**Crocheting** a process that involves using a hooked noodle to interlock loops of yarn or thread together.

**Cross-stitch** a specific type of embroidery that uses stitches that cross each other to form X-shaped patterns.

**Dyeing** a process of coloring fibers, yarns, cloth, or fabrics with either a natural or synthetic dye.

**Embroidery** the broad activity of decorating fabric, cloth, or other materials using a needle and thread to stitch.

**Fabric** a generic term to describe a piece of material made by the interweaving of fibers. Rather than cloth, fabric refers to the resulting material from textile processes, such as weaving.

**Felt** a fabric made by matting, condensing, and compressing fibers using moisture and heat.

**Fiber** a thread-like substance, either natural or synthetic, that can be combined to create fabric or spun to make yarn. In American English, it is also used more broadly as a category to describe works made by fiber, such as "fiber art."

**Knitting** a process where loops of yarn (called stitches) are created in a line using two long needles or a knitting machine.

**Knotting** the act of making a fastening by looping material and tightening it (creating a knot).

**Loom** a machine used to weave fabric that allows threads to be interwoven across (the weft) and the threads that run lengthwise (the warp). There are many different types of looms. The most common include floor looms (a floor-based loom used for weaving long and wide swathes of fabric), backstrap looms (a smaller, portable, and lightweight loom), and jacquard looms (uses a card-punching mechanism allowing for many threads to be woven, allowing for the weaving of detailed and intricate patterns  now primarily a digital process).

**Lacemaking** the making of an openwork fabric (lace) by the manipulation of a single thread (needle lace) or multiple threads (bobbin lace) by hand.

**Macramé** a form of textile produced by using decorative knotting techniques, known as a series of hitches.

**Needlepoint** the general term given to a technique of covering the canvas with stitches.

**Needlework** a broad category that includes any processes that are constructed using a needle, such as sewing and embroidery.

**Patchwork** a form of sewing where multiple pieces of fabric is sewn together to create a more significant piece. The term is primarily used within textiles, especially quilting, but it can also designate wider uses of *patching* and bringing disparate elements together, such as in collage.

**Petit point** a specific type of embroidery on canvas, comprised of very fine and small "petit" needlepoint stitches, which are usually tightly packed together to create intricate detail and decoration.

**Quilting** a form of patchwork where multiple pieces of fabric are sewn together, usually with padding or "batting" placed in between the layers.

**Resist dying** a process of dyeing where the maker actively prevents dye from touching certain areas of the fabric, usually to create patterns or decorations. Various techniques are used to "resist" the dye, such as applying wax (as in wax resist) or tying (as in tie-dye).

**Sampler** refers to a piece of needlework, traditionally used as a demonstration or "sampling" of needlework skills, such as embroidery and cross-stitch.

**Shuttle** a wooden tool used for weaving on a loom. It stores a bobbin carrying the weft thread and is passed back and forth between the warp threads.

**Sewing** the act of joining or mending fabric using stitches, either by hand with a needle and thread, or by a sewing machine.

**Stitch** a single turn or loop of thread created by passing a needle through the fabric. It also refers to a single loop of thread or yarn created through processes such as knitting and crochet.

**Tapestry** a form of textile, usually image-based, traditionally woven by hand or on a loom.

**Tatting** a technique for handcrafting a particularly durable lace using a series of knots and loops, usually with a small shuttle.

**Textile** cloth or fabric that is created using processes such as knitting or weaving. In British English, it is also used more broadly as a category to describe works made by fiber, such as "textile art."

**Thread** a slender, strong strand or cord, especially one designed for sewing or other needlework.

**Warp** the yarn that runs lengthwise on a loom.

**Weaving** the process of making fabric by interlacing a series of warp yarns with weft yarns, traditionally with a loom and shuttle.

**Weft** the yarns that run crosswise on a loom.

**Yarn** strand of fibers, filaments, or other material suitable for knitting, weaving, braiding, sewing or any other process that involves intertwining yarn to produce textiles.


## Ceramic

**Bisque** pottery that has been fired once, without glaze, and cannot be recycled. Sometimes, slips are used in a bisque firing.

**Bone china** a translucent porcelain containing bone ash.

**Burnishing** the ancient rubbing process of burnishing polishes the outside skin of a clay pot while significantly reducing its porosity.

**Centering** a technique used in wheel-thrown pottery that involves moving and shaping the clay into the middle of the wheel.

**Ceramic** a hard natural substance and the general name given to all fired clay forms.

**Clay** a fine-grained natural soil material containing clay minerals that transitions into ceramic when fired at high temperatures.

**Coiling** a hand-building technique that involves making pots by building up long pieces or "coils" of clay.

**Contraction** a decrease in size due to a temperature change that is reversible.

**Delftware** a general term used for Dutch tin-glazed earthenware, often recognizable by its blue and white ornamental aesthetic.

**Earthenware** a coarse, usually tan or reddish type of pottery, that is fired at a low temperature.

**Enamel** colored glass-like decoration applied to ceramics.

**Extruder** a tool that includes a die, through which clay can be passed through to create a uniform shape.

**Faience** a term for fine tin-glazed pottery.

**Firing** describes the process of heating a clay object to a specific temperature.

**Fluting** a decorating technique involving carving or forming vertical grooves or "flutes."

**Glaze** the surface coating of pottery that provides a decorative and usually smooth surface, giving increased strength to the pot.

**Grog** a sand-like substance added to clay to give it greater workability and strength.

**Handbuilding** where an object is assembled by hand, typically without specialist equipment like a pottery wheel.

**Impressing** a decorating technique where a textured or patterned material or object is pressed into a clay surface.

**Incising** a decorating technique where a design is formed by cutting or carving shallow lines on clay surface.

**Kiln** a thermally insulated chamber, a type of oven, that produces temperatures sufficient to make ceramic.

**Luster** a metallic surface made by coating glazed-fired ware in precious metals that are suspended in liquid formulations.

**Patina** an overall thin wash of glaze or oxide stain, allowing the color and texture of the clay body to show through.

**Pinch** manipulating clay by hand and fingers. It describes the specific technique of making "pinch pots" and other objects by forcing into the center of a ball of clay with a thumb and gradually pinching outwards.

**Pit firing** a type of bonfire firing where wares are buried in sawdust in a pit in the ground, and a bonfire is built on top so that the fire and coals slowly burn away the sawdust and fire the wares.

**Plasticity** the quality of moldable flexibility in damp clay.

**Polishing** as compared to burnishing, the act of creating a shiny surface on terra sigillata (or any clay or slip) by rubbing with a soft cloth, a soft brush, or a piece of plastic film.

**Porcelain** a hard, usually translucent and white ceramic that is fired at a high temperature.

**Potter's wheel** a device with either a manual (foot-powered) or an electric rotating wheel typically used to make pottery forms.

**Pottery** the process and the products of forming vessels and other objects with clay and other raw materials, fired at high temperatures to give them a hard and durable form.

**Reduction** refers to the reduction of oxygen from glazes.

**Resist** decorating technique where resist materials are applied to prevent other layers from adhering to some areas, such as slip resist, glaze resist, or wax resist.

**Rib tool** a wide, flat handheld tool used to shape, smooth, and/or scrape clay surfaces.

**Scoring** the process of incising the surface of wet or leather-hard clay in a crosshatch pattern before applying slurry and joining pieces.

**Shrinkage** a decrease in size during the irreversible drying and firing process.

**Slab** pressed or rolled flat sections of clay used in hand building.

**Slip** liquid clay slurry, usually used for slip casting, glazing, or decorating.

**Slip casting** the forming of ceramics by pouring or pumping water-reduced clay slurry (slip) into plaster molds.

**Stoneware** a type of durable pottery primarily made from stoneware clay and fired at a high temperature.

**Terracotta** a form of hard, unglazed, brown-red earthenware clay, most often used for ceramic sculpture, including small figures and architectural ornaments.

**Underglaze** any decoration applied to the bare (usually bisque-fired) clay surface directly before glazing.

**Ware** a generic term for any ceramic objects.

**Warping** distortion of clay forms caused by uneven stresses within the clay. This can be caused by the forming method, uneven drying, uneven support in firing, and irregular or excessive heat in firing.

**Wax resist** melted wax or wax emulsion used to prevent slip or glaze from adhering to a clay surface, either in decorating or in preparing work for glazing.

**Wheel thrown** describes a type of pottery made using a potter's wheel.

## Wood

**Band saw** a mechanical saw with a continuous, flexible blade with teeth on one side.

**Bark** the outer layer of a tree and other woody plants.

**Bending** a process creating curves, usually by softening the wood with hot water or steam (steam bending) to make it pliable. Once softened, the wood is bent and clamped into the desired shape so that it retains that shape once it has dried and cooled.

**Bow** a deviation or curvature in the flat of the timber from one end to the other.

**Burl** wood that has grown in a non-typical way, creating a rounded bulbous growth. This produces a complex, intricate grain pattern and structure which looks like a clustered group of knots. Burled wood is typically challenging to work with, but it is prized for its decorative potential and is mainly used in turning. In British English, it is called burr.

**Butt joint** the most basic joining technique where two pieces of wood are joined together with a square joint.

**Cabinetry** the craft and trade of making furniture, especially cabinets.

**Caning** a furniture technique that involves weaving rattan vine.

**Carpentry** the craft and trade of cutting, working, and joining wood, especially timber. The term includes both structural timberwork and domestic objects.

**Carving** the act of using tools to shape something from a material by scraping away portions of that material, usually by means of a cutting tool or chisel.

**Chamfered** edges have been removed lengthwise at an angle.

**Chiseling** cutting or shaping using a chisel, a long-bladed hand tool with a beveled, sharp edge and a handle usually struck with a hammer or mallet.

**Computer-aided design (CAD)** a digital drafting mode typically used to create 2D and 3D designs.

**Cupping** the bending of wood across its grain.

**Doweling** cylindrical piece or length of wood. They are also known as rounded wood.

**Fabrication** making an object in parts and assembling it to form a whole.

**File** a tool to remove fine amounts of material from a workpiece.

**Filing** a process of shaping or smoothing the material, usually with a combination of rasps and files.

**Furniture** objects intended to support various human activities such as sitting, sleeping, or eating. Furniture making is a broad category that describes the act of creating furniture, including processes such as cabinetry, carpentry, and woodworking.

**Grain** the arrangement of a wood's fibers resulting from the growth of a tree, usually used to refer to the visual pattern resulting from such an arrangement.

**Groove** a long, narrow channel.

**Hardwood** wood from deciduous trees (a group of trees that shed their foliage annually).

**Inlay** inserting or applying material layers on an object's surface, usually for a decorative function.

**Jig** a tool that helps keep wood in a fixed place so that it does not move during processes like cutting or drilling.

**Joinery** the method for joining pieces of wood together to produce more complex items.

**Joist** typically a length of timber that supports a structural building.

**Knot** a circular pattern in timber caused by a dead branch that was not fully integrated into the tree before it was cut down.

**Laminated** several thin layers of wood and adhesives that are built up to make a single board.

**Live edge** the outside of the tree, which may be left intact in some designs.

**Maquette** a three-dimensional object made as a preparatory study before construction.

**Marquetry** decorative patterns created by inlaying veneers and sometimes thin layers of other materials such as metal, shell, or pearl into the surface.

**Mitre** two pieces forming an angle, or a joint formed between two pieces of wood by cutting bevels of equal angles at the ends of each piece.

**Modular** consisting of several separate parts (modules) as the basis of its design and construction.

**Planing** removing thin layers of wood from the surface of a workpiece to create a smooth, even finish, usually with a tool called a plane.

**Rasp** a coarse form of file used for coarsely shaping wood or other material.

**Sanding** smoothing the surface with an abrasive, such as sandpaper.

**Sawing** to cut through or divide material, usually with a saw or other bladed tool.

**Softwood** wood from gymnosperm trees (a group of seed-producing trees).

**Species** the botanical classification of trees and timber.

**Square** two straightedges at a right angle, as in a square joint. It is also used to measure the angle, as in a woodworking square.

**Tongue** a reduction of the thickness of the edge of a board.

**Turning** a form of woodworking involving using a motor-driven lathe and hand-held tools to cut a symmetrical shape around the rotation axis.

**Varnish** a translucent or colored hard coating that protects and enhances the appearance of wood.

**Veneer** thin slices of wood and sometimes bark that are typically applied to a thicker and coarser wood base, most often used in marquetry, cabinetry and furniture making.

**Warp** to bend or twist because of dampness or heat.

**Whipsaw** a large, long saw that cuts in one direction and usually requires two people to use it.

**Wood** an organic material sourced from trees and other "woody" plants.

**Woodworking** the activity or skill of making items from wood. It includes many categories and sub-disciplines, such as cabinetry and furniture making, wood carving, joinery, carpentry, and woodturning.

## *Paper*

**Adhesive** a substance capable of holding separate materials together.

**Assemblage** broadly used to describe a collection or gathering of objects that are then "assembled" together. The term is most often used to describe a three-dimensional collage, usually made from disparate found objects.

**Book arts** a wide-ranging category that describes various practices and traditional skills such as papermaking, letterpress printing, and bookbinding.

**Bookbinding** the process of creating a book, usually in the form of stacked paper sheets, which are bound together and then placed in a cover.

**Cellulose** plant tissue, the primary substance of paper manufacture.

**Chine-collé** a technique in printing where a thin sheet of paper is sandwiched between the printing paper and the printed image.

**Collage** a broad term that describes a whole made up of different pieces. From the French word "coller" meaning "to glue" or "to stick together" and most commonly designates the act of cutting and sticking paper (or other materials) to create a composition.

**Crease** a line, mark, or "crease" caused by bending, folding, or pressing paper.

**Décollage** the opposite of collage, a process that involves deconstructing and tearing apart different pieces from a whole. It is a French term that loosely translates as "take-off" or "to become unstuck."

**Fiber** these are used in papermaking and are typically a range of plant fibers (which contain cellulose), though other fibers may be added such as animal fibers like hair or wool.

**Folding** bending one part of the paper to cover another part.

**Glaze** gloss or polish coating on a sheet of paper that has a shiny finish.

**Letterpress printing** a technique of relief printing using a letterpress that creates a direct impression of an inked, raised surface (such as type) against sheets of paper.

**Matte** a satin-like coating on a sheet of paper that has a smooth finish.

**Montage** a specific form of collaging that is specifically used to refer to an assembly of materials that relate to one another or relate to a particular theme, as opposed to a more random selection of images.

**Mould** rectangular wooden frame covered with either a laid or wove wire surface used for forming sheets of paper by hand.

**Newsprint** name for paper used for printing newspapers, the cheapest type made.

**Opacity** quality of a paper related to the amount of light transmitted through its surface.

**Paper** a thin sheet material that can be made from a range of cellulose fibers, trees being the most common source of cellulose fiber (wood pulp).

**Paper weaving** a way of taking several strips of paper and interlacing them either "over" or "under" a base piece of paper.

**Papercutting** the act of cutting paper, usually with scissors or a scalpel.

**Papermaking** the process and trade of making paper. Paper is made by mechanically or chemically processing cellulose fibers in water, draining the water through a fine mesh to leave the fibers. This is then evenly distributed on a surface, followed by pressing and drying.

**Papier collé** a specific form of collage that refers to the exclusive use of paper in a composition. It is a French term that loosely translates as "pasted paper."

**Photomontage** a collage constructed from photographs.

**Printmaking** a process that involves transferring an image onto another surface, most often paper. It is broadly used to describe a category of different printing techniques, such as woodcut, etching, engraving, and lithography.

**Pulp** the aqueous substance containing disintegrated cellulose fiber from which paper is made.

**Ream** a term used for a number of sheets of paper.

**Scalpel** a type of sharp knife typically used in paper crafts when detailed work or neat cutouts are needed.

**Scissors** a pair of blades with sharpened edges used for cutting thin material such as paper.

**Scoring** the creation of a specific type of crease, usually by using a blunt knife and ruler, that allows the paper to be easily folded and ensures a cleaner line.

**Scrap** a small piece or amount of something, especially one left over after the more significant part has been used.

**Sheet** a piece of paper or board, generally rectangular.

**Tearing** separating something by ripping, as opposed to cutting.separating something by ripping, as opposed to cutting.


## *Metal*

**Abrasion** the process of rubbing, grinding, or wearing away by friction.

**Alloy** a substance with metallic properties that is composed of two or more elements (of which at least one is a metal), such as bronze, which is made from both copper and tin.

**Anvil** a heavy object of durable material that can support material and resist hammering, usually used in blacksmithing.

**Base metals** more common naturally occurring metallic elements compared to precious metals, such as copper. Base metals oxidize when heated in air.

**Blacksmithing** a trade and a specific type of metalsmith who creates objects primarily from wrought iron or steel, but sometimes from other metals, by forging the metal, using tools to hammer, bend, and cut.

**Boring** enlarging a hole that already has been drilled or cored.

**Brittleness** the tendency of a metal or material to fracture.

**Burr** a rough area on a piece of metal that is left after the metal is cut, which is usually then filed and polished.

**Chainmail** a type of armor consisting of small metal rings linked together in a pattern to form a mesh.

**Chroming** chrome plating or "chroming" is a technique of electroplating a thin layer of chromium onto a metal object. It creates a decorative, shiny finish and can help improve the object's resistance and durability.

**Corrosion** deterioration of a metal by chemical or electrochemical reaction with its environment.

**Embossing** raising or indenting a design in relief.

**Engraving** a decorative technique in which lines or patterns are carved or cut into the metal surface.

**Ferrous** related to iron (derived from the Latin ferrum). Ferrous alloys are, therefore, iron base alloys.

**Filing** a process in which a tool with numerous small teeth is applied manually to round off sharp corners and shoulders and remove burrs.

**Forge** typically used to describe a blacksmith's workshop but is sometimes used to describe the place of work for various metalsmiths, including specialist equipment.

**Forging** refers to a set of metalworking processes in which metal is formed into different forms using compressive forces such as hammering or pressing.

**Jig** a piece of stationary apparatus that enables the holding of metal while it is being worked upon, such as being filed.

**Lathe** turning machine capable of numerous processes.

**Metal** any of a class of substances characterized by high electrical and thermal conductivity and malleability, ductility, and high reflectivity of light.

**Metalsmith** broadly describes someone who makes objects using metal. There are different types of metalsmiths, or "smiths," who work with specific metals (such as a goldsmith, who works with gold), or specific objects (such as a bladesmith, who works with knives, swords, and blades).

**Metalworking** any process in which metal is processed to give it a new form.

**Oxidization** the reaction of metal and oxygen.

**Polishing** abrasive process that improves surface finish.

**Powder coating** a dry finishing process created by an electric charge that causes a dry powder to fuse to the surface of the metal.

**Powder metallurgy** processes in which metallic particles are fused under various combinations of heat and pressure to create solid metals.

**Precious metals** rare naturally occurring metallic elements with high economic value, such as gold. Precious metals are less chemically reactive than base metals.

**Sawing** using a blade with teeth to cut a piece of material or give it a new shape.

**Soldering** joining metal pieces by heating and flowing an alloy with a lower melting point than the components to fill the seam.

**Temper** the condition of substance, usually adjustable.

**Welding** a method of joining metal by using high temperatures to melt the parts together.

## *Glass*

**Blown glass** objects that are made by using glassblowing techniques.

**Blowpipe** a hollow steel rod with a mouthpiece on one end that the artist blows through to expand a bubble through the hot glass.

**Cast glass** objects that are made by using casting techniques.

**Casting** the process in which glass objects are cast by directing molten glass into a mould where it then cools and solidifies.

**Clear glass** standard transparent glass.

**Cold glass** the practice of working with glass to decorate it or alter its appearance once it has cooled. Cold glass or "coldworking" is also used as a broad category that encompasses different techniques of working with glass after it has cooled, often including etching, engraving, polishing, sandblasting, and similar techniques.

**Crackle glass** a decorative technique that gives the glass a deliberately fractured appearance. The hot glass is plunged into cold water during blowing, creating a network of cracks and fissures that grow during successive blowing and reheating.

**Engraving** a technique that includes creating a shallow surface decoration by rubbing the surface of cold glass, usually with a sharp tool or hand drill.

**Etching** creating designs and patterns on glass surfaces using acidic, caustic, or abrasive substances.

**Flameworking** the technique of forming glass using a bench top or handheld heat source, such as a torch. It offers greater flexibility for shaping and manipulating glass.

**Furnace** designed to melt raw materials into a liquid state, producing glass.

**Annealing oven** a specific type of oven used to relieve stresses in the glass created during the glassblowing process by slow cooling.

**Frit** crushed glass often melted onto other glass to produce patterns and colors.

**Fused glass** where individual pieces of glass are fired to melt the glass and fuse pieces together.

**Glass** a hard, brittle, inorganic substance, typically transparent or translucent, made by melting raw materials (such as sand, soda ash, and limestone) at a high temperature and then cooling rapidly.

**Glassblowing** the process of blowing air into glass that has been softened by heat, using a blowpipe to inflate and form it into desired shapes and sizes.

**Glory hole** the opening in a furnace used to keep glass hot and workable.

**Hot glass** the practice of working with glass by heating it with a direct flame.

**Kiln** a thermally insulated chamber, a type of oven, that produces temperatures sufficient to heat glass.

**Mirrored glass** a metal coating is applied to one side of the glass and sealed with a protective layer to create a mirrored effect.

**Patterned glass** also known as textured glass, patterned glass is a type of rolled glass that has patterns embedded into it by a roller while the glass is still soft.

**Polishing** abrasive process that improves surface finish.

**Rotary tool** a handheld power tool with a rotating head that spins at high speed. The versatile tool can be fitted with various attachments or drill bits.

**Sandblasting** a technique used to create a translucent frosted-like effect that still allows light to pass through the glass, but obscures visibility through the glass. It includes spraying particles of sand at high velocities over the surface of the glass. It is usually used for forms of decoration by using stencils.

**Satin etch** glass that has been chemically treated to give it a satin or frosted finish on one or two sides.

**Stained glass** is a mosaic of colored and clear glass made from individually cut glass pieces traditionally joined together by soldering strips of lead.

**Studio glass** refers to glass made by an individual or small workshop, usually for aesthetic or creative purposes as opposed to functionality.

**Tempered glass** a type of safety glass that has been subjected to a thermal or chemical process to increase its strength. As a result, it may also be called "toughened" glass.

**Warm glass** the practice of working with glass by heating it in a kiln.